Beginning App Development with Parse and PhoneGap

Wilkins Fernandez
Stephan Alber

Apress®

Beginning App Development with Parse and Phonegap

ISBN-13 (pbk): 978-1-4842-0236-4

ISBN-13 (electronic): 978-1-4842-0235-7

Managing Director: Welmoed Spahr
Acquisitions Editor: Louise Corrigan
Developmental Editor: Chris Nelson
Technical Reviewer: Zeeshan Chawdhary
Editorial Board: Steve Anglin, Mark Beckner, Gary Cornell, Louise Corrigan, James DeWolf,
    Jonathan Gennick, Robert Hutchinson, Celestin Suresh John, Michelle Lowman, James Markham,
    Susan McDermott, Matthew Moodie, Jeffrey Pepper, Douglas Pundick, Ben Renow-Clarke,
    Gwenan Spearing, Matt Wade, Steve Weiss
Coordinating Editor: Rita Fernando
Copy Editor: Ann Dickson, Mary Behr
Compositor: SPi Global
Indexer: SPi Global

Distributed to the book trade worldwide by Springer Science+Business Media New York, 233 Spring Street, 6th Floor, New York, NY 10013. Phone 1-800-SPRINGER, fax (201) 348-4505, e-mail orders-ny@springer-sbm.com, or visit www.springeronline.com. Apress Media, LLC is a California LLC and the sole member (owner) is Springer Science + Business Media Finance Inc (SSBM Finance Inc). SSBM Finance Inc is a Delaware corporation.

For information on translations, please e-mail rights@apress.com, or visit www.apress.com.

Apress and friends of ED books may be purchased in bulk for academic, corporate, or promotional use. eBook versions and licenses are also available for most titles. For more information, reference our Special Bulk Sales–eBook Licensing web page at www.apress.com/bulk-sales.

Any source code or other supplementary material referenced by the author in this text is available to readers at www.apress.com. For detailed information about how to locate your book's source code, go to www.apress.com/source-code/.

*This is dedicated to people who want to get their app ideas
out of their heads and into the hands of many.*

Contents at a Glance

Contents

xvi

About the Authors

Wilkins Fernandez is a software and hardware engineer with a passion to create. Software development started as a personal hobby in 2002, but soon turned into a career for Wilkins. He now works for major companies and media agencies across NYC. When he's not soldering or coding, he enjoys writing in third person.

Stephan Alber is an engineer and product manager for digital content and apps, counting over 15 years of relevant industry experience. After completing his work on this publication, Stephan joined Facebook to manage their developer documentation. In the past, he was active as a blogger, book author, panelist (TV), and conference speaker covering Parse and Facebook technology. He also worked for digital agencies in New York City and Germany and founded a couple of small start-ups. (Disclaimer: This book is not endorsed by Facebook. Inc.)

About the Technical Reviewer

Zeeshan Chawdhary is an avid techie with interests in everything related to technology. He started coding in the days of BASIC and has been hooked ever since. Professionally, with over ten years of experience, he has worked in the gaming, education, travel, automotive, and eCommerce spaces. He enjoys working with start-ups that challenge the conventional ways of business.

Zeeshan enjoys reading, writing, and reviewing technology books. Currently, he is working as the chief technology officer for a self-drive car rental start-up in India. He can be reached on Google at imzeeshanc@gmail.com.

Acknowledgments

Throughout the process of writing this book, many friends have taken time to help us out. We'd like to give a special thanks to Inge Terwindt and Nick Smolney, who were reviewing our content early on and providing invaluable feedback. Thanks to Stephanie Carino for getting this book started. We'd like to thank Andrew Suzuka, Ricky Bacon, and Greg Ratner for enabling us to execute this project.

Stephan would like to thank his mom for creating him.

Wilkins would like to thank his wife, Cristina, and his dog, Ada—both whose support made this possible.

We would also like to thank the PhoneGap community and the Parse team for building such amazing products, enabling people to prototype and execute their ideas.

And finally, we thank you!

Preface

Hello, World! Welcome to *Beginning App Development with Parse and PhoneGap*. We wrote this book to help anyone who wants to build native mobile applications, but may be missing knowledge about advanced programming languages and techniques that are required to do so.

Traditionally, building a native mobile application involved learning multiple programming languages: Objective C (iOS) or Java (Android) for building your program logic and a server language such as PHP or .NET to build your application server. You also needed to learn a database language like MySQL. With Parse and PhoneGap, you use a single language to conquer all aspects: JavaScript.

Similar rules apply to the user interface. Instead of learning a new UI editor or language, you can use the well-known web technologies CSS and HTML to design your user interface.

With Parse and PhoneGap combined, you'll be able to build a robust application in a fraction of the time it would take you to do it in the traditional way. In the pages that follow, you'll be using Parse to manage programming logic, user administration, database creation and analysis, and other great out-of-the-box features. With PhoneGap, you will learn how to access a device's native features such as camera access, geolocation, UI customizations, and much more using powerful plug-ins that can greatly enhance your applications' user experience.

The code in this book can be reused for projects outside of this book. We encourage you to extend the code, debug errors, and—simply put—build something awesome.

■ ■ ■

CHAPTER 1

Introduction

Let's start with the basics! What is PhoneGap? What is Parse? Even if you already know about PhoneGap or Parse, you will still find it worthwhile to read this section, as we'll explain the motivation behind and benefits of combining the two.

After providing a brief description of PhoneGap and Parse, we will talk about previous knowledge and requirements, discuss some code standards, and present a general overview of what you will learn about PhoneGap and Parse.

What Is PhoneGap?

PhoneGap is an open source project used to build mobile applications. It takes your JavaScript, HTML, and CSS code, and packages them into an executable program that can run an array of mobile devices.

PhoneGap does this by exposing access to a device's native features such as file and camera access, using what is known as *Foreign Function Interface* (FFI). This interface lets you invoke platform specific native code using JavaScript. This allows background tasks to send data from JavaScript to native code and vice versa. FFI also allows developers access to native user interface features, such as showing the system's dialog.

PhoneGap makes writing native applications possible by using a plug-in system. This system permits developers to add custom features to their applications. Plug-ins are both maintained by the PhoneGap team and the open source community. We'll be exploring some of them later in this book.

History

The PhoneGap project history and its naming are somewhat bewildering. The project was born at a hackathon in 2008 at the iPhoneDevCamp, which was later renamed iOSDevCamp. In the following years, a company named Nitobi, located in Vancouver, Canada, further developed the software.

In 2011, Nitobi was acquired by Adobe. As a part of the acquisition, the source code of the project was donated to the *Apache Software Foundation* (ASF), allowing the core of the PhoneGap project to remain open sourced. This open source part of the project is named *Apache Cordova* (see Figure 1-1).

Figure 1-1. *Apache Cordova homepage: cordova.apache.org*

This begs the question: What's the difference between PhoneGap and Cordova? In short, PhoneGap is Cordova plus Adobe services and extensions that further enhance its capabilities. Cordova can still be used independently.

How PhoneGap Works

The first task is rather easy to understand by imagining your device's browser without header and footer bars, history, bookmarks, windows, and so forth. What's left is the WebView, your playground that you can use in full-screen mode to build an application using the web technologies HTML, CSS, and JavaScript.

The second part—exposing the device's native features—is a more complex subject. Using code samples is the best way to explain this concept. Before we look at code samples, let's come back to the original issue, which is that while we can do many things in JavaScript, there are some things we still cannot do. For example, let's say you want to use the Parse iOS *Software Development Kit* (SDK) in your application. How can you use this SDK in JavaScript? You can't. PhoneGap closes this gap, making native device and operating system capabilities accessible.

Foreign Function Interface

The FFI system enables developers to build a bridge between JavaScript and native code for a very specific task. Collections of these foreign function calls are commonly bundled in plug-ins, while a wide set of basic features comes shipped with the Cordova or PhoneGap base package.

PhoneGap offers a broader feature set, which is required to build your mobile application. For example, in Chapter 2, you will learn about the PhoneGap *command line interface* (CLI). This tool set allows you to build and maintain PhoneGap applications by executing terminal commands.

Using the CLI, you'll be able to package and compile your application files, as well as test your application using virtual emulators or physical devices. These tools will help you to prepare your application for distribution on marketplaces such as the Apple Store or Google Play.

Supported Platforms

PhoneGap applications are able to run on many platforms using only one code base. This book focuses on developing with the most popular platforms—iOS and Android. Although PhoneGap is primarily used for mobile devices, it is possible to apply the concepts covered here to a desktop platform such as Windows 8.

As you have already learned, PhoneGap projects can be extended with the use of *plug-ins*: concise scripts designed to add extra functionality to an application. As wonderful as they are, plug-ins must be used responsibly due to the possibility of quirks between devices.

For example, the *battery status* application programming interface (API) for Windows Phone 7 and 8 does not yet provide a way to determine the battery level of the device. It *does,* however, provide a way to tell if the device is plugged in or not. You may often run into situations such as this one where it will take some creativity to get the behavior you want.

The examples in this book will demonstrate some of the core plug-ins that come standard with PhoneGap; these features cover all supported platforms, as shown in Figure 1-2.

  TIZEN

Firefox OS

Figure 1-2. Compatible PhoneGap devices starting from the left: Android, iPhone and Apple devices, Tizen (formally bada), BlackBerry OS, Firefox OS, ubuntu, webOS, Windows Phone

---

■ **Note** In 2014, PhoneGap stopped actively supporting webOS, Symbian, BlackBerry, and Windows Phone 7 platforms that use Cordova versions below 3.0 (currently v5.0.0) in favor of supporting current and widely used platforms. If you want to use PhoneGap to target these platforms, you can install older versions of Cordova to build your application.

PhoneGap vs. Web Applications

Writing a PhoneGap application isn't the same as building a web site. PhoneGap believes that writing code in the languages that make up web pages should also be used to communicate with hardware devices.

When programming with PhoneGap, we intend to interface with a mobile device. A PhoneGap application shouldn't just be a packaged static web site that doesn't take advantage of its API capabilities. In fact, Apple may refuse your application to the App Store if they feel your application is just a bundled web site that provides no entertainment value. In light of this, there are many examples of successful PhoneGap applications available on the market today.

Building and Testing PhoneGap Applications

Mobile devices typically have a web browser out of the box. The basic technology that renders a web page can also be used to create an installable application with PhoneGap.

The PhoneGap API was designed specifically for interfacing with hardware on mobile devices. This means that PhoneGap applications will not work on a typical web browser, as you would expect on a personal computer.

Web browsers use HTML and CSS for styling, positioning, and animating content elements (such as text, buttons, images, and so forth). JavaScript is used for adding dynamic interactivity, giving the user a unique experience. In this trio of languages, JavaScript arguably plays the most important role.

There are a variety of ways to build and test PhoneGap applications. The good news is that you only need one code base to create an installable package for each compatible device. We will be looking at different ways to test your applications, such as using device emulators and live testing on a compatible mobile device.

For example, if you plan on developing an application for an Apple device such as iPhone, you will need to use a program called *Xcode* installed on a Mac computer. Using the developer tools that Xcode comes with, combined with additional CLI tools, developers can test applications using the *iOS simulator*.

As you may expect, developers face several challenges when writing mobile applications for multiple device platforms. Programming and testing applications natively typically requires its own development tools and setup.

Does this mean you need to have a custom set development environment for *each* platform when using PhoneGap? Yes. For proper testing of your user interface and application behavior, you need to test each platform's version of your application in its proper environment. This applies in particular to plug-ins accessing native device capabilities.

In any case, developing PhoneGap applications for multiple platforms only requires one code base. With that in mind, you may find yourself having to make adjustments to your code in order to provide the best experience for users across operating systems or devices.

Once you are ready to release your application to the world, each marketplace expects you to provide a package type that is unique to its store. The only way to do so is to have PhoneGap compile your application in the environment that it is intended for. For example, if you are developing in an iOS environment and want to release your application to Google Play, you'll need to build your application using Android-based IDE tools Android Studio.

The Adobe PhoneGap Build Service (Optional)

Since teaming up with PhoneGap, Adobe now offers a service that enables developers to build their mobile applications for multiple devices all in one shot. As you know, there are many platforms that PhoneGap can compile to. There is also a unique development environment for each platform; things can get messy quickly.

There are some potential pitfalls with using this service, which we'll examine next. First, lets go over some of the benefits of using Adobe PhoneGap Build.

If you are like most people, you may not have access to the devices and development environments needed for compiling a PhoneGap application. Because of this, Adobe offers the build process in the cloud, allowing developers to package mobile applications simultaneously for all available platforms. This ensures that your application is updated with the latest native SDKs.

With new mobile devices coming out every few months, you can imagine the complexities involved with developers maintaining and supporting new, current, and legacy operating systems. With PhoneGap applications, you can maintain your code with confidence, knowing that you're using open standards that are supported by major platforms.

PhoneGap Build expands your application's audience reach by providing multiple packaged platform builds. This means you no longer need to write software in proprietary vendor code.

Without having to maintain multiple native SDKs, the Adobe PhoneGap build service does it all for you. This optional service allows you to focus more on writing great software, not worrying about how to get it to your users.

Adobe offers a three-tiered plan, each tier offering unique options. Figure 1-3 illustrates each plan in detail, as of this writing. Learn more at `build.phonegap.com/plans`.

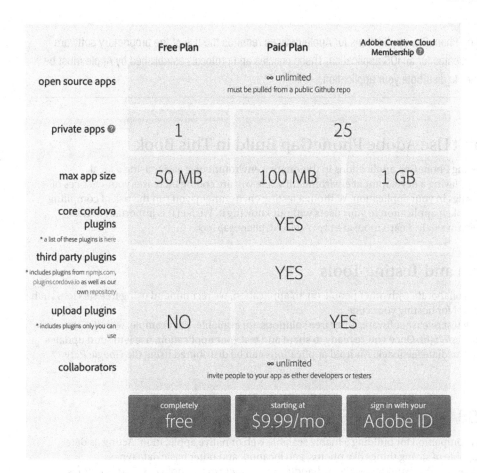

	Free Plan	Paid Plan	Adobe Creative Cloud Membership ?
open source apps		∞ unlimited must be pulled from a public Github repo	
private apps ?	1	25	
max app size	50 MB	100 MB	1 GB
core cordova plugins * a list of these plugins is here		YES	
third party plugins * includes plugins from npmjs.com, plugins.cordova.io as well as our own repository		YES	
upload plugins * includes plugins only you can use	NO	YES	
collaborators		∞ unlimited invite people to your app as either developers or testers	
	completely free	starting at $9.99/mo	sign in with your Adobe ID

Figure 1-3. *Adobe PhoneGap Build services*

When developing a PhoneGap application on your computer, you still need a way to actively test what you're building. Chapter 2 focuses on the tools and software you'll need for the targeted platform.

Caveats

There are some things to consider before using the Adobe PhoneGap Build service. Technically, you don't *need* to install any platform-specific development environment, such as Xcode, to develop PhoneGap applications. Following this logic, because this service builds your application for you, there is no need to install software locally. Although this may be true, we recommend, at least if you're getting started, using the software that is designed to build your application locally. This can give you a better understanding of the platform and its capabilities.

The Adobe PhoneGap Build service compiles your HTML, CSS, and JS code into the appropriate packages for operating systems. It is your responsibility as a developer to submit your compiled application to its respective app store for distribution.

> ■ **Note** Developing PhoneGap applications for Apple devices requires the use of the proprietary software Xcode to create certificates for an iOS application. These policies and protocols established by Apple must be implemented in order to distribute your application.

Why We Don't Use Adobe PhoneGap Build in This Book

Debugging and testing PhoneGap applications in their native environment is easier using a local development setup. Having a development environment while you are coding increases your chances of avoiding potential bugs in your application. Without a testing environment, you run the risk of compiling and distributing a broken application to your users without knowing it. We feel it is important to use discretion and program safely. Learn more at http://build.phonegap.com.

Collaboration and Testing Tools

If you would like to collaborate with other people on an application, we recommend using free services such as Github or Bitbucket for hosting your code.

For distributing test release software, other free solutions are available. For example, with iOS you can use a service called *TestFlight*. Once you're ready to share and test your application, use it to send updates to beta testers for immediate feedback. Android applications can be distributed using the *Google Play Developer Console*.

Using Parse

Parse is the perfect companion for building a highly scalable web or native application. Acting as data storage, Parse is capable of saving things like photos, geo location, and other basic data types.

By providing features that would typically be handled by a variety of technologies, Parse bundles together features such as push notifications and scheduled tasks using its intuitive API. Gone are the days when you need to host your own databases and sync them to your applications. Now that everything can be handled "in the cloud," saving and managing data have never been easier.

Parse was created by a group of developers who got together to create a set of back-end tools and services to help manage all the facets of mobile development. In 2013, Facebook acquired Parse with the intent of further expanding its already amazing feature set.

Developing Applications with Parse

Parse offers its services for use with many different programming languages. For this book, we'll be using the JavaScript SDK, as it's perfect for using with PhoneGap.

Parse offers different tiers of free and paid services based on your needs. When your application reaches the point where your users are making more than 30 requests per second, Parse offers to extend the free service by providing more file storage, as well as a higher data transfer rate.

For our purposes, a free account will suffice. In fact, this would be the case for most new applications. A free account gives you up to 20 gigs of data and file storage respectively for *each* Parse application you create. That's a lot of data! Not only that, it also offers the ability to run what it calls "background jobs." These are programs that you can write to run on the cloud at any given time. This is helpful for things like providing mass updates to your app or introducing new features to your users in real time.

Features

We'll be exploring different aspects of Parse throughout this book. To give you an idea of how awesome Parse is, here are just a few cool things that come with a registered account:

- *Analytics*: Instead of just having to rely on third-party scripts to track your apps usage, Parse offers an analytics tool without your having to configure anything.

- *Parse push*: Using any of the SDKs, you'll be able to send up to one million unique recipients push notifications a month.

- *User management*: In place of creating your own database structure and code for user accounts, Parse offers this functionality right out of the box. This includes things like resetting passwords, linking accounts with Facebook, and many other conveniences.

- *Data browser*: Using the web interface, you can browse all of your application's data with just a few clicks. It also allows you to create new data objects that allow you to save custom data sets, while also providing pre-defined data structures such as the User or Product classes.

Why Parse and PhoneGap?

Of all the frameworks, in all the languages, why did we choose to go with Parse and PhoneGap? The answer is easy: To build a successful application, you need a user interface technology—the *front end*—and a data infrastructure—the *back-end*. While PhoneGap is doing a good job on the front end, the project doesn't cover back-end needs.

With PhoneGap alone, you are forced to learn another programming language and design your back-end system on your own. If you want to save data to the back end, you needed to write a front-end module to prepare the data, connect to a server, and send the data to it. In the back-end tier, the request needs to be authenticated, processed, and then stored to a database. This is typically done using another system with its own language, such as MySQL. The same applies to the task of reading data.

With Parse, this approach is a thing of the past. Using PhoneGap *together* with Parse will enable you to use only *one* programming language—JavaScript—to manage all your data needs: reading, saving, deleting, defining schemas, authentication, querying, and so forth.

To demonstrate how easy it is to save data in Parse, we'll use a simple code example: In Listing 1-1, we initialize the Parse JavaScript SDK, which opens a connection to the Parse backend. This back-end service will store your data securely and efficiently "in the cloud."

To get an idea of how data is stored using Parse, Listing 1-1 demonstrates creating a class that we save a new record to. We start by defining a new Parse class named Toy, then create a new *instance* of the class, set some sample values, and finally save the object to the database using myToy.save().

Listing 1-1. Saving a Simple Object to the Parse Cloud in JavaScript

```
// Initialize Parse JavaScript SDK
Parse.initialize("APPLICATION ID", "JAVASCRIPT KEY");
// Define a new Parse class named "Toy"
var Toy = Parse.Object.extend("Toy");
// Create a new Instance of the Toy Parse Class
var myToy = new Toy();
```

```
// Set some Example Values
myToy.set("name", "Rocking Horse");
myToy.set("color", "brown");
// Save Object to Parse Cloud Database
myToy.save();
```

That's it! Saving data has never been easier. In a production application, we *could* add more complexity to these tasks, like success and error callbacks, but in a perfect world this code will actually work as is. Figure 1-4 shows how the result from Listing 1-1 would look when it is executed and viewed in Parse's data browser.

Figure 1-4. *The result of Listing 1-1*

Yet saving data is just one example how Parse and PhoneGap complement each other. We show a wider span of applications in Table 1-1. These samples will assure you that joining these two forces just seems natural.

Table 1-1. *Complementary Functionality between PhoneGap and Parse*

PhoneGap	Parse
Access camera and audio functionality of the native operating systems	Has a database field that is specifically used for media such as images, video, and audio files
Get the geo position of a device, pinpointing a user's location anywhere in the world	Has a data field for geo location, allowing you to save the latitude and longitude and query data by location and distance
Access the contact list a user has on his or her phone, providing information that can enhance your application	Stores media, text, and all basic database field types in the cloud. Can store user profiles, content, and any other associated data for your needs
Access the native (push) notification system of Android and iOS devices via PhoneGap plug-ins	Offers a push notification service for both Android and iOS devices
Compiles your application code for multiple platforms	Allows to share data between platforms (iOS, Android, Web)

Make Your Application Social

Humans have a need to communicate with each other. Using Parse and PhoneGap together to create an application allows you to facilitate this need by allowing you to share. This social component can be very important in the success of your application. After all, it's *Words with Friends*, not *Words with Myself*. Building static, nonsocial applications is a thing of the past.

PhoneGap and Parse together stand by your side when building social applications. As an example, you can use the Parse Facebook single sign-on login feature to sign up to an application and connect with friends. You can then use PhoneGap's technology to capture a picture and use Parse again to store it to the cloud and share it with your friends.

Adding a social element to your application does more than expose your work to new users. It can also add a personal touch that can make your application feel special. We'll show you how to build a full social application starting in Chapter 6 that will demonstrate how to keep people connected. We'll be doing all sorts of cool things like accessing media, location sharing, and providing real-time updates.

Previous Knowledge and Requirements

There are a few core concepts in modern front-end web development that need to be understood before continuing. These will provide you with a foundation that you can build upon while developing multiple skills. There are plenty of approaches you can take for creating a PhoneGap application, and you don't have to decide on anything *before* starting a new project. However, knowing the fundamentals will aid you in taking the best approach for each application.

There are many books that cover the delicate intricacies of HTML, JavaScript, and CSS. Because of this, we'll only highlight some of the key concepts that you'll need to get the most out of this book. We encourage you to do further research on any topics you find challenging.

Whatever level of programming you are at right now, consider the following section a refresher on some of the concepts that need to be understood to get the most out of this book.

JavaScript Object Literals

If you're just getting into programming, the phrase *object-oriented programming* can sound frightening. Objects in programming are analogous to real-world tangible objects that have properties and values. If you were to consider yourself as an object, the *value* of your firstName property would be *your* first name.

An object literal can be thought of in the same way, with some rules: *the value of a property name must fall within a predefined type of data.* This basically means you need to use valid data. All values in JavaScript are considered objects, so anything can be stored into an object. An object literal is enclosed in a set of curly braces, like this { key: value }. An empty set of braces ({}) is considered a valid object; it has zero properties and values. The following code demonstrates JavaScript's primitive types of data by assigning them to an object that is referenced in the variable named obj:

```
var obj = {
  name: "value",
  array: [4,2,0],
  boolean: true,
  type: "string",
  number: 0,
  emptyObject: {},
  fn: function(){
    var declaredButNoValueAssigned;
    console.log("fn scoped variable: " + declaredButNoValueAssigned);
    var emptyValue = null;
    // This function returns a null value
    return emptyValue;
  }
};
```

```
console.log(obj.name);           // value
console.log(obj["name"]);        // value
console.log(typeof obj.name);    // string
console.log(typeof obj.type);    // string
console.log(obj.type);           // string
console.log(obj.array);          // [4,2,0]
console.log(typeof obj.boolean);// boolean
console.log(typeof {});          // object
console.log(obj.fn());
  // fn scoped variable: undefined
  // null
```

Namespaces with Object Literals

Object literals are a great way to organize related functionality. The way programmers write JavaScript applications has developed over the years since its creation in 1995. A common and powerful concept that JavaScript shares with other programming languages is that of *namespaces*. From server-side scripting with Node.js, to client-side and installable applications with PhoneGap, namespaces allow developers to communicate concepts into understandable programmatic interfaces.

All programming languages have unique ways of expressing objects and ideas. Each has its own syntactical rules that need be followed in order to use it. What all programming languages have in common is the use of language itself: strict syntax that is used to communicate concepts that a machine can understand. In JavaScript, *object literals* help developers encapsulate logic in an expressive and organized way that can be understood by others. In Chapter 2, you'll see this put to use in a full example using PhoneGap. Listing 1-2 demonstrates how a fictional JavaScript program may be written using namespaces.

Listing 1-2. Creating a Simple JavaScript Using Namespaces

```
var app = {
  settings: {
    version: "0.0.1"
  }
};
app.user = {};
app.user.register = function(){};
```

To get an even deeper understanding of namespaces, we recommend reading a great article by engineer and developer advocate Addy Osmani titled "Essential JavaScript Namespacing Patterns."[1]

Organizing Code for Projects in This Book

The code samples and concepts in this book can be combined with many JavaScript projects, libraries, and frameworks. As a matter of fact, a part of the JavaScript Parse SDK is forked from Backbone.js; existing developers will find converting existing applications intuitive. Some demonstrations in this book use third-party libraries such as jQuery. However, we do also use plain ole' JavaScript as well. With each chapter, we explore both the PhoneGap and Parse APIs by demonstrating functionality that you could use in your next application.

---

[1]Read the "Essential JavaScript Namespacing Patterns" article at http://addyosmani.com/blog/essential-js-namespacing/.

All projects use some form of file structure for organizing different aspects of an application. Chapter 2 explores what a typical PhoneGap application looks like by using the "Hello World" starter application. Parse also has a starter application that we dig into in Chapter 3.

Aside from the default folder structures found in starter Parse and PhoneGap projects, we'll be using intuitive naming conventions in an attempt to keep things simple, clear, and concise. The following snippet demonstrates a typical folder structure for web-based projects with index.html located at the root of the folder:

```
img/
js/
css/
index.html
```

The example structure above contains three directories and one HTML file, the home page. The folders are named in an obvious way as to make it clear what it's responsible for containing. In Chapter 6, you will start creating a Parse and PhoneGap application that will have a similar structure, while still respecting the required directory structure needed for compiling PhoneGap applications.

Loading Scripts with LABjs

There are many ways to load scripts in JavaScript. From using classic `<script>` tags to building complex modular compiler systems, loading scripts in JavaScript is always an important task. We decided to go with what we find is one of the most straightforward and simple ways of loading scripts: a library named LABjs. LABjs is an open source project written by Open Web Evangelist, Kyle Simpson.

Chapter 6 demonstrates the necessity of using a script loader, in which we'll begin building an entire application from scratch. There will be *lots* of scripts in this application, and in order to manage them, we will use LABjs to do the hard work.

You can see a comparison of traditional loading vs. loading using LABjs in Listings 1-3 and 1-4.

Listing 1-3. Traditional Script Loading Using the <script> Tag

```
<script src="framework.js"></script>
<script src="plugin.framework.js"></script>
<script src="myplugin.framework.js"></script>
<script src="init.js"></script>
```

Listing 1-4. Script Loading using LABjs

```
<script>
        $LAB
        .script("framework.js").wait()
        .script("plugin.framework.js")
        .script("myplugin.framework.js").wait()
        .script("init.js").wait();
</script>
```

Although it may not look like much, using this script loader is an efficient way to load scripts and, more importantly, manage dependencies using the wait() method. We'll be going through this in extensive detail as the application progresses in the chapters following Chapter 6.

Build Process

A *build process* is a series of automated operations that aids developers in outputting production-ready applications. We will not be covering this topic in this book, but thought we'd acknowledge its use and efficiency.

Again, when it concerns JavaScript, everyone has an opinion. What the JavaScript community *can* agree on is trying our hardest to deliver the best experience for our users. In doing so, there have been a few popular tools that aid in this process, including the following:

- Grunt.js
- Gulp.js
- Yeoman.io
- Brunch.io

There are numerous plug-ins for each of these tools designed to make your life as a developer run more smoothly. Processes such as JSHint, SASS/LESS compilation, minification, image compression, and many more are available with build-processing tools.

Debugging

Software that has yet to be written is the only kind without bugs. This means that every time you write code is an opportunity for a bug to appear. We will be introducing some basic debugging techniques that are specific to PhoneGap development. PhoneGap applications aren't like typical web applications and need special attention when it comes to debugging issues. We'll be going through a few ways of testing PhoneGap applications in Chapter 4. Additionally, we'll be covering ways of testing database interactions with Parse by using their Data Browser, among other tools and techniques.

Basic knowledge of web developer tools such as the browser inspector should be understood. It's OK if you're new to it; we'll be covering what you need to know to make the most out of each application you build. The most common and basic way to see what's going on during code execution is to log statements to the console. This technique is often used for building web sites.

Command-Line Interface Tools

A command-line user interface allows programmers to communicate with a computer by executing statements using an interactive console. If you're not familiar with executing code from the command line, we have got you covered. After installing a few command-line based tools for using Parse and PhoneGap, you'll be experienced in no time. All tools will both work in Terminal (Mac) and Command Prompt (Windows).

After installing packages for Parse and PhoneGap development, we'll be experimenting with various aspects of each API, like syncing Parse apps to your local environment for publishing, as well as compiling and previewing PhoneGap applications using an emulator.

Integrated Development Environment (IDE)

An IDE is where all the magic happens. And by *magic*, we mean coding. It's the software you use to *write* software. There are a plethora of options to choose from. From command-line interface editors like *vim*, to basic text editors like Notepad or textEdit, practically anything can be used to create a web site.

While some are more powerful and fully featured than others, the IDE you use is up to you. Some of our recommendations include the following:

- Atom.io

- Sublime Text 2

- NotePad++

Any of these IDEs will get the job done. If you already use an editor you know and love, great! But if you haven't found one, here are some things to consider:

- Is it free? Is paying for one worth it?

- Are there plug-ins that can extend its functionality?

- Does it contain any built-in features like code collapsing, autofill, or syntax highlighting?

What You Will Learn about PhoneGap and Parse

Chapter 2 will provide you with everything you need to begin application development with PhoneGap. From installing and setting up, to previewing and editing an example application, to implementing real-world scenarios that demonstrate some of PhoneGap's core functionality, we'll attempt to cover as much of their API as possible.

We'll also be covering some cool plug-ins that extend the functionality of your applications, as well as some debugging and development tools that you can start using immediately.

Using Parse as our main data storage, we'll be covering everything from creating an account to setting up your first Parse application. As the book progresses, we'll introduce some core features of Parse. We'll be covering the Parse JavaScript SDK, which we'll tie into PhoneGap applications. This will enable you to do things like take a picture using the native camera on a mobile device and saving it to a database.

Going Further

The code and concepts used for examples in this book can be applied to any PhoneGap or Parse application you create. Because we are using the language of the web (HTML, JS, CSS), there is opportunity to build a variety of different experiences for your users per application. For example:

- Storing media with Parse: audio, image, and video storage

- Accessing media content with PhoneGap

- Creating user accounts with Parse

- Sync Facebook accounts with your Parse app

- Using PhoneGap plug-ins to extend device features

- Structuring your application data using the Parse Data Browser

We are convinced that this book contains enough information to get you building applications that you have only imagined. Aside from the hands-on projects that we'll be walking you through, we encourage you to take everything you learn and apply it to your next project.

CHAPTER 2

■ ■ ■

Beginning PhoneGap

Configuring your Development Environment

In this chapter, you'll learn the essentials of PhoneGap. First, we will walk you through the installation process of PhoneGap and its dependencies. Then you'll be creating, debugging, and testing your first "Hello World" PhoneGap application.

We get underway with setting up your development environment for the two most popular mobile platforms, iOS and Android. You'll install the package manager for Node.js, which will lead to the PhoneGap installation process.

Platform Setup and Restrictions

While PhoneGap is designed to use one codebase to handle multiple platforms, you still need to prepare your system for *each* platform you wish to support. For example, with *Android* you'll need to install the Android SDK, with the *Windows Phone* you will need to install the Windows Phone SDK, and so forth.

Each platform may have further dependencies or operating system restrictions. For instance, you need a Windows system to build Windows Phone applications and a Mac OS X system to build iOS applications. While the Android SDK can run on Windows and Mac, it requires the installation of the Java Development Kit (JDK). Requirements and installation procedures will be covered in the following sections.

Installing Node.js and Node Package Manager

Before installing PhoneGap and its dependencies, you need to install Node.js. Node.js is a server side JavaScript programming environment used to build fast, scalable network applications. When Node.js is installed on your computer, it includes a JavaScript package manager called node package manager (npm), which we'll be using to install PhoneGap and other tools.

Even though npm was intended for use with Node.js and JavaScript, it may be used for source files using other programming languages as well. You can install JavaScript packages, called *node modules*, by using the `npm install <package-name>` terminal command. Download Node.js from `http://nodejs.org/download/` and follow the installation instructions.

Node.js is available for both Windows and Mac. To ensure you have installed Node.js properly, in your terminal, run `node -v`. This should return the currently installed version of Node.js on your system.

iOS Environment Setup

If you want to develop iOS applications, you need a Mac OS X computer. If you are a Windows user, this doesn't necessarily mean you need run to the nearest Apple store and buy a Mac. It is possible, but *not* recommended, to simulate an installation of Mac OS X on Windows using virtualization software like *VMWare*, or the open source alternative *VirtualBox*.

Once you either have a Mac or virtual machine configured and running, you need to install Apple's IDE software called *Xcode*. With Xcode, you can build applications for OS X and iOS. You'll only need the iOS portion for this book.

Figure 2-1 shows the Xcode IDE for Mac. It also shows how the iOS simulator looks when running the starter project that comes with all PhoneGap applications.

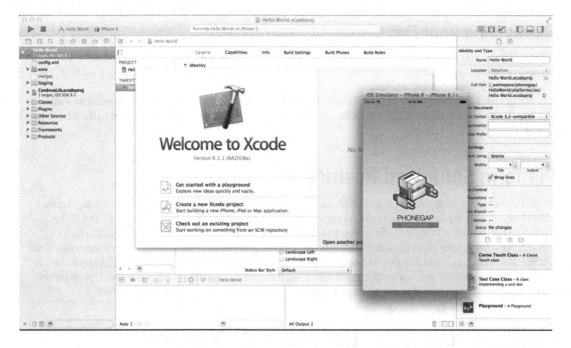

Figure 2-1. *Xcode, the IDE for iOS, and the iOS simulator*

The fastest way to download and install Xcode is by searching for "Xcode" in the App Store desktop application. After it's installed, it will either be listed in the Mac's dock or in the Launcher. You can also find it using the Spotlight Search.

Alternatively, you may download Xcode (and more) in the *Apple Developer Member Center*. The Member Center requires you have an *Apple ID* and register as an Apple Developer. This can be done for free at https://developer.apple.com/register/. After you have registered as a developer, visit https://developer.apple.com/downloads/ to download Xcode.

If you intend on releasing your applications to the Apple App Store, you will need to enroll in the *iOS Developer Program* ($99/year). With that said, you won't need it right now.

■ **Note** Setting up things like Certificates, Identifiers, and Provisioning Profiles (things you'll need to publish your applications) are outside of the scope of this book. For a complete guide on setting this up, visit developer.apple.com/library/ios/documentation/IDEs/Conceptual/AppDistributionGuide/ MaintainingCertificates/MaintainingCertificates.html.

Command Line Tools for Xcode

The Command Line Tools package allows you to do command-line development in OS X. PhoneGap uses this package to build the iOS version of your application. For OS X 10.9 and greater, Xcode comes bundled with all command-line tools.

If you're using an older version of OS X, you can install the Command Line Tools package from the main menu in Xcode. Select *Preferences* and then click the Downloads tab. From the Components panel, click the Install button next to the Command Line Tools listing. If Xcode does not show an option to install the package or if it's missing for any other reason, you can download the package from the Apple Developers downloads page at https://developer.apple.com/downloads. Note that in order to view the downloads page, you must be logged in with your Apple Developer credentials.

iOS Launcher Packages

To be able to install and run PhoneGap applications using the iOS simulator or an iOS device from the command line, you need to install two more JavaScript packages using npm. The command ios-deploy launches iOS apps to a physical iOS device, and ios-sim executes the application using the iOS simulator provided by Xcode. Install the packages via the following commands, adding the sudo prefix if needed. The following code lines demonstrate two separate commands for installing the packages used for testing PhoneGap applications.

```
npm install -g ios-sim
npm install -g ios-deploy
```

At this point, you should have everything you need for iOS development with PhoneGap. If you do *not* wish to develop for Android, skip the next section and continue to *PhoneGap Installation*.

■ **Note** You don't have to use Xcode as your code editor. You also don't need to use it to build PhoneGap applications; the latter happens using the command line. However, Xcode is a good tool for testing your application on different types of iOS devices. You can download more iOS simulators using Xcode via Preferences from the main menu (in the Downloads tab).

Android Environment Setup

Setting up your environment for Android development differs greatly from that of iOS. Figure 2-2 illustrates where it all starts—the Android Developer Portal.

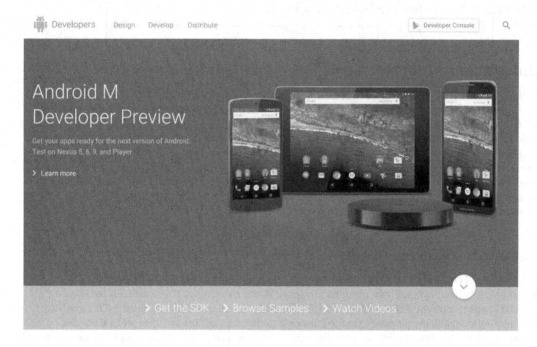

Figure 2-2. *The Android Developer Portal at* `http://developer.android.com`

To build applications for the Android platform, you need to install the *Android SDK*. As previously mentioned, there are no OS restrictions—you can use either Windows or Mac to build Android applications. The Android environment setup is slightly more involved than the iOS setup. But fear not, you will be guided through the setup process step-by-step.

There are theoretically two ways to install the Android SDK: via the Android Studio software or with the Android standalone SDK. Because Android Studio is not needed to build PhoneGap applications, we don't cover it in this book, but stick to the stand-alone SDK.

Java Development Kit (JDK)

Android is closely tied to the Java programming language. It's no surprise that you'll need to install the JDK to be able to use the Android SDK. This applies in particular to Windows systems; you have to install the JDK *prior* to running Android installations. For older Mac systems (< 10.7), you may skip this step.

Identify the JDK package fitting your system configuration on the Oracle Java Downloads page: `www.oracle.com/technetwork/java/javase/downloads/`.

Android SDK Installation

As previously stated, we will use the Android SDK Tools only to build the Android version of our PhoneGap applications. You should also be able to navigate to the SDK package download from `developer.android.com/sdk/index.html`.

In case something has changed since this writing, head over to the Android Developer site (`http://developer.android.com`) and choose Get the SDK link (as shown in Figure 2-2) to navigate to the latest Android SDK download instructions. Next, choose the Installing the Android SDK link from the main navigation. This will take you to a new page where you will click the Stand-alone SDK Tools button.

Pick either Windows or Mac and accept the terms and conditions on the following page to initiate the download. For Windows, we recommend using the executable installer package.

Windows

Double-click the executable (`.exe`) file to start the installation process. Write down the location where you saved the SDK on your system—you will need it to refer to the SDK directory later when using the SDK tools from the command line. Once the installation completes, the installer starts the *Android SDK Manager*. Skip the following Mac paragraph and continue at Android SDK Manager.

Mac

Unpack the ZIP file you've downloaded. By default, it's unpacked into a directory named `android-sdk-mac_x86`. Move it to an appropriate location on your machine, for example, to the directory `/Users/{YOUR_USERNAME}/Library/Android/sdk/`.

Android SDK Manager

As you may know, there are many different versions of Android. The latest version 5.0 is named *Lollipop*, yet more common are the older releases *KitKat* (4.4) and *Jelly Bean* (4.3, 4.2, 4.1). To install the SDKs for these different platform versions, use the Android SDK Manager. There are some other tools, like the Android SDK Build Tools, that you need to install. These will be installed via the Android SDK Manager as well.

To start the SDK Manager on Windows, double-click the `SDK Manager.exe` file at the root of the Android SDK directory.

On Mac, open a terminal and navigate to the `/tools` directory in the Android SDK directory (for example, `/Users/{YOUR_USERNAME}/Library/Android/sdk/tools`). Then execute the command `android sdk`. This will open a new window, the Android SDK Manager.

Once the Android SDK Manager starts, it will look for packages available for download. This will include both the latest releases as well as older or common packages. See Figure 2-3 for reference. By checking the boxes right next to the packages and hitting the Install button, you can download and install the selected packages.

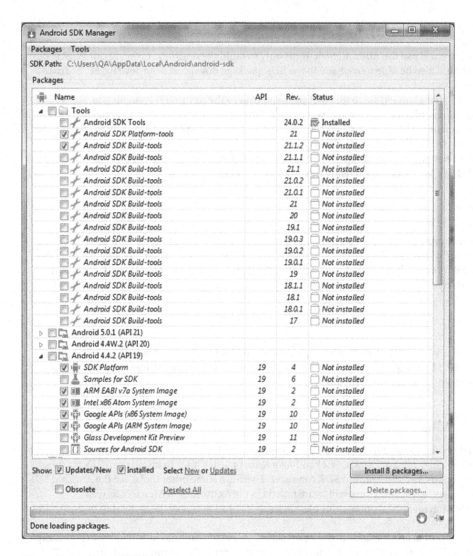

Figure 2-3. *Android SDK Manager*

At minimum, you should download the latest tools and Android platform:

- Android SDK Tools

- Android SDK Platform-tools

- Android SDK Build-tools *(highest version)*

Next, you need to add each platform version you want to test your application on. We recommend starting on the most common version (as of this writing), *KitKat (4.4)*, first. You can later verify that your application is working on other platforms as well.

Open the folder *Android 4.4.22 (API 19)* and select the following:

- SDK Platform

- A system image for the emulator, such as `ARM EABI v7a System Image`

Choosing an Android Emulator Image

Emulation on Android is a tricky thing. And by tricky, we mean it's slow. To speed up your emulator, install the package, use the `android sdk` manager, and select "Intel x86 Emulator Accelerator" from the Extras menu. Also select a corresponding emulator image (for example, Intel x86 Atom System Image).

You can find more information about this topic in the article "Speeding Up the Android* Emulator on Intel Architecture" at `https://software.intel.com/en-us/android/articles/speeding-up-the-android-emulator-on-intel-architecture`.

As an alternative, you can use a physical Android device connected via USB cable as a test system. Even though it's an external device, it will speed up the process of installing and testing your application significantly.

There are also third-party services, such as Genymotion (`www.genymotion.com`), that can assist you in testing your Android applications.

Managing Virtual Devices

Once you have downloaded and installed all Android packages, it's time to add a *virtual device*. A virtual device is an emulator configuration defined by hardware and software options. This means you can combine any emulator image you downloaded in the previous step with a range of devices, operating system versions, and so forth.

Virtual devices are managed via the Android Virtual Device (AVD) Manager. To start the manager, run the command `android avd` in the `tools` directory. Add a new virtual device via the Create button. You will need to configure the following:

- *A hardware profile*: The hardware profile defines the hardware features of the virtual device, including how much memory the device holds, whether it has a camera, and so on.

- *A mapping to a system image*: In the previous step, you downloaded at least one image using the Android SDK Manager. Assign one of the images you downloaded.

- *Other options*: You can specify the screen dimensions, appearance, and other options of the device, including the size of the device's internal storage in which it saves the user's data (installed applications, settings, and so on) as well as a virtual SD card memory.

Once you have finished your configuration, confirm via the OK button, as shown in Figure 2-4.

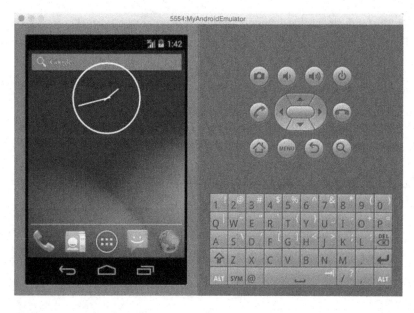

Figure 2-4. *The Android Virtual Device Manager (AVD Manager)*

You can test your virtual device by selecting it and clicking the Start... button. It may take some time to launch the emulator. If you have major speed issues, please refer back to the preceding section, "Choosing an Android Emulator Image." Figure 2-5 shows an example of the emulator.

Figure 2-5. *Android emulator*

Adding Android SDK Paths

To make the Android SDK accessible for PhoneGap, you need to add SDK paths to your system's settings. Among other things, adding these paths will allow PhoneGap to compile your application.

On Windows systems, execute the commands shown in Listing 2-1 in the command prompt. On Mac systems, execute Listing 2-2 in the terminal. Replace the placeholder {INSTALLATION-LOCATION} with the path you picked at the beginning of the Android SDK installation process.

Listing 2-1. Adding Android SDK Paths on Windows

```
set ANDROID_HOME=C:\{INSTALLATION-LOCATION}\android-sdk
set PATH=%PATH%;%ANDROID_HOME%\tools;%ANDROID_HOME%\platform-tools
```

Listing 2-2. Adding Android SDK Paths on Mac

```
export ANDROID_HOME=/{INSTALLATION-LOCATION}/android-sdk-macosx
export PATH=${PATH}:$ANDROID_HOME/tools:$ANDROID_HOME/platform-tools
```

Installing Apache Ant

On most systems, you need to install Apache Ant (http://ant.apache.org) as a last step. If you own a Mac and use Homebrew, you can run brew install ant.

■ **Note** Homebrew is a package manager for Mac OS X. If you don't yet use it, you should! You can find download and install instructions on http://brew.sh/.

You can also pick and download a fitting Ant binary from www.apache.org/dist/ant/binaries/. As Ant is built with Java, the files for Mac and Windows are the same. Extract the ZIP file (for example, apache-ant-1.9.4-bin.zip) somewhere on your computer. Add the full path to the contained bin/ folder to the end of your PATH environment variable as shown in Listings 2-3 and 2-4. You can find more instructions and help how to install Apache Ant on ant.apache.org/manual/install.html.

Listing 2-3. Adding the Apache Ant Path on Windows

```
set PATH=%PATH%;C:\{YOUR-PATH}\apache-ant-1.9.4\bin
```

Listing 2-4. Adding the Apache Ant Path on Mac

```
export PATH=${PATH}:{YOUR-PATH}\apache-ant-1.9.4\bin
```

Installing PhoneGap

Next, you'll be installing PhoneGap via the node package manager. The PhoneGap command-line tool will allow you to install plug-ins, build your application, or install and run your application using a simulator.

Windows

To install PhoneGap on Windows, open the command prompt. You can find the command prompt via the Windows search using "cmd" as your search term or via the Start button in *All Programs* ➤ *Accessories* ➤ *Command Prompt*. Execute npm install -g phonegap. It does not matter in which directory you execute this command.

Mac

Open the Terminal application. You can find it using Spotlight Search. As on Windows, execute npm install -g phonegap. If you run into a permission error, you may need to run this as a *superuser* (sudo), since the installation requires authorization. In this case, execute sudo npm install -g phonegap instead.

■ **Tip** The -g flag installs npm packages globally, making the command available to run in any directory on your computer. This is why the location of where you execute this command is irrelevant. Without using -g, the package will only install in the directory that npm install is executed.

During the installation process, you will see several requests to npm logged in the terminal; this retrieves all the packages used for PhoneGap. To ensure it's properly installed, run phonegap -v once. This will return the version of PhoneGap you have installed.

Updating PhoneGap

When installing PhoneGap the first time, you'll always have the latest version. You can stay up-to-date with npm packages by using the update command before the name of the package, for example, npm update -g phonegap or respectively sudo npm update -g phonegap. Follow the PhoneGap blog to stay up-to-date with new releases and information at http://phonegap.com/blog/.

Using the PhoneGap CLI Tools

You'll be using the CLI throughout this book to run an array of commands such as compiling PhoneGap applications and running your application using emulation software. To get an idea of what is in store when using phonegap commands, in your terminal execute phonegap help. This will show all the commands available in the PhoneGap CLI, as shown in Figure 2-6.

```
Usage: phonegap [options] [commands]

Description:

  PhoneGap command-line tool.

Commands:

  help [command]       output usage information
  create <path>        create a phonegap project
  build <platforms>    build the project for a specific platform
  install <platforms>  install the project on for a specific platform
  run <platforms>      build and install the project for a specific platform
  platform [command]   update a platform version
  plugin [command]     add, remove, and list plugins
  info                 display information about the project
  serve                serve a phonegap project
  version              output version number

Additional Commands:

  local [command]      development on local system
  remote [command]     development in cloud with phonegap/build
  prepare <platforms>  copies www/ into platform project before compiling
  compile <platforms>  compiles platform project without preparing it
  emulate <platforms>  runs the project with the flag --emulator
  cordova              execute of any cordova command

Experimental Commands:

  Requires the --experimental flag to use the command

  save                 save installed platforms and plugins
  restore              restores saved platforms and plugins

Options:

  -d, --verbose        allow verbose output
  -v, --version        output version number
  -h, --help           output usage information

Examples:

  $ phonegap help create
  $ phonegap create path/to/my-app
  $ cd my-app/
  $ phonegap run ios
```

Figure 2-6. *PhoneGap help menu used in the command-line interface*

For even more information from the command line, run phonegap help <command>. For example, phonegap help create provides a full description of how to use the create command.

Creating a New PhoneGap Application

It's time to create your first PhoneGap application. All new PhoneGap projects start by using the create keyword. Before you get started, select a location on your computer where you intend on saving projects associated with this book. You can develop from any directory just as long as you keep it consistent and easy find. For example:

Windows

```
C:\Users\%USERNAME%\Apress\Chapter-2\
```

Mac

```
/Users/<username>/Documents/Apress/Chapter-2/
```

When you have a location that you're happy with, navigate to that folder in your terminal and execute `phonegap create <project name>` to create a new PhoneGap application. You can see an example for creating an application named `HelloWorld` in Listing 2-5.

Listing 2-5. Terminal Command for Creating a New PhoneGap Application Named "HelloWorld"

```
phonegap create HelloWorld
```

Executing the code in Listing 2-5 will create a new folder of the same name, for example, `C:\Users\%USERNAME%\Apress\Chapter-2\HelloWorld`. The contents inside are files and folders PhoneGap uses to build and compile the application. You'll need to navigate into this folder through the terminal to be able to run phonegap commands. You can do so by executing the change directory command followed by the folder name: `cd HelloWorld` (Windows and Mac).

PhoneGap "Hello World" Application

The `create` command will add a small sample application to your project folder. You can find the application files in the directory `HelloWorld/`**www**. Further details about files and folders inside the "Hello World" application will be described later. For the moment, the goal is to run this application on an Android and/or iOS simulator.

After creating a PhoneGap application, it's time to add a testing platform. To do so, run the command `phonegap platform add <platform>`. To add iOS and Android to your project, run the commands shown in Listing 2-6.

Listing 2-6. Adding Platforms to Existing PhoneGap Projects (iOS, Android)

```
phonegap platform add ios
phonegap platform add android
```

The command will create a directory for each platform in `./HelloWorld/platforms`. These directories will contain platform specific code and libraries as well as your JavaScript application, HTML, CSS, and image files.

Important rule for the `platforms` directory in advance: You should *never* change the contained files, or bad things may happen.

You can get a list of all installed and available platforms using `phonegap platform list`. Other `phonegap platform` commands include `update` and `remove` respectively. For more information, run `phonegap platform help`.

Building Applications

As explained in the introductory chapter, PhoneGap will compile your web application into a program that can run natively on a device. Executing `phonegap` **build** `<platform>` performs this operation. You will need to use the `build` command every time you change your web application code or when you add or remove a PhoneGap plug-in.

The first time you add a platform to a PhoneGap project, the application is ready to run. However, for testing purposes, use the build command for all platforms you added in the previous section, as shown in Listing 2-7.

Listing 2-7. Build the Application for the Targeted Operating System

```
phonegap build ios
phonegap build android
```

Running Applications

There are generally two different ways to run a PhoneGap application: using a simulator or a physical device. Because running your application on a device will require some additional work, let's focus on using a simulator for now. To install and run your application using a simulator, use the emulate command, as shown in Listing 2-8.

Listing 2-8. Start the Emulator from the Command Line Using the Targeted Device Name

```
phonegap emulate ios
phonegap emulate android
```

After a few moments, your system will do a few things:

1. Launch the simulator for the targeted platform

2. Compile and install the application on the simulator

3. Start the application

The application will show the PhoneGap icon followed by the message *Connecting to Device*. Once the app is fully loaded, the message will switch to *Device is Ready*. Figure 2-7 shows that the device is ready.

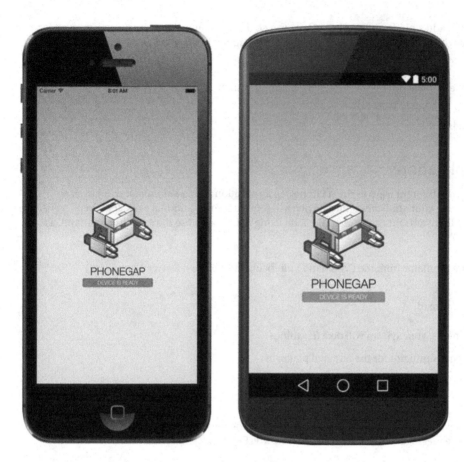

Figure 2-7. *The PhoneGap "Hello World" application on iPhone (left) and Android (right)*

Device Selection

If you have multiple virtual device configurations, you can pick one of them by running phonegap emulate android --target "{virtual-device-name}". Replace {virtual-device-name} with the name you picked in the AVD Manager.

To see a list of available simulators for iOS, execute ./platforms/ios/cordova/lib/list-emulator-images in the root of the project's directory. Common simulators are shown in Listing 2-9. Executing phonegap emulate android --target "{virtual-device-name}" will select which device simulator to launch.

Listing 2-9. Common List of Available Simulators for iOS

```
iPhone-4s
iPhone-5
iPhone-5s
iPhone-6-Plus
iPhone-6
iPad-2
```

```
iPad-Retina
iPad-Air
Resizable-iPhone
Resizable-iPad
```

Inside PhoneGap's "Hello World" Application

All PhoneGap projects created via the phonegap create command provide an introductory Hello World project.

This project contains the files and directory structures that PhoneGap uses to compile web application to platform specific applications. Each directory—and subdirectory—has its purpose. We'll explore the more important aspects of each directory in the following list. For detailed information, please refer to the official PhoneGap documentation http://docs.phonegap.com/en/edge.

- config.xml The config.xml file is used to define general project settings like the name of you application, the bundle ID for the app store, and author information. Listing 2-10 shows an example of this file. Check out an interactive guide by Developer Evangelist Holly Schinsky here: http://devgirl.org/files/config-app.

  For even more information, you can always visit the PhoneGap documentation at http://docs.phonegap.com/en/edge/guide_project-settings_index.md.html.

- hooks: The hooks directory is used to execute custom processes that occur **before** *and* **after** certain PhoneGap commands. As this is an advanced topic, it will not be covered in this book.

- platforms: Once you create a new PhoneGap project, the platforms folder is empty. Adding a new platform creates a directory of the same name, such as platforms/android for **Android**. Each subdirectory contains the code for its respective platform. Unless you know what you are doing or are instructed to do so, you should never change anything in the platforms directory.

- plugins: The plugins directory is used to add third-party plug-ins into your application. This can be used for enhancing your application's appearance or functionality. Plug-ins are typically platform-specific and should be used responsibly. It's always good to read a plug-in's documentation before introducing it into your project.

- www: The www folder is reserved for the application source code; it's where you'll write custom HTML, CSS, and JS.

Listing 2-10. An Example of a config.xml for PhoneGap Projects

```
<?xml version='1.0' encoding='utf-8'?>
<widget id="com.phonegap.helloworld" version="1.0.0" xmlns="http://www.w3.org/ns/widgets"
xmlns:gap="http://phonegap.com/ns/1.0">
    <name>Hello World</name>
    <description>
        Hello World sample application that responds to the deviceready event.
    </description>
    <author email="support@phonegap.com" href="http://phonegap.com">
        PhoneGap Team
    </author>
```

```
<content src="index.html" />
<preference name="target-device" value="universal" />
...
<access origin="*" />
</widget>
```

After creating a new PhoneGap project, a predefined set of files and folders are created for you. Figure 2-8 illustrates how a new PhoneGap application is structured.

Figure 2-8. *Directory structure the PhoneGap CLI creates when starting a new PhoneGap application*

To understand what is going on in this application, we turn our attention to index.html; this is where the scripts are used for this PhoneGap application. Just before the closing </body> tag, there are some script references to JavaScript files, as shown in Listing 2-11. There is also a call to a method named initialize on the app namespace.

Listing 2-11. Script Tags Used in the index.html File for the Sample Application Created with New PhoneGap Applications.

```
<script type="text/javascript" src="cordova.js"></script>
<script type="text/javascript" src="js/index.js"></script>
<script type="text/javascript">
app.initialize();
</script>
```

The first script tag reference is to a file named cordova.js. If you take a look at the files in the www folder (where you'd expect this file to be, given the path relative to index.html), cordova.js is missing. This is normal and expected.

After adding a platform to your application, the file will be located and accessed by PhoneGap inside one of the folders of the chosen platform, for example, ios/CordovaLib/cordova.js. This is one of the reasons that PhoneGap applications will not run inside a browser; PhoneGap uses this file internally after building platform specific files.

The next script tag is a reference to js/index.js that contains application code. Directly after this file reference is a call to an initialize method on the app namespace. This begins the application.

Main Application Script (index.js)

The index.js file in the "Hello World" application demonstrates the use of PhoneGap's most basic *event* function, deviceready. Listing 2-12 shows the full script (with original comments, beginning with forward slashes) used for the *Hello World* app.

Listing 2-12. The Code for Hello World That PhoneGap Provides When Creating a New Application

```
var app = {
    // Application Constructor
    initialize: function() {
        this.bindEvents();
    },
    // Bind Event Listeners
    //
    // Bind any events that are required on startup. Common events are:
    // 'load', 'deviceready', 'offline', and 'online'.
    bindEvents: function() {
        document.addEventListener('deviceready', this.onDeviceReady, false);
    },
    // deviceready Event Handler
    //
    // The scope of 'this' is the event. In order to call the 'receivedEvent'
    // function, we must explicitly call 'app.receivedEvent(...);'
    onDeviceReady: function() {
        app.receivedEvent('deviceready');
    },
    // Update DOM on a Received Event
    receivedEvent: function(id) {
        var parentElement = document.getElementById(id);
        var listeningElement = parentElement.querySelector('.listening');
        var receivedElement = parentElement.querySelector('.received');

        listeningElement.setAttribute('style', 'display:none;');
        receivedElement.setAttribute('style', 'display:block;');

        console.log('Received Event: ' + id);
    }
};
```

Although this code provides some helpful comments, let's dig a bit deeper and understand what's really going on.

To begin, notice that all the application code is contained within a variable of *type* object named app, the main namespace of this application. There are four functions that are *properties* of the app object. The order of the functions executed, beginning with the app.initialize() call from index.html, goes like this:

1. app.initialize: calls a function named bindEvents that is located on the app namespace (reference by this).

2. The bindEvents function adds an *event listener* to the document for the PhoneGap event deviceready.

3. When this event is triggered, it calls a function named onDeviceReady, located in the currently scoped object (app).

4. In onDeviceReady, a function named receiveEvent, which is a property of app, is executed. It is passed a single argument (of type *String*) deviceready.

5. The receivedEvent function then updates the appearance of the user interface to indicate that the program has loaded.

The visual representation is demonstrated in Figure 2-9.

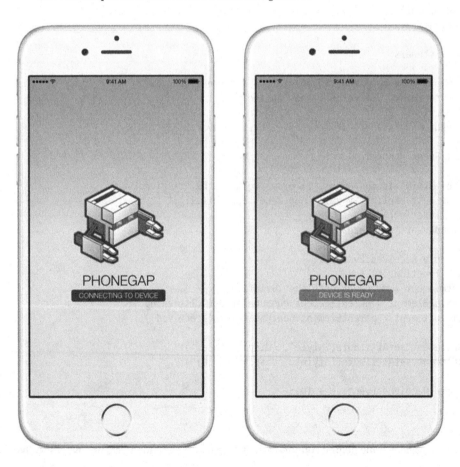

Figure 2-9. *The before-and-after appearance once the receivedEvent function executes*

Debugging PhoneGap Applications

An important part of any software development is the ability to debug: a process for finding flaws that affect a feature of a program. If there is an error, you'll want to know about it to be able to fix it.

PhoneGap offers a special challenge: debugging in more than one programming environment at the same time. Even though you'll be building your application in JavaScript, the use of plug-ins, invalid parameters, or any other mysterious bug might cause an issue inside your application's *native* layer (respectively Objective C [iOS] or Java [Android] for our purposes). Using tools like the console can provide you with important information about different areas of your program.

The native portions of PhoneGap applications already come with a built-in debugging system. Let's do the same for JavaScript debugging by installing the console plug-in.

Because we are building a PhoneGap application, we won't have access to the API programmatically as you normally would a global variable in a classic browser or web application.

While there are other elements we might want to debug, like the user interface, the first step focuses on the WebView's console API. After all, PhoneGap does run inside a native WebView. As you may already know from modern web browsers, the console.log command is available to developers for debugging JavaScript applications.

As with other PhoneGap plug-ins, you add them by navigating to the root directory of the project and executing phonegap plugin add <plugin name>.

In your terminal, add the console project to the *Hello World* application by navigating to the project root in your terminal and running phonegap plugin add org.apache.cordova.console.

This will download and install the plug-in from the cordova plug-in repository. Once installed, you can use it to debug your program during development. The following code demonstrates its usage:

```
var i = 0;
console.log(i); // Logs '0' to the console
```

You can also log multiple values at a time in one line by separating the values with commas:

```
var noun = 'world';
console.log('Hello', noun); // Logs 'Hello world' to the console
```

Using log messages is not a requirement of software development and is intended to aid you, the author, in debugging during development. Next, you will see the console plug-in in action with the *Hello World* app.

■ **Tip** Execute phonegap plugin ls to list all of the plug-ins installed in a PhoneGap project.

For platform quirks and other helpful information about the console plug-in, check out build. phonegap.com/plugins/1171.

Summary

This chapter focused on getting your development environment set up to program PhoneGap applications. Developing for iOS or Android applications has their own unique setup. Once everything is up and running, you'll be using a single code base to target multiple devices.

When creating a new PhoneGap application, a base project is automatically set up for you. Using the iOS or Android emulator, you were able to run this demo application.

CHAPTER 3

■ ■ ■

Beginning Parse

A cloud-based service that provides everything you need to build an app

With features like data storage, web hosting, push notifications, and SDKs ranging from iOS to Android, Parse (Figure 3-1) offers a complete infrastructure for developing dynamic applications. Other development kits include Windows/Windows Phone 8, Unity, and OS X. Using their PHP or JavaScript SDKs as a REST API can additionally provide an interface for data that can be used for CMS tools, middleware, or any database-driven application.

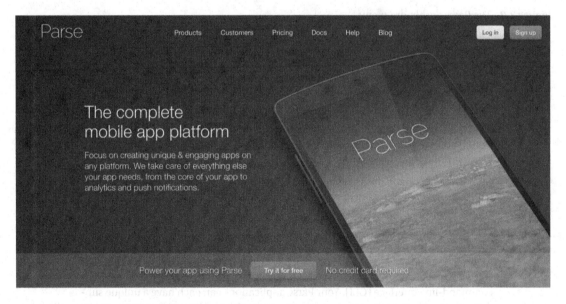

Figure 3-1. *The Parse home page*

Accessing and using data from a REST API using JavaScript isn't anything new. Creating API endpoints for delivering JSON objects is possible in virtually all programming languages. For example, using PHP you can create an API endpoint, for example, app/users/, that returns queried data as JSON strings, allowing JavaScript to consume it for a client application.

What makes Parse special is its ability to perform common database processes, like creating users and querying data, which allows developers to focus on manipulating application data. With all this power on the back end and an intuitive API, Parse makes a great choice for application development.

With the growing popularity of Node.js and npm modules, JavaScript is on its way to being the most flexible language for building native and web-based applications. You'll explore Parse's JavaScript API to build real-world applications, and you'll learn some tricks and techniques that you can integrate with PhoneGap.

Parse Features at a Glance

There are tons of awesome things about Parse that make it a unique platform to use to write applications. The following list highlights Parse's main features.

- *Cloud-based Service*: Internet connection required! Everything in Parse happens in the cloud. Instead of on a personal server, Parse securely stores your data in a high-performance and scalable manner.

- *Parse Dashboard*: Each Parse application you create has its own dashboard. This gives you access to things like browsing data and configuring settings (Figure 3-2). We'll go into more details later.

Figure 3-2. *The Parse dashboard menu*

- *Easy User Registration*: With just a few lines of code, you can quickly add users to your application. The Parse API comes standard with rich features like registration, user roles, logging in and out, email verification, a forgot password link, and a host of security features that can be tailored to your needs.

- *Cloud Code*: Creating recurring or scheduled executable scripts with Parse is a snap. If you take advantage of this feature, you can run server-side scripts without using the dashboard. You can send emails, push notifications, and run any server-side logic all while you're asleep.

- *Data Browser (Core)*: This is where you can create and view all of your application's data. You can create custom queries to filter out data as well as configure security setting for client permissions. The data browser is located in the ***Core*** section of the main menu, as depicted in Figure 3-2.

- *Hosting*: All web-based applications need a place to live. While you'll be building native mobile applications, which do not require any hosting space like classic web sites, Parse optionally provides the ability to host projects created with Parse's command-line interface (CLI). Your Parse applications can each have a unique sub-domain name that you can configure in the app's settings. Hosting is *not* required for using the Parse SDKs.

  Parse applications have a base domain name of parseapp.com. So your application's domain name would look something like *my-parse-app.parseapp.com*. Don't want users seeing the base domain? You can configure your application to use a custom domain name in your applications *Hosting* section.

- *Analytics*: Curious about how well your application is doing? Each Parse application you create has its own analytics suite so you can keep track of what's going on (Figure 3-3). In order for an application to be successful, it's important to understand how people are using it. Using the Analytics tool, you can keep track of things like crashes and API requests.

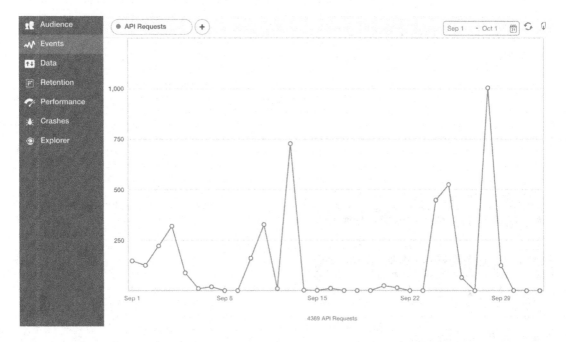

Figure 3-3. *Parse analytics*

- *Push Notifications*: Sending information to your users immediately with push notifications is a great way to directly engage them individually. This can add a new layer of interactivity to your next application. Parse offers this service through all their native and client SDKs, as well a REST API and web console interface.

  Using the Push Composer, anyone who can send an email can tactically distribute the message to their users via advanced message filters and scheduling options. You will also be able to create A/B tests among your users to get the best results for your applications services.

- *Background Jobs*: Let your application work behind the scenes by executing predefined functions exactly when you want to. This is useful for adding new products in batches, altering an existing data-sensitive Parse object, or even sending push notifications. Background jobs are also useful for data-heavy transactions associated with third-party resources such as importing external data.

- *Explorer*: Get a detailed, searchable analysis of your applications' API requests using the Parse Explorer. This tool allows you to visualize and query up-to-date API requests that have been made by your application's users. This level of understanding can help you improve your application's performance.

Creating and Setting Up a Parse Project

The first thing you need to get started with Parse is perhaps the most obvious: a new Parse account. Head over to `www.parse.com` and sign up (Figure 3-4) for your free account to begin. You can create one using your email address or using one of their single sign-on services, including Facebook, Google Plus, and GitHub.

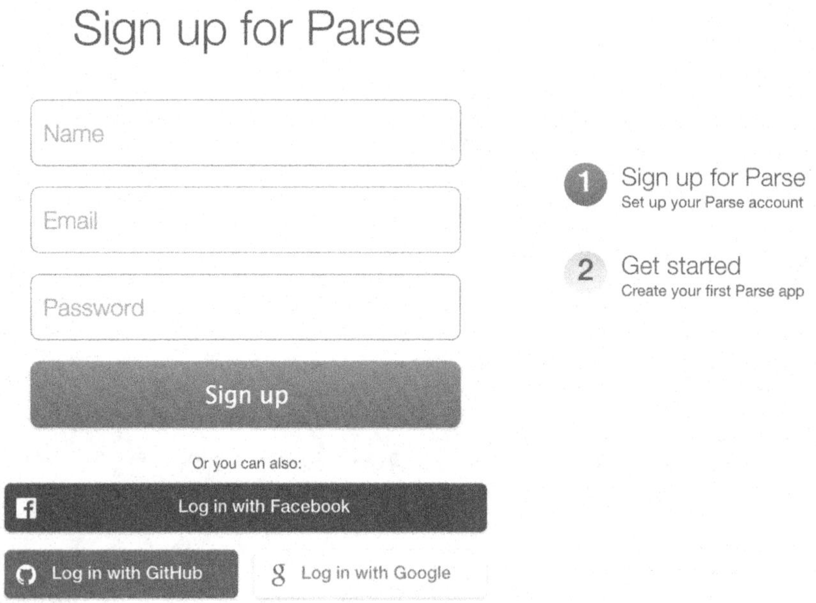

Sign up for Parse

Name

Email

Password

Sign up

Or you can also:

Log in with Facebook

Log in with GitHub   Log in with Google

1 Sign up for Parse
   Set up your Parse account

2 Get started
   Create your first Parse app

Figure 3-4. *Parse signup page*

After logging in, you will have the option to create a new Parse app. You can also visit `parse.com/apps` to create and manage Parse applications. This is where you access each of your application's settings and details, such as Analytics and Cloud Code.

You will be asked to pick a name for your app. As you'll soon notice on your journey into programming (or if you already have programming experience, you already know), naming things can be hard. To help things move along, name your application "CRUD" because we'll be using this application to demonstrate the basics of relational database actions using Parse. There are four major database operations: **C**reate, **R**ead, **U**pdate, **D**elete (CRUD).

Once you create the app, click its name (Figure 3-5) to view its details. This will take you into a view that has everything associated with your newly created app. From the main navigation, select the *Settings* icon, as previously shown in Figure 3-2, and examine the configuration options.

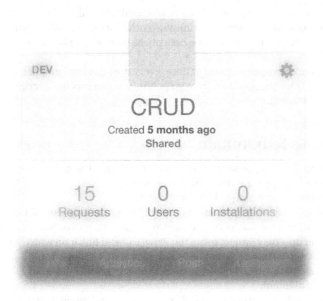

Figure 3-5. *A Parse application named CRUD*

Web Hosting

There are many important sections in the *Settings* area of your Parse application. For now, you are interested in the *Hosting* (Figure 3-6) section. Although not required for Parse applications, Parse offers the ability to host your applications for you. This is a great opportunity for you to experiment and publish applications live to the Web. An advantage to using this feature is if your application is installed on a user's phone. Once installed, updates can be made without having to update the application.

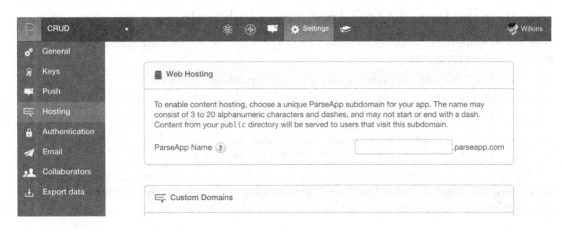

Figure 3-6. *The Web Hosting section of a Parse app*

Frictionless updates are done by executing code on the server side through Cloud Code, all while the application code is running locally on a device. For example, if you are running a private beta release of your app using a project hosted on Parse, you can inform the app whether the beta phase is public or private by executing a script from Parse's Cloud Code.

Each state can trigger a unique user experience you create ahead of time. Every time the app launches, it can check the beta status via an HTTP request. Once the app is ready to go public, you can execute a script hosted on Parse that will do the job and make the switch.

Configuring a Parse Application's Subdomain

Let's first configure your application's URL in the Web Hosting section of your app's settings. Once you publish your code using the Parse command line interface, the *ParseApp Name* (see Figure 3-6) you choose will be associated with your Parse application. An example URL would look like this: your-custom-subdomain.parseapp.com. Pick a name for this application that will be used as a subdomain.

If you visit the domain for your application right now, you will see a blank page. You haven't published any code yet! In the next section, you'll locally set up a new project using the Parse CLI and link it up with your newly created Parse application. Just as PhoneGap has a starter application, Parse's CLI allows you to quickly start a default project using its own base template. It should be noted that Parse and PhoneGap starter projects and their contents are *completely* different.

After creating an application at parse.com, you have the option to link its data from a folder on your computer. When using the Parse CLI to link to an existing Parse application, you can deploy the project right from the command line.

■ **Note**   Linking your project locally using the Parse CLI isn't required for using the Parse API. However, it is a great starting point for exploring Parse and some of the cool functions available with the command line interface.

Installing the Parse CLI for Application Publishing

Next, you install the Parse command-line tools. This will enable you to do things like generate sample projects and deploy applications.

- *Max/Linux*: Run the following code to install the command line dev tools:

  ```
  curl -s https://www.parse.com/downloads/cloud_code/installer.sh |
  sudo /bin/bash
  ```

- *Windows*: Download an executable file that installs the tools for you from http://parse.com/downloads/windows/console/parse.zip.

Now that you've successfully installed the Parse CLI, you'll create a new project and build on it in this chapter. To ensure that you have the Parse CLI properly installed, run the following script in the command line:

```
parse help
```

The help command will bring up a list of available commands based on the version of Parse you are running. If you have previously installed Parse, you can run parse update to get the latest version of the tool.

Setting Up Folders

The Parse JavaScript library is just like any third-party JS library in that it needs to be referenced in your HTML page in order to use. However, Parse also offers a command-line tool that has some cool features that you'll explore next.

When starting a new web-based project, there are numerous ways to organize the structure of files. As with the starter PhoneGap application, Parse has a pre-defined folder structure that is created when starting a new project using the CLI.

Before getting started, select or create a folder on your computer where you'll keep projects associated with this book. For example,

- *Windows*: `C:\Users\%USERNAME%\Apress\Chapter-3\`

- *Mac*: `/Users/<username>/Documents/Apress/Chapter-3`

Creating a New Project

As you did in Chapter 2, navigate to the path you want to use in your terminal. Now create a new Parse project in the current directory, using the CRUD application created earlier. Create a new project by executing the following code:

```
parse new CRUD
```

This will create a new folder named CRUD in your current directory. The command prompt will then ask you to log into Parse using your credentials. You will be presented a list of Parse applications that are associated with your account (Figure 3-7).

```
→ apress  parse new CRUD
Creating a new project in directory /Users/Wil/Documents/Sites/apress/CRUD
Creating directory /Users/Wil/Documents/Sites/apress/CRUD/config
Creating config file /Users/Wil/Documents/Sites/apress/CRUD/config/global.json
Creating directory /Users/Wil/Documents/Sites/apress/CRUD/cloud
Writing out sample file /Users/Wil/Documents/Sites/apress/CRUD/cloud/main.js
Creating directory /Users/Wil/Documents/Sites/apress/CRUD/public
Writing out sample file /Users/Wil/Documents/Sites/apress/CRUD/public/index.html
Email: █
```

Figure 3-7. *Creating and authenticating a new Parse project using the CLI*

You are interested in syncing the CRUD application. Once you have completed this process, navigate into the new folder through your terminal using the *change directory* command, followed by the name of the folder, like so:

```
cd CRUD
```

Once inside this folder, list the folders using the terminal and see what just happened. On Windows, the command is `dir`. On Mac, it's `ls`.

Running the command from inside the newly created Parse project will reveal three directories with files in them, as shown in Figure 3-8.

Figure 3-8. *The file and directory structure of a starter Parse project*

About Parse Project Files and Folders

When creating a new Parse project from the command line, three folders are automatically created for you. You'll edit these to create and publish a custom application.

- Configuration: The config/global.json (json is pronounced like the first name "Jason") file (see Figure 3-8) contains automatically populated details about the current project, like the name and the associated keys. You can also find these values in your Parse account in the Application Keys section of an application.

- Cloud Code: There is a folder called cloud with a sample file in it. The code in this folder is used for Parse's Cloud Code. It is exactly what you might expect: code that runs in the cloud. The word *cloud* here refers to Parse's servers on the Internet. Parse handles all of your app's server-side processes using files in this folder.

- Public: The public folder is associated with your application code. The index.html file is the default page for the current directory. The URL associated with the current Parse application will redirect to the public directory, making the index file the home page.

Deploying a Parse Project

Because you choose to use the Parse CLI to create and sync your application, you now have the ability to publish it to the live URL you configured in the *Web Hosting* section of the app.

To deploy a Parse project, ensure that you are located at the root (the parent folder named CRUD). In the command line, execute the following:

```
parse deploy
```

This will start an upload sequence that will send your project files to Parse. After it is complete, navigate to the URL that you created for this application and test it. See Figure 3-9.

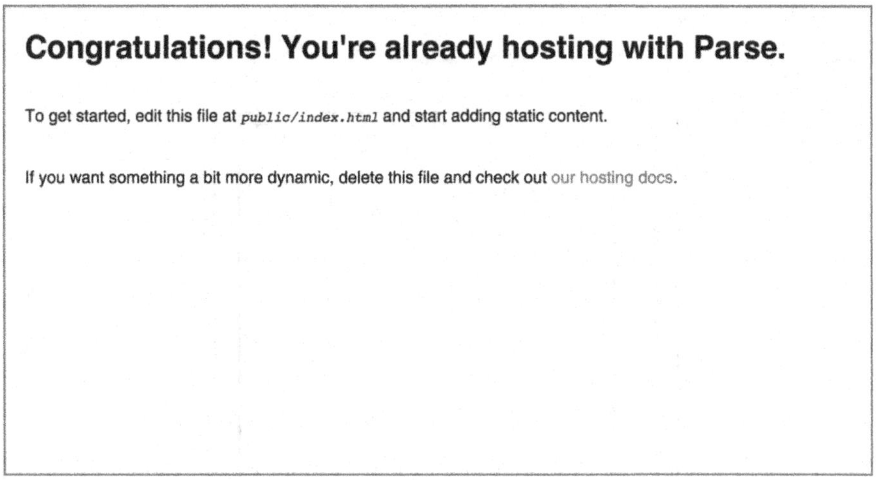

Figure 3-9. *The home page that comes with Parse projects created using the CLI*

For the rest of this chapter, you'll build an HTML5-based web site that will help illustrate the four core database operations using Parse.

Building a CRUD Application

The next project you'll create involves basic data entry and editing of content. You will use the Parse starter project as a base template. After removing some boilerplate code from index.html, you'll populate it with custom elements and styles. The user interface will need to display existing records and also provide the ability to create new and edit existing database records.

After all HTML objects load, you'll want to initialize the program and sync the application to Parse. You then will bind the form elements to functions that will communicate with Parse and update the user interface with new content.

There are four primary database functions that this application will demonstrate:

- *Creating*: See "Creating a new Record"

- *Retrieving*: See "Retrieving Existing Records"

- *Updating*: See "Updating Records"

- *Deleting*: see "Deleting Records"

Once the form is submitted, the UI will update by adding the form's value to an unordered list tag (<ul>) as a list item (<li>). At this point, you will then attempt to save the entry to Parse.

Why update the display, and then save to Parse? Because doing so provides a better user experience and gives the feeling of a quick and snappy application. Whether the data is saved successfully or not, you will update the list item style with a CSS class that will indicate the status of the record.

You'll be using the HTML5 contentEditable attribute on the li so that when an item is selected, it will toggle the main menu to reveal a secondary menu for editing. Figure 3-10 demonstrates the before and after states.

Figure 3-10. *Screens for reading and creating new records (left), and editing view (right) when an item is selected*

Updating index.html of the Parse Starter Project

Before getting into the JavaScript, let's first update the index.html file by adding some custom user interface elements. This demo project will have minimal style and is designed mobile-first.

You will optimize for mobile devices but won't affect the display on non-mobile browsers by adding a custom meta tag to the head of the HTML document. The values you use for the content attribute of the meta tag scales the width of the screen in CSS pixels to 100%.

Add a meta tag after the <title> tag in the index.html page with the following code:

```
<meta name="viewport" content="width=device-width, initial-scale=1">
```

■ **Tip** There are other properties that can be added to control the viewport (see "Creating a New PhoneGap Application" in Chapter 2 for comparison). For example, you can disable pinching and zooming on a touchscreen device by adding maximum-scale=1 to the existing **width** value.

Remove all of the custom styles contained within the `<style>` tag. You will add minimal custom styles later. Start from scratch and remove everything inside the body tag.

Adding Custom UI Elements

The HTML5 `section` and `footer` tags contain your UI elements. The section contains your list of editable records, while the footer houses the form and its elements. Replace the contents of the body tag in the `index.html` file with the code in Listing 3-1.

Listing 3-1. The HTML Used for the User Interface

```
<section>
  <ul class="record-list"></ul>
</section>

<section class="form-container">
  <form>
    <textarea id="test-input" placeholder="Create a new record!"></textarea>
    <button id="btn-add">Create</button>
    <div id="edit-panel" class="hide">
      <button id="btn-update">Update</button>
      <button id="btn-delete">Delete</button>
      <button id="btn-cancel">Cancel</button>
    </div>
  </form>
</section>
```

Adding Script References

To use the Parse API, you need to include it in your HTML page as a script source. You also want some custom JavaScript, so you include a reference to a file that has *yet* to be created.

Instead of saving the Parse JavaScript library to your project and referencing it locally, you use the Parse CDN to deliver the script. Add the following snippet just before the body tag:

```
<script type="text/javascript" src="http://www.parsecdn.com/js/parse-1.4.2.min.js"></script>
<script type="text/javascript" src="js/app.js"></script>
```

Customizing CSS

Before creating the `js/app.js` file, let's get the presentation layer out of the way. After adding the HTML elements and script references to `index.html`, preview this page in your web browser. Notice two things:

1. The page looks boring.

2. There is a script reference error (`js/app.js` doesn't exist yet).

Add the CSS (Listing 3-2) styles for the CRUD application between the head tags of `index.html`.

Listing 3-2. CSS Styles for the CRUD Application

```
<style>
  body {
    font-family: Helvetica, Arial, sans-serif;
    margin: 0;
  }
  ul li:nth-child(2n) {
    background: #f9f9f9;
  }
  ul {
    padding: 0;
    margin: 0;
  }
  li {
    padding: 10px;
  }
  section.form-container {
    position: absolute;
    bottom: 0;
    background-color: #F7F7F7;
    border-top: 1px solid #000;
    width: 100%;
    height: 40%;
  }
  section {
    position: absolute;
    height: 60%;
    overflow: scroll;
    width: 100%;
  }
  form {
    margin: 3%;
  }
  textarea {
    margin-bottom: 2%;
    width: 50%;
    display: block;
  }
  .msg-processing {
    color: #ccc;
  }
  #btn-delete,
  .msg-warn {
    color: red;
  }
  button {
    padding: 2%;
  }
  #btn-update {
    color: green;
  }
```

```
    .hide {
      display: none;
    }
    .show {
      display: block;
    }
</style>
```

After saving your styles, refresh this page in your browser to make sure it all looks OK. At this point, nothing exciting is happening yet. In the next section, you'll start adding some custom JavaScript and communicating with Parse.

Creating a JavaScript Application File

You will only use one JavaScript file for this application. Create a new folder inside the public folder named js with a file called app.js. For example, public/js/app.js.

Start off by creating an initialize function. This function is called when the elements on the page have loaded. The following code snippet is an empty initialize function gets called when the DOMContentLoaded event is triggered:

```
function initialize() {
    // Intentionally empty
}
document.addEventListener('DOMContentLoaded', function (event) {
  initialize();
});
```

Initializing Parse

The first thing you need to do in any Parse application is *initialize* it. Use the Parse.initialize function from the Parse API to sync the code with your application. The Parse.initialize() function takes two parameters: Application ID and JavaScript Key.

The values used for this function can be found in the Settings ➤ Keys section of your application on parse.com. Each key is unique per Parse application. Because the initialize function is the first thing that gets called when the application starts, you want to put your Parse.initialize function call there. The following code updates the initialize function with a call to the Parse.initialize function:

```
function initialize() {
  // Initialize Parse application
  Parse.initialize('your-application-id','your-javascript-key');
}
```

At this point in the application, when the DOMContentLoaded event is triggered, you call the initialize function that uses the Parse API to connect to your application. Next, you create and save a new record to Parse, and then preview it using the *Data Browser*.

Extending a Parse.Object

Parse.Object is the essential interface for storing and reading data. It allows you to execute an AJAX request and other methods to write or read data from the database. A Parse.Object is mostly identical to a classic database schema that has tables, columns, and rows. However, Parse objects are *schemaless*, meaning they have no predefined structure. When you add a property to an instance of a Parse object, it will infer upon the data and create it for you.

For example, if you only have one field, as you do in this application, and you later want to add a new field, Parse will automatically add the field to the subclass. Records without the new field will be empty, but can be populated by updating the record.

Properties of Parse objects are synonymous to field names in a traditional database. Create a new instance of Parse.Object and name it ParseObject; this can be considered the name of a table:

```
var TestObject = Parse.Object.extend('ParseObject');
```

■ **Tip**   The TestObject variable should be available to all functions inside the app.js file. To do this, make sure to declare it outside the scope of any functions, like at the top of the file for example.

Saving to Parse

A newly-created Parse object inherits all abilities of the Parse.Object class, like saving, deleting, fetching, and updating records. It also simultaneously creates a reference to your ParseObject table.

For this application, you'll only deal with one subclass in your database. You can create new subclasses on the fly with Parse by default. This is helpful when users (such as yourself while writing this application) need to create a new class.

■ **Note**   When you're ready to share your application with the world in a production environment, you may not want your application to create unauthorized classes because it's an easy way for malicious code to be executed and possibly corrupt existing data. To prevent this, update the App Permissions (Figure 3-11) in the General section of your application's Settings.

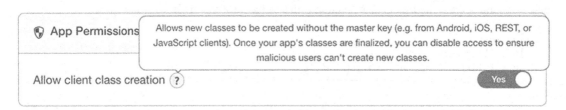

Figure 3-11. *App Permissions*

After creating a reference to your class, follow up with a new variable reference to the input form field that will contain the content for each record. The input variable should also be made global and thus available to other functions in app.js:

```
var input = document.getElementById('test-input');
```

CRUD Preparation

As stated, this application will demonstrate the four primary database operations. Let's create another variable and assign it four properties to empty functions. You'll populate this variable as you continue. Create a new variable below input named crud, a placeholder variable (Listing 3-3) that is an object literal that will be used for database functions.

Listing 3-3. An Object with Placeholder Function Names

```
var crud = {
  create: function () {
  },
  retrieve: function () {
  },
  update: function () {
  },
  delete: function () {
  }
};
```

Adding Event Listener

To submit the form data to Parse, you need to bind an action to the click event of the form's add button (#btn-add). Place all form bindings in your initialize function. The following code is a call to the function crud.create to btn-add:

```
document.getElementById('btn-add').addEventListener('click', function(event) {
    event.preventDefault();
    crud.create();
});
```

The Event [event] interface represents any event of the DOM. It contains common properties and methods to any event. To prevent the form from submitting and refreshing the page, use the preventDefault method of the event.

Creating a New Record

There are two main sections to the crud.**create** function: updating the user interface with the addition of a list item, and then saving the data to Parse. Before getting to any of that, first make sure it's worth the effort by checking to see if there is a value in the form input field.

Adding Safeguard Before Creating New Record

To ensure that you have something to save to Parse, only execute the create function if there is a value in the input field. The following code stops the function from continuing if there is no value in the input field:

```
create: function () {
  if (input.value === '') {
    return;
  }
}
```

■ **Note** The word "create" is a reserved word for JavaScript objects. In this code, you are overwriting this method with your own. It normally isn't good practice to do this in a real-world application because the effects may be damaging. It's done here for demonstration purposes only: to emphasize the *create* functionality of CRUD commands.

Updating the User Interface

If there *is* a value in the field, the script will continue on executing anything *after* the if condition blocks. Here you instantiate a new Parse object. You then update the ul by adding a child element, an li, with the contents of the value property on the input element.

Using the CSS classes defined earlier, you also add the msg-processing style to indicate to the user that the content is waiting to be saved to Parse. Using the HTML5 contentEditable attribute, you use the list item as an input field for updating and destroying records.

■ **Tip** The contentEditable attribute turns any HTML element into an editable piece of content.

The following snippet creates a new list item with the contents of the form input and appends it to the list. Update the create function with the following:

```
var li = document.createElement('li');
li.innerHTML = input.value;
li.className = 'msg-processing';
li.contentEditable = true;
document.querySelector('.record-list').appendChild(li);
```

Test this out right now and see what happens. When you create a new item, it is added to the list and styled using a CSS class. The value in the input field is still populated with content. For a better experience, you want to clear the form after an item is added.

After adding a few items to the list, refreshing the page will reveal that the content you added wasn't persistently stored anywhere. Let's change that next by saving the data to Parse.

Instantiating Parse Object

To save the input data to Parse, you instantiate a new TestObject (created earlier), which is associated with your ParseObject subclass, and assign it to the variable testObject.

Notice the differences in the spelling of the first character of the test object variable(s). Parse recommends naming references to subclasses beginning with an *UpperCase*, versus an instantiated reference ("keys") to it in *lowerCase*. The following instantiates TestObject with a variable of the same name, but starting with a lowercase letter. Declare a new variable testObject (the following snippet) outside of the create function scope, like so:

```
var testObject = new TestObject();
```

Saving to Parse

The variable testObject now has a *save* method. It takes three parameters, and the last two are always the same: success and error callback functions. The first parameter depends on how you plan on setting the values you want to save.

There are a few ways to *set* a property on a Parse object. The most basic way is by using the inherited set method with the name of the property and its value as parameters:

```
testObject.set('foo', input.value);
```

Setting the data doesn't mean it is saved to Parse yet. The save method must be called on testObject in order to actually save the data.

The save method also has way to set and save the property in one function call. In this version, you use a JavaScript object literal as the first parameter of save that represent the data to be saved. The remaining two parameters are, as expected, the success and error functions. Use this method to save the form data.

Success and Error Callback Functions

If the object is successfully saved to Parse, you want to clear the class of the list item and add an id attribute equal to the automatically generated Parse ID. At this point in the program, you want to clear the input field so that a user can enter a new record.

In an event of an error, you log it to the console and update the list item's class to indicate there was an error saving the record. Use the value of the list item (HTML5 editable element) as the value for the property foo. Edit the create function with code in Listing 3-4.

Listing 3-4. CSS Styles for the CRUD Application

```
testObject.save({
  foo: li.innerHTML
}, {
  success: function (object) {
    console.log('success!', object);
    // Reset the ID to the Parse object ID
    li.setAttribute('id', object.id);
    // Reset class, and make editable, and clear form value
    li.className = '';
    li.contentEditable = true;
    input.value = '';        },
```

```
  error: function (object, error) {
    console.warn('Could not create object.');
    console.warn(object, error);
    li.className = 'msg-warn';
  }
```

Error Handling

It's often good to know what the error was so you can properly respond to the user. You can do that by inspecting the second argument of the error function, error. It has a property named code where you can compare the error **code** to predefined Parse Error codes and display a custom message if desired. The following code can be appended to the error function:

```
if (error.code === Parse.Error.CONNECTION_FAILED) {
  console.warn('Could not connect to Parse Cloud.');
}
```

Try refreshing the page. There's nothing new on the unordered list. However, the console logs reveal that the data was saved to a Parse object. You need to retrieve the records in order display them to the user. First, let's check out the Data Browser and see the test records.

Data Browser

While logged into your Parse account, go to the Core section of the CRUD app. This will open a view of all the data for the application. See Figure 3-12 as an example.

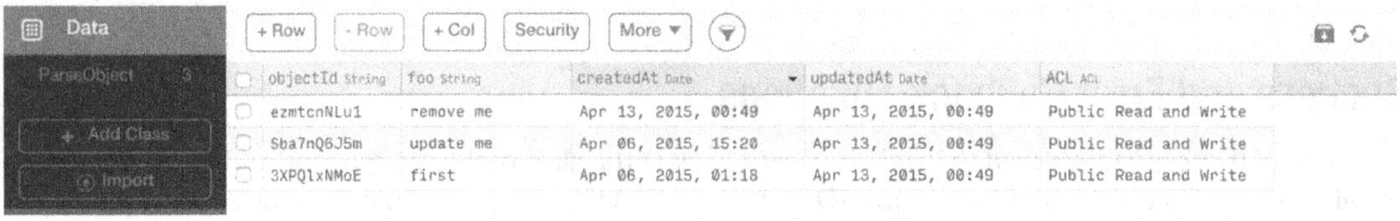

Figure 3-12. *View of the content for the CRUD application using Parse's Data Browser*

Within this section, you can add, remove, and edit records directly in the browser. This is useful if you want to structure the data scheme of an application before any coding. You can create new classes, along with custom fields.

When creating a new record for the first time, Parse adds a set of fields in your database automatically:

- objectId: A unique identifier for each saved entry

- createdAt: Represents when the record was created

- updatedAt: Represents when the record was modified

- ACL: Permissions attached to the record. This is used for security purposes.

Having these fields created for you is added by Parse as a convenience. The objectId will ensure that each record in your class is uniquely identifiable. This can be used for things like displaying data for a single product of many products that are part of a collection. The createdAt and updatedAt fields can be used for querying data like sorting by dates, date ranges of records, and much more.

■ **Tip** Importing and exporting data into an existing Parse application is simple. You can export your application's data from the Export data section in the Settings page of your application on `Parse.com`. Importing is done from the Data Browser (see Figure 3-12)

CLASS TYPES

There are five unique types of Parse classes. The `ParseObject` class created for the CRUD application is the most complex, as it is a custom class created by you.

The remaining default classes are as follows:

- `Installation`: The `Installation` class is a special class that stores push notification subscriptions for each device running your app.

- `Product`: The `Product` class is a special class that stores your in-app product data.

- `Role`: The `Role` class is a special class that allows you to specify groups of users with shared permissions.

- `User`: The `User` class is a special class that can be authenticated, allowing users of your app to log in, sign up, and more.

Retrieving Existing Records

Now it's time to populate the user interface so that when the page loads, the data saved in Parse will be retrieved. The data browser allowed you to confirm that the form input was saving, so that's a good. You'll use this data to populate the app's interface next.

It starts by creating a new *query* for the data. If Parse successfully connects and retrieves the content, you will update the HTML `<ul>` tag by adding child nodes (`<li>`) with data returned from the query.

The `crud.`**`retrieve`** function will be called when the application loads. It will also serve the purpose of repopulating the user interface after the user updates a record.

Parse.Query Object

There are several types of queries that you can run against your application data. In order to search for any data, a Parse object must be instantiated. You created one earlier using `Parse.Object.extend()` and referenced it using the variable `TestObject`.

The `Parse.Query` function takes one parameter: a Parse object class. Creating a new `Parse.Query` object allows you to put conditions on it and retrieve an array of records that match the query.

To create a new query object, declare and assign a new variable named **query**. You will use it again in another function call, so it needs to be declared *outside* of the `crud.create` function scope.

■ **Tip** Variables that you intend to be available for functions declared inside a parent scope should be declared at the top of the function.

After the declaration and assignment of TestObject, create a new Parse.Query object using TestObject:

```
var query = new Parse.Query(TestObject);
```

Here you use the Parse object TestObject to run query functions on. The variable query now has methods that enable you to find and filter data on the ParseObject class.

You will use the find method to query records in your database. It will return an object that you will refer to inside the success function scope as object.

Updating crud.retrieve

Using the find query method, you iterate through the returned object and populate the UI with the records from the ParseObject class. Listing 3-5 shows the code for crud.retrieve, which adds new list items to the unordered list based on the query.

Listing 3-5. Adding New List Items to the Unordered List Based on the Query

```
query.find({
  success: function (records) {
    var frag = document.createDocumentFragment();
    records.forEach(function (record) {
      var li = document.createElement('li');
      li.innerHTML = record.get('foo');
      li.id = record.id;
      li.contentEditable = true;
      frag.appendChild(li);
    });
    ul.appendChild(frag);
  },
  error: function (object, error) {
    console.warn('Could not retrieve records.', error);
  }
});
```

First, you create a new document fragment that will contain the data for each record. A document fragment can be thought of as a branch with leaves that can be appended to a tree. The forEach array method will iterate through each of the records. You use record as a reference to the current Parse object inside the loop. Inside the loop, you create a new list element and assign some properties to it.

You use the get method of the returned object to get the value of the 'foo' attribute. This is used to populate the list item's content.

Within the forEach loop, you create a new list element and apply add the id attribute equal to the unique Parse object id (objectId). You will use the object id later to update and delete a record.

Testing Record Retrieval

Now that you have a way to retrieve records from your Parse class, you need to update the initialize function to call the retrieve function so the UI can populate when the page loads. Add the following function call inside initialize, after Parse.initialize():

```
crud.retrieve();
```

Extending Queries

The CRUD application at this point only has a few test records in the ParseObject class. Querying data from such a small sample is great for demoing and testing code. Let's explore how to query data on a handful of objects out of hundreds, thousands, or even millions of records!

Parse's JavaScript API makes searching for data feel intuitive, using methods that make sense for what you're trying to accomplish. You use the query variable, an instance of Parse.Query, to call upon methods that will help you find data. In crud.retrieve, you use the find method to execute a query.

Query Methods

In Structured Query Language (SQL, pronounced "sequel"), a "where" clause allows you to query for specific data based on a key and value. For example, if you want to return all records from the Products table where the price is less than 100, the code looks as follows:

```
SELECT *
FROM Products
WHERE price < 100;
```

The previous SQL statement can be written in Parse like this:

```
var Products = new Parse.Object.extend('Products');
var queryProducts = new Parse.Query(Products);
queryProducts.lessThan('price', 100);
```

When using an instance of Parse.Query there are tons of methods available that will help you get the exact data you want. Some other "equal" style Parse.Query methods include

- lessThanOrEqualTo

- greaterThanOrEqualTo

- notEqualTo

The following exercise requires the CRUD application to have more than one test record in the database. Add some sample content and get ready to query!

Querying for Data

This will demonstrate how to search example data using Parse. Use the value first as the key value to search in the database.

Add a new test record to the database where 'foo' is set to string value 'first'. In the crud.**retrieve** function, update the query by using the contains method. Add this before the call to query.find:

```
retrieve: function () {
  query.contains('foo', 'first');
  query.find({
    success: function(results){
    // 'results' is an array of Parse.Object
    },
```

```
    error: function(errorObject, errorMsg){
      // errorObject is an instance of Parse.Error
    }
  });
}
```

Refresh the page and observe the results. Records that contain the substring 'first' for the key 'foo' are returned. Add a new record with the string 'first' in it (for example, 'who is first?'), and then refresh and observe that more than one record contains the substring 'first'.

Comment out the query.contains function call, save, and then refresh. Observe all the records are now returned.

You used one of the methods available on Parse.Query, contains, to narrow the results of your dataset. For a complete list of available query methods (over 30!), check out the full documentation at http://www.parse.com/docs/js/api/symbols/Parse.Query.html.

Sorting Results

There may come a time when you want to sort the returned results from a query. The Parse.Query object has some convenient methods that do just that.

As you saw with the contains method, query methods are used before the call to find records. Using the ascending or descending methods on a query, you're able to return query results in order. For example, to sort records by the time the record was created, you can use query.ascending('createdAt').

■ **Tip** By default, Parse returns a limit of 100 records. You can increase this limit up to 1,000 by using the limit method, like so:

query.limit(10);

Updating Records

A record first needs to exist before it can be edited. After adding a few sample objects to the database, it's time to **update** them.

You know that there is an update button (#btn-update) in the HTML form; it's located inside a hidden div tag with other edit buttons. Before you add an event handler to it, create a new function to perform a function on a Parse object. This will allow you to select and update a record from the list.

Create a new function named getParseObject. It will take two arguments: a Parse object ID, and a callback function that will use the returned Parse object as a parameter. Use the get method of Parse.Query to select a single record:

```
function getParseObject(parseObjectId, fn) {
  query.get(parseObjectId, {
    success: function (object) {
      fn(object);
    },
    error: function (data, error) {
      console.warn(data, error);
    }
  });
}
```

Use the id that you set in `crud.retrieve` to pass to `getParseObject` for record selection. First, you add an event listener to the update button. When clicked, the current value for the data attribute `parseid` from the input is passed to `crud.update`. It is used to update the currently selected record:

```
document.getElementById('btn-update').addEventListener('click', function (event) {
  event.preventDefault();
  getParseObject(input.dataset.parseid, crud.update);
});
```

Reset the Form

Next, create a simple utility function to restore the form back to its original view. Since it will be used a few times in your application, breaking out the functionality into its own function provides you an easy way to reset the view.

Create a new function named `resetForm`, as demonstrated in the following listing. It simply updates the class names on a few DOM elements, as well as clears the input value and the data attribute that you use to associate with a selected record:

```
function resetForm() {
  editPanel.className = 'hide';
  btnAdd.className = 'show';
  input.className = 'show';
  input.dataset.parseid = '';
  input.value = '';
}
```

Update crud.update

Updating Parse objects couldn't be simpler. All you need to do is save a Parse object with new properties or values. Next, *update* the update method using the code in Listing 3-6.

Listing 3-6. Updating an Existing Record with the Content From the List Item

```
update: function (parseObject) {
  var li = document.getElementById(parseObject.id);
  parseObject.save({
    'foo': li.textContent
  }, {
    success: function () {
      removeDOMNode(parseObject.id);
      // Repopulate list items
      crud.retrieve();
      resetForm();
      li.contentEditable = true;
    },
    error: function (data, error) {
      document.getElementById(parseObject.id).className = 'msg-warn';
      console.warn('Could not update.', error);
    }
  });
}
```

Using the save method as you did in crud.create, you do the same, except this time you use the returned Parse object from the get method used in getParseObject function.

The crud.update function takes one argument: a Parse object. If the update is successful, you repopulate the list elements by calling crud.retrieve, and then reset the form so the user can start over.

If there is an error when updating the record, the error function will add a class to the DOM node to indicate to the user that the update has failed.

Editing an Item

In order to properly select an item from the list for editing, you need to add some code to handle it. Create a new function named editItem and populate it with the following code:

```
function editItem(event) {
  if (event.target.parentNode.className === 'record-list') {
    input.dataset.parseid = event.target.id;
    btnAdd.className = 'hide';
    input.className = 'hide';
    editPanel.className = 'show';
  }
}
```

In order to put this function to use, you need to bind it to an event. Adding the following event listener to the initialize function listens for events on items that get added to the list:

```
document.querySelector('body').addEventListener('click', function (event) {
  event.preventDefault();
  editItem(event);
});
```

Before continuing, let's get an understanding of what the two previous code snippets are actually doing. In the previous snippet, you add an event to the body tag. Although it may seem odd, it allows you to listen to all click events that *may* occur at a later time in the life of the application (versus its state when the page loads). Inside this function, you call the editItem function and pass the current event as an argument.

Now turn your attention to the editItem function call. Using the passed-in argument event, you determine what the parent node is by checking if it has a specific class name assigned to it. If the parent node has a class of record-list, then you continue with the function.

When a user selects a list element, you use the current records ID and store it in a data attribute of the input. This way, you can keep track of what record the user intends on updating.

Why all the fuss for this particular event? If you were to add an event listener using a CSS selector for a li element in your list (and not the body tag), it will only bind to what currently exists at the time of the binding.

Because you are dynamically populating the list, you need a way to bind an event to *future* li elements. By listening to the body tag for clicks, and narrowing your scope by checking the parent node, you can bind your function to current *and* future elements that have yet to be on the page. Pretty nifty, huh?

Testing the Update Function

Try updating any existing records using your HTML interface. Everything *seems* to work fine; however, after successfully updating a record, a duplicate of the updated entry still exists in the DOM. The success function calls crud.retrieve to get the latest results, but a local copy of the item still exists after the user creates a new record. So let's create a small function that will remove an element from the DOM.

■ **Note** Repopulating the entire DOM isn't always the best approach when dealing with updating content. There are numerous frameworks, libraries, and techniques to go about gracefully updating content in real time. For instance, frameworks like React JS use what's known as virtual DOM to quickly compare the updated DOM versus the one in memory, allowing only the element required to update. This is a huge performance gain versus repopulating the DOM. If you are curious to learn more, Parse also implements ReactJS seamlessly! Learn more at `https://github.com/ParsePlatform/ParseReact`

Removing DOM Node

This function's only purpose is to delete a DOM node based on its id. It will take only one parameter, the id of the element to be removed:

```
function removeDOMNode(id) {
  var node = document.getElementById(id);
  if (node.parentNode) {
    node.parentNode.removeChild(node);
  }
}
```

Finishing Touches

Now that you have a function that will help clean up the DOM, call it from success function of the save method in crud.update as follows. The following code adds a call to removeDOMNode and passes the Parse object id as a parameter:

```
// ...
success: function (data) {
  removeDOMNode(parseObject.id);
  // Repopulate list items
  crud.retrieve();
  resetForm();
},
// ...
```

Deleting Records

All things must come to an end, and to complete the four essential database operations using Parse, you need the ability to *delete* records.

Just like crud.update, you need to know which record is being requested for deletion. You will reuse the getParseObject function again to return the record you want to delete. Because the editItem function keeps track of which record is selected, you only need to add a few more lines to finish this application.

To begin, add an event listener to the delete button to call your *yet-to-be* populated crud.delete function. This will look identical to the one used for updating, except this one calls your delete function.

Add an event listener to the delete button in the `initialize` function, like so:

```
document.getElementById('btn-delete').addEventListener('click', function (event) {
  event.preventDefault();
  getParseObject(input.dataset.parseid, crud.delete);
});
```

Using the passed-in argument (Parse object), call upon Parse's `destroy` method to remove the record from the database. Use your utility functions to clean up after the record is successfully deleted. The following code uses the `destroy` method on a Parse object to remove it from the database:

```
delete: function (parseObject) {
  parseObject.destroy({
    success: function (parseObject) {
      console.log(parseObject.id + ' destroyed');
      removeDOMNode(parseObject.id);
      resetForm();
    },
    error: function (parseObject, error) {
      console.info('Error deleting: ', parseObject);
      console.warn(error);
    }
  });
}
```

Cloud Code

We'd be remiss if we didn't cover Parse's Cloud Code. This section *briefly* covers how Cloud Code works. As mentioned, Cloud Code is code that runs on Parse's servers–in the cloud. Cloud Code is just like the code that runs inside your main application, except that it runs on the Internet. This is great for things like running code that is process-heavy, or adding new features to your application on the fly.

When creating a Parse application using their CLI, a folder named `cloud` is automatically created. All code in this folder is intended to execute over the Internet and is intentionally separated from your main application code. Cloud Code can be used by all of Parse's SDK's and the REST API.

There are two ways to use execute Cloud Code processes:

- *Cloud Functions*: Named functions that you define, which can be called inside your main application.

- *Triggers*: Code that runs when a particular action is triggered.

Cloud Functions

The following code is the function signature, or general information, on how to structure and create a custom cloud function:

```
Parse.Cloud.define('customFn', function (request, response) {
  // ...
});
```

All Cloud Code functions use the Cloud namespace. To *define* a function, use the define method. The first parameter is a user-defined name used to call the function. In this case, the function is named customFn. The second parameter is a function that uses two parameters, request and response. You'll learn more about these next.

To call this function inside application code, use the run method as demonstrated in the following code:

```
Parse.Cloud.run('customFn', {foo: 'test'}, {
  success: function (result) {

  },
  error: function (error) {

  }
});
```

The Parse.Cloud.**run** method takes three parameters:

- The name of the function
- Parameters to be used for the function
- An object that contains a success and error callback function

The second parameter is an important one; it's what the custom function uses for processing. In the exercise that follows, you will pass an object with a property of foo equal to the string test. The following code demonstrates how this is used:

```
Parse.Cloud.define('customFn', function (request, response) {
     console.log(request.params.foo);        // test
});
```

The response parameter is an object that has two methods: success and error. Whatever is passed into these functions is what is returned when it is called from your application code.

Trigger Events

Instead of calling custom functions directly, Parse also offers a way to automatically call functions based on how they're triggered. There are four events that can be used to trigger functions, all self-explanatory:

- beforeSave
- afterSave
- beforeDelete
- afterDelete

The first parameter of each of these functions can either be a Parse class name or a Parse.User object (more on Parse.User later in the book). The second parameter is a callback function.

The following will demonstrate how the beforeSave works. We'll use it in the CRUD application to show you how you could use it in your next application. Although the following won't be used for any "real" application, we hope it demonstrates the functionality of how to use Cloud Code to automatically execute functions based on an event.

This next example uses the beforeSave function to prevent users from creating a new record with the value of 'test'. It triggers an error, ultimately putting to use the msg-warn CSS style.

Open cloud/main.js file, erase the contents, and update the file with the following code:

```
Parse.Cloud.beforeSave('ParseObject', function (request, response) {
  if (request.object.get('foo') === 'test') {
    response.error('Use another test value.');
  } else {
    response.success();
  }
});
```

Save the file and deploy your application by running parse deploy in your terminal. Locally, or on your hosted application, try creating a new record with the value of 'test' (without quotations).

Observe that the record does not save and the CSS class msg-warn is applied to the <li>. This demonstrates how you could use Parse's Cloud code to automatically run a function based on a specific event that is fired throughout the lifecycle of your application.

Complete Code

In the event you got lost along the way, or if you want to see the code in all its glory, the following is the complete code for this project. As a bonus, this code (Listing 3-7) is wrapped in an immediately invoked function expression (IIFE) to prevent polluting the global namespace.

Listing 3-7. The Complete Code for This Application

```
(function () {
// User Interface elements
var input = document.getElementById('test-input');
var editPanel = document.getElementById('edit-panel');
var btnAdd = document.getElementById('btn-add');
var ul = document.querySelector('.record-list');

// Create new Parse Object and instantiate it
var TestObject = Parse.Object.extend('ParseObject');
var query = new Parse.Query(TestObject);

// Used when editing a record after the user selects a record from the list
function editItem(event) {
  if (event.target.parentNode.className === 'record-list') {
    input.dataset.parseid = event.target.id;
    btnAdd.className = 'hide';
    input.className = 'hide';
    editPanel.className = 'show';
  }
}

// Executes a function on a returned Parse object
function getParseObject(parseObjectId, fn) {
  query.get(parseObjectId, {
    success: fn,
```

```
      error: function (data, error) {
        console.warn(data, error);
      }
  });
}


// Removes an element from the DOM based on id
function removeDOMNode(id) {
  var node = document.getElementById(id);
  if (node.parentNode) {
    node.parentNode.removeChild(node);
  }
}


// Resets the interface to it's initial view
function resetForm() {
 editPanel.className = 'hide';
  btnAdd.className = 'show';
  input.className = 'show';
  input.dataset.parseid = '';
  input.value = '';
}


// Object containing CRUD methods
var crud = {
  create: function (id) {
    if (input.value === '') {
      return;
    }
    // Create a new <li> element, set the value, then append it to the list
    var li = document.createElement('li');
    li.innerHTML = input.value;
    li.className = 'msg-processing';
    document.querySelector('.record-list').appendChild(li);

    // Create new Parse Object then save
    var testObject = new TestObject();
    testObject.save({
      foo: li.innerHTML
    }, {
      success: function (object) {
        console.log('success!', object);
        // Reset the ID to the Parse object ID
        li.setAttribute('id', object.id);
        // Reset class, and make editable, and clear form value
        li.className = '';
        li.contentEditable = true;
        input.value = '';
      },
      error: function (object, error) {
        console.warn('Could not create object.');
        console.warn(object, error);
```

```
        if (error.code === Parse.Error.CONNECTION_FAILED) {
          console.warn('Could not connect to Parse Cloud.');
        }
        li.className = 'msg-warn';
      }
    });
  },
  retrieve: function () {
    // query.contains('foo', 'first');
    // query.ascending('createdAt');
    query.find({
      success: function (records) {
        var frag = document.createDocumentFragment();
        records.forEach(function (record) {
          var li = document.createElement('li');
          li.innerHTML = record.get('foo');
          li.id = record.id;
          li.contentEditable = true;
          frag.appendChild(li);
        });
        ul.appendChild(frag);
      },
      error: function (object, error) {
        console.warn('Could not retrieve records.', error);
      }
    });
  },
  update: function (parseObject) {
    var li = document.getElementById(parseObject.id);
    parseObject.save({
      'foo': li.textContent
    }, {
      success: function () {
        removeDOMNode(parseObject.id);
        // Repopulate list items
        crud.retrieve();
        resetForm();
        li.contentEditable = true;
      },
      error: function (data, error) {
        document.getElementById(parseObject.id).className = 'msg-warn';
        console.warn('Could not update.', error);
      }
    });
  },
  delete: function (parseObject) {
    parseObject.destroy({
      success: function (parseObject) {
        console.log(parseObject.id + ' destroyed');
        removeDOMNode(parseObject.id);
        resetForm();
      },
```

```javascript
      error: function (parseObject, error) {
        console.info('Error deleting: ', parseObject);
        console.warn(error);
      }
    });
  }
};

function initialize() {
  // Initialize Parse application
  Parse.initialize(' your-application-id ', 'your-javascript-key');

  // Populate with existing records
  crud.retrieve();

  // Bind UI elements

  // Add
  document.getElementById('btn-add').addEventListener('click', function (event) {
    event.preventDefault();
    crud.create();
  });

  // Edit
  document.querySelector('body').addEventListener('click', function (event) {
    event.preventDefault();
    editItem(event);
  });

  // Update
  document.getElementById('btn-update').addEventListener('click', function (event) {
    event.preventDefault();
    getParseObject(input.dataset.parseid, crud.update);
  });

  // Delete
  document.getElementById('btn-delete').addEventListener('click', function (event) {
    event.preventDefault();
    getParseObject(input.dataset.parseid, crud.delete);
  });

  // Cancel
  document.getElementById('btn-cancel').addEventListener('click', function (event) {
    event.preventDefault();
    resetForm();
  });
}

document.addEventListener('DOMContentLoaded', function () {
  initialize();
});
})();
```

Summary

This chapter acted as an introduction to the world of Parse. After getting an overview of some of the features Parse offers, you created a new account and configured your first application.

The Parse CLI tools are used to interface with Parse using the command line. With it, you created a new local project and linked it to an application that was first created using the Parse web site.

You used the Parse base project as a starting point for creating a custom application that demonstrated the CRUD commands: Create, Read, Update, and Delete. Using the CLI, you deployed code using Parse's hosting solutions.

All Parse applications need to be initialized using a unique application ID and JavaScript key. With it, you connected to your Parse app when it initialized.

Most Parse functions have a `success` and `error` callback functions. With them, you were able to execute specific functions based on the outcome of the request. After creating some test records, you used the data browser to see the contents of each record.

In your CRUD methods, you were able to query for specific records to edit and update them. There are over 30 query methods that Parse provides to help find exactly what you need.

With the aid of some helper functions and event listeners, you were able to bind events to user interface elements.

Using Cloud Code, you were able to run code independently from your main application code. There are many things you can do with this, and exploration of the API is encouraged.

CHAPTER 4

■ ■ ■

Tools and Helpers

Picking the right tool for the right job

This chapter discusses some of the tools you'll be using throughout the rest of this book. Our goal is get you up to speed with some great resources that will help you build your next application.

jQuery to the Rescue

Perhaps the most important thing to realize about jQuery is that it's *written in JavaScript*. Although there is no special magic behind the most popular JS framework, it is often the go-to choice for developers.

jQuery is a free open source JavaScript library that abstracts complex logic into an expressive and easy to use API. From DOM manipulations to simple animations, jQuery is packed with lots of convenience methods you can use for everyday development.

jQuery is the perfect place to start learning JavaScript if you're just starting out, aside, of course, from just learning the language on its own. Released in August 2006, jQuery's approach to JavaScript programming opened the door to new JS developers from all corners of the world by helping those new to the language quickly grasp how it works. Whether it's the simple intuitive syntax, the relentless cross-browser compatibility, or any of the jQuery Foundation's other projects such as *QUnit* or *jQueryUI*, jQuery is pretty amazing.

Perhaps some of the true powers of jQuery are its users. There are tons of community-written plug-ins that offer a variety of functions that extend the use of jQuery. With such a rich ecosystem, jQuery is a great way to improve and build on your JavaScript skills.

There are two versions of jQuery that you should know about:

- v1.x: Good for legacy sites that require support for Internet Explorer versions 6–8

- v2.x: Smaller than v1 and does *not* support IE <= 8

You'll be using 2.x later in this book because supporting old IE browsers isn't applicable to PhoneGap applications (thankfully!).

Use jQuery Responsibly

It's usually a good idea to start a new project from scratch, adding dependencies only as needed. Using a library like jQuery isn't necessary if you only plan to use a few functions from it. Often, there is either a smaller library that can do what you want, or you can just do it yourself with a few custom lines of JavaScript. You don't always need jQuery. Check out youmightnotneedjquery.com for more information.

Why jQuery Matters for This Book

Beginning in Chapter 6, you'll be building a Parse and PhoneGap application from scratch. Using jQuery will allow you to focus on application code, rather than AJAX, DOM manipulation, and other niceties that jQuery provides.

We wanted this book to get into the hands of as many developers as possible. Because jQuery is such a popular library, we figured it'd be best to cast a wide net to demonstrate real-world applications powered by Parse and PhoneGap.

It should be noted that jQuery is not required for using Parse or PhoneGap; they are all independent entities that are awesome on their own.

If you already know jQuery, then sweet! If not, it's time to find out what all the fuss is about. You can find excellent documentation at `api.jquery.com` as well as a huge online community that can help you with any issues you run into while using the library.

Twitter Bootstrap

Developing a customized application takes time. For the purpose of rapid prototyping and experimentation, you'll be using Twitter Bootstrap (TB).

In 2010, a small team at Twitter created TB. Its purpose was to encourage *consistency* across internal web tools. A year later, they open-sourced the project and its popularity quickly rose.

Tools such as TB make putting an idea, layout, and/or application together quickly. TB is a collection of HTML, JavaScript, and CSS design templates used for creating engaging web sites for all screen sizes. It uses CSS grids to proportionately size and style web page elements such as buttons and forms.

As of version 3, its mobile-first philosophy promotes responsive design, using discrete interchangeable modules. TB offers compact components that provide an array of out-of-the-box functionality such as progress bars and drop-down menus (see Figure 4-1). Using jQuery as a dependency, TB is a great resource for quickly getting your ideas out of you head and onto the screen. You can also create custom builds, so you can only include the scripts, styles, and components (such as icons and media) that you need for a given application.

Figure 4-1. *The TB documentation for the drop-down menu component*

Using their predefined CSS classes and HTML structuring, you can add style and functionality to your app with little effort. Developers find this very appealing about TB, and it is why you'll be using it a bit later.

Use Bootstrap Responsibly

Not every application you build will need TB. It is used here as a teaching tool to get you building applications quickly while not having to deal with the specificity that is typically involved in creating custom applications.

One important note to realize is that the look and feel of TB is easily recognizable at this point. If you intend on using it for all your projects, you'll notice that they'll all look the same. This will limit your potential in making something unique for your users.

With enough experience, you can override core styles or functionality, but at a cost. What if you break something that it depends on? Be wary of introducing any custom functionality into its core. TB is great for getting your ideas and concepts developed fast. This will help you quickly envision how your application will look and function without having to roll out custom code.

Why Twitter Bootstrap Matters for This Book

Using TB will allow you to focus on PhoneGap and Parse, instead of customizing styles, widgets, and other tasks involved with application development.

As with most web tools, there are other projects similar to Bootstrap. Just as jQuery is the most popular JavaScript library, Twitter Bootstrap is one of the most widely used starter frameworks today. That said, just because the "cool kids" use it, you don't have to. It works for the purpose of this book: getting those beginning web development a head start into programming for the web.

JavaScript Templates with Handlebars.js

Often in an application, you'll want to render some data based on a variety of different factors. This is where content templates come into play.

Handlebars.js is a dynamic templating library that helps you construct HTML pages. They are likely used in a variety of web sites without your even being aware. For example, when you shop online at your favorite web site, you'll see that the content is tailored specifically to you. This typically occurs when you are logged into the site, or if an action you take has an effect on the content being displayed. Dynamic templates are programmed to populate content on the fly.

Static vs. Dynamic Web Sites

We all visit the same web sites (Amazon, Google, and so forth) and have different experiences based on how we use them. *Unique* content is rendered, but behind the scenes, each web site stills uses the same HTML structure and styles. This is an example of a *dynamic* web site.

Conversely, *static* web sites do *not* change. Examples of content that may not change are things like links on a footer or content on an About page. It can be argued that such content *can* be populated from a database, which is technically dynamic content, but I digress.

Large applications benefit from reusing snippets, as it helps organize code and source files. Later in this book, we'll introduce the usage of dynamic templates using Handlebars.js. This will allow users who sign into your application to have a unique experience based on their interactions. Figure 4-2 shows an example of how Handlebars.js can be used.

```
<div class="entry">
  <h1>{{title}}</h1>
  <div class="body">
    {{{body}}}
  </div>
</div>
```

with this context:

```
{
  title: "All about <p> Tags",
  body: "<p>This is a post about &lt;p&gt; tags</p>"
}
```

results in:

```
<div class="entry">
  <h1>All About &lt;p&gt; Tags</h1>
  <div class="body">
    <p>This is a post about &lt;p&gt; tags</p>
  </div>
</div>
```

Figure 4-2. A handlebarsjs.com example demonstrating the API

When to Use Dynamic Templates

When developing a front-end-only application, it's helpful to have a way of displaying content dynamically. Dynamic programming languages such as PHP already use dynamic templates to render unique content based on data. Handlebars.js provides the same functionality, but it uses JavaScript.

If you find that you're constantly mixing JavaScript and HTML code together, it's best to isolate concerns into their own functionalities. This will help tremendously with keeping code not only organized but, more importantly, *maintainable*. Isolating functionality into discreet structures is common in programming. By organizing your application's scripts and templates in a modular fashion, you will be able build upon them and integrate with other features.

There are a few instances when using a templating engine is a good idea:

- *Large applications*: An application with many files and folders can get messy quickly. Having dynamic template can help organize the chaos. Having reusable snippets allows you to combine multiple interfaces in many combinations.

- *Working with a team*: When on a project with multiple people, having separation of concerns is important, as it allows for multiple people to work on the same feature. It makes for consistent, predictable patterns that everyone can follow.

- *Lots of dynamic data*: If you're dealing with large amounts of different kinds of data, dynamic templates are the way to go. User-generated, content-rich web sites such as *Reddit* would be an example of template usage. Theming content and page templates allows for multiple reuse and extensibility.

Let's use a search engine's results page as an example. All the content rendered is based on a search term or phrase, which in turn can display in a variety of ways. For example, each of the following can be its own user interface template:

- Sponsored links on the header

- Sponsored links on the side of the results

- A preview of image results

- Definitions associated with searched content

- Related search terms

- Map information (if the search term/phrase is a location)

- Pagination on the footer to jump directly to a result page

Why Handlebars.js Matters for This Book

Applications typically have a lot of independent parts that come together to form the entire application. This is a great way for beginners to understand code organization and the impact it has on the maintainability of an application. Templates are simple to understand and implement, and yet provide a powerful feature set that enables you to customize different states in your application.

Loading JavaScript Files

As discussed, the more code you write or add to an application, the bigger your application code is (in file size), and the more you need to maintain.

Each JavaScript file you add means that users will need to wait that much longer until all the scripts load *before* using your web site. Loading scripts for a web site vs. scripts for PhoneGap application is different, as you'll see in a moment.

Traditionally on a web page, JavaScript files are loaded in the head tag of an HTML file. Loading multiple JavaScript files in the head will give the appearance of a slow, sluggish web site to the end user. Because the scripts are above the content (the body), they need to load first, *and then* the content is displayed.

After much experimentation, web performance guru Steve Sauders figured out that by loading scripts before the closing body tag, page speed loading increased dramatically. This isn't a silver bullet for every case, as sometimes scripts (such as *Modernizr*) still need to be loaded in the head.

Script Loading Today

As applications grow, which they always tend to, JavaScript files can become harder to manage. If you have a static web site with ten pages, you'd have to add a script file reference to every single page. What if you want to add some new functionality that needs to be on *each* page? As you can imagine, this isn't good practice.

There are many ways to improve this process. Here are just a few that you may or may not have already heard of:

- Minifying and combining scripts into a single file

- Breaking up your code logically into modules using something such as the following:

  - Asynchronous Module Definition (AMD)

  - CommonJS

- Using build processes such a *gruntjs*, *gulpjs*, *brunch.io*, and *webpack* that aid developers in bundling applications for production

- Using a Content Delivery Network (CDN) for serving large files

However you slice it, it's all JavaScript in the end. Whatever method you choose *after* this book is up to you. Just keep in mind that on your end, you want your code maintainable; from the user's perspective, the application has to load as fast as possible and perform well.

Script Loading in PhoneGap

Why do we need a script loader if PhoneGap compiles our application anyway? Simply put, code organization and reusability. The application you'll build later will be extendable, allowing you to reuse the code or add to it however you wish. Having scripts in their own discreet files allows you to keep things tidy.

LABjs Script Loader

Because there are so many options for beginners to wrap their head around, we decided to go with the most straightforward approach and use a script loader called LABjs, an open source project created by Open Web Evangelist Kyle Simpson.

LABjs uses *one* file to manage the loading of *multiple* JavaScript files, making coding complex applications a breeze. Often when working with multiple scripts, you will have one or more scripts depend on another. This is very common with large applications. Third-party libraries like RequireJS have looked to solve this problem using AMD modules. Environments like Node.js use the CommonJS format.

As an example, if script-b depends on script-a in order to work, then script-a needs to completely load in order for it to be used by script-b.

Later in this book, we'll be using jQuery as a dependency. Before loading our custom application code, jQuery needs to load first. LABjs helps us manage this with elegance. Take the following snippet from the LABjs documentation as an example:

```
<script>
    $LAB
    .script("framework.js").wait()
    .script("plugin.framework.js")
    .script("myplugin.framework.js").wait()
    .script("init.js").wait();
</script>
```

LABjs will load your scripts in sequential order and optionally wait until the queued file is loaded before moving onto the next. We'll be using a similar approach later when we build an application from scratch.

PhoneGap Testing Tools

In the early days of PhoneGap, testing applications was possible, but painful. Today, there are many tools available for testing and debugging your applications. The tools discussed in this section provide some ways you can test PhoneGap applications.

PhoneGap Developer App

This amazing application offers developers a chance to see changes in *real time* on a physical device. It works by running your application on a web server from your computer, and then using a mobile app to connect to it. No more rebuilding your project to see updates—you can simply save your files and see updates as they happen. One of the coolest features of this app is that you can see your `console` statements in the terminal as they are happening.

Install instructions for the PhoneGap Developer App can be found at app.phonegap.com.

Using the PhoneGap Developer App

You will need the PhoneGap Developer App installed on your mobile device and your computer in order to continue. Your physical mobile device *must be connected to the same network* your host computer is on.

You can use the *Hello World* application from Chapter 2 to test this out. In your terminal, navigate to the root directory of the project and execute phonegap serve. You should see a similar print out in your terminal as depicted in Figure 4-3.

```
→  HelloWorld   phonegap serve
[phonegap] starting app server...
[phonegap] listening on 192.168.0.5:3000
[phonegap]
[phonegap] ctrl-c to stop the server
[phonegap]
```

Figure 4-3. *The terminal when the PhoneGap Developer App starts. Note that your IP address may be different*

Live Testing

Once the server is running on your computer, use the PhoneGap Developer mobile application to connect to it. Figure 4-4 shows the app's interface.

Figure 4-4. *The PhoneGap Developer App interface*

After inputting the IP address provided by the phonegap serve command (depicted in Figure 4-4) into the PhoneGap Developer App, you will have the ability to preview code changes *live*.

PhoneGap's create command does a lot of work behind the scenes. Most importantly, it creates a folder named www. The www folder is similar to Parse's public folder in that it is where you will write your custom code. For sanity's sake, update some code to experience the workflow.

1. Have the PhoneGap Developer App on your mobile device running and synced with your host PC using the generated IP address.

2. Open up the index.html file located in the www folder created by PhoneGap.

3. Update the "PhoneGap" text surrounded by heading (h1) tags to say "Hello PhoneGap". The style of the text is controlled via CSS. Save the file and witness the magic, as shown in Figure 4-5.

Figure 4-5. *The result of the updated index.html file located in the www folder*

As you continue to save any file in the www directory, the PhoneGap Developer App will update on your mobile device automatically.

PhoneGap App Desktop Beta

The PhoneGap App Desktop is an optional companion app that works with the PhoneGap Developer App. As of version 0.1.2, this application is now easily installable for Windows and Mac and will notify you when updates are available. Check out https://github.com/phonegap/phonegap-app-desktop/releases for the most current version and install it on your computer.

Since you've already experimented with the Developer App, this should feel familiar. The user interface is fairly straightforward (Figure 4-6). Once you select which PhoneGap application you want to test, it starts a server, just like phonegap serve does, allowing you to pair it with your mobile device via the generated IP address.

Figure 4-6. PhoneGap App Desktop home screen

Also similar to the PhoneGap Developer App is the log. Using the Server Log tab located on the left-hand side of the app, you can quickly see what's going on while your application is running (see Figure 4-7).

Figure 4-7. *PhoneGap App Desktop Server Log screen*

Using these two applications are just the thing to get you debugging and testing your next PhoneGap application.

Summary

This chapter provided a general overview of some of the tools web developers use to build applications. jQuery is a respected and dependable codebase that covers many cross browser issues that you probably don't even know exist. Combined with other tool sets like Twitter Bootstrap, you will be able to quickly prototype your ideas.

Building a dynamic and extendable user interface is an important element when building an interactive application. Using Handlebars.js, you will populate templates using dynamic content while separating concerns logically using clear and maintainable templates.

As scripts pile up, libraries like LABjs help make loading multiple scripts easy. Once your scripts are in order, using the PhoneGap Developer App and other testing tools will aid you in building an awesome application.

CHAPTER 5

Facebook API

Getting Social with the Facebook API

Parse provides an easy way to integrate the Facebook authentication system into your Parse user management. But before getting to this, it's important to learn about the Facebook Platform itself, as well as integrating it into a PhoneGap application.

We'll begin by discussing the features of the Facebook Platform and the benefits of using them. You'll then set up a Facebook Developer account and a Facebook application, and you'll create a simple PhoneGap application to test the Facebook API.

The Facebook Developer Platform

Besides the intersection points between Facebook and Parse, using the Facebook Platform for a mobile application is generally a good idea. Using the platform, you'll be able to build more social and feature-rich applications. Other developers do this as well.

> *An average eight of the top-ten-grossing iOS apps and nine of the top-ten-grossing Android apps are integrated with Facebook.*

> — Facebook, developers.facebook.com/docs/games/overview

But how does it help you? Depending on your application concept, the implementation of some features will make sense, while others may be useless. The Facebook Platform offers so many different API endpoints, plug-ins, and so forth that it's not easy to summarize *all* of the features. In short, the following are the most common use cases for using the Facebook Platform:

- Sharing
- User management and permissions
- Friends
- Monetization
- Audience network
- Insights

Sharing

The first feature that will help your app audience grow is usually the implementation of sharing your application or your application's content. A subset of features for this task includes

- Dialogs to share a link or message on a user's timeline

- Sharing using a private message

- The infamous *Like* button

- Posting of messages, links, and pictures via the Facebook Graph API

- Using custom open graph stories

This chapter will cover some of these features, but for more, please consult the "Sharing" section of the Facebook Developer documentation at `developers.facebook.com/docs/sharing`.

User Management and Permissions

Using the Facebook Login system, you can identify users and provide exclusive access to certain elements of your application. This will also enable you to save settings per user via their account, instead of a device. This is essential if a single user uses the application across multiple devices.

Friends

Finding friends using the same application and interacting with them is probably the feature that can have the biggest impact on your product's design. It makes a huge difference whether your customers are betting on the next sporting event in a silo or in competition with their friends. The same can apply to running, shopping, fashion, and many other application concepts.

Among other features, the Facebook Platform offers you opportunities to invite friends and send requests. You can then use friends' data to personalize the experience of your application. This could be any element of your application that is somehow related to a user's friends. For example, pictures taken by a user can be shared with friends and or *their* friends, thus expanding the reach of your application.

Monetization

In the first phase of building your application(s), monetization may play a less important role, but at a certain point you'll want to create revenue to finance your project. The Facebook Platform offers two ways to monetize your apps, by using a payment service and an advertising platform called *Audience Network*.

Payment Services

Due to legal restrictions, you cannot use Facebook's payment service in iOS applications, so you should only consider this option if you are building a web application in parallel with a web portion.

The system can enable you to support over 80 payment methods including Visa, MasterCard, and PayPal in more than 50 countries. You can use it to sell subscriptions or virtual goods. You can find more information about the Facebook payment service in the developer documentation at `developers.facebook.com/docs/payments/`.

For *in-app* purchases, you should consider using the Apple Pay service, Google Play's in-app billing, or a certified third-party payment service like Stripe (stripe.com/). Of course, there are PhoneGap plug-ins for all of these services:

- Apple Pay plug-in: github.com/jbeuckm/cordova-plugin-applepay

- Android in-app billing plug-in: github.com/poiuytrez/AndroidInAppBilling

- Stripe plug-in: github.com/Telerik-Verified-Plugins/Stripe

Audience Network

The situation for the Audience Network is luckily a different one; you can use the service both in Android and iOS applications. The service does three jobs for you:

- Offers a way to place ads in your application

- Sells and fills these spaces for you

- Handles all billing questions and concerns you or your customers have

You just have to add the service and start collecting money. An example ad is pictured in Figure 5-1.

Figure 5-1. A test ad created by the Facebook Audience Network

There is, however, one little barrier: you need to apply to use the service. You can find more information about the service and apply via the Facebook Developer web site at `developers.facebook.com/products/audience-network`.

To implement the service to a PhoneGap application, I recommend using the Cordova Plug-in for Facebook Audience Network, available at `github.com/floatinghotpot/cordova-plugin-facebookads`.

Due to its complexity, this book will not cover the implementation of monetization services. The hope is that after finishing this book, you will be in a very good place to manage this task independently.

Insights

One by-product you'll gain by using the Facebook Platform is usage and user data. Once the Facebook SDK is implemented in your application and being used by your users, Facebook will start collecting data about them. This includes how many users are using your application, where they are from, and other interesting statistics that you can use to improve your application.

Besides passive tracking, you can use the Insights API to track custom user events. You can learn more about this at `developers.facebook.com/docs/app-events`. An example of a custom user action could be someone adding a picture or joining a group.

Goals and Requirements for This Chapter

As you can imagine, this chapter cannot introduce an entire platform in just a few pages. Instead, it will focus on the basic setup as well as the most common use cases like logging in users via Facebook. You will need this knowledge to connect the Facebook Login process with Parse's user management, which will be covered a little later.

Next, you'll learn how to share a link on a user's timeline, read user data like their email address, and upload a picture to Facebook.

To create a Facebook-enabled PhoneGap application, you need to complete the following steps.

1. Create a new PhoneGap application.

2. Create a Facebook Developer account.

3. Create a Facebook application instance.

4. Install the Facebook PhoneGap plug-in.

Creating a New PhoneGap Application

Before starting the Facebook application setup, you should create a new PhoneGap application. The reason for doing this step first is the need to name bundle identifiers for PhoneGap and Facebook.

Both the name and the bundle identifier of your PhoneGap app are very important for this step. They need to match the Facebook configuration, which you'll be concerned with in a moment.

Create a new PhoneGap app and write down the name of your application, as well as the namespace.

An example for an app named MySocialApp and the bundle identifier com.apress.mySocialApp is in Listing 5-1.

Listing 5-1. Creating a New PhoneGap Application Named MySocialApp. This Includes Adding a Bundle Identifier That You'll Use for Facebook.

```
phonegap create ./mySocialApp-path/ com.apress.mySocialApp MySocialApp
```

For existing applications, you can find and adjust the values in the file `www/config.xml`, as shown in Listing 5-2.

Listing 5-2. Updating the Bundle Identifier for an Existing PhoneGap Application Using the config.xml File

```xml
<?xml version='1.0' encoding='utf-8'?>
<widget id="com.apress.mySocialApp" version="1.0.0" xmlns="http://www.w3.org/ns/widgets"
xmlns:gap="http://phonegap.com/ns/1.0">
    <name>MySocialApp</name>
    <description>...
```

Creating a Facebook Developer Account

If you currently do not have a Facebook account, please sign up on `Facebook.com` before continuing. After logging into Facebook with your account, visit `https://developers.facebook.com/` (Figure 5-2).

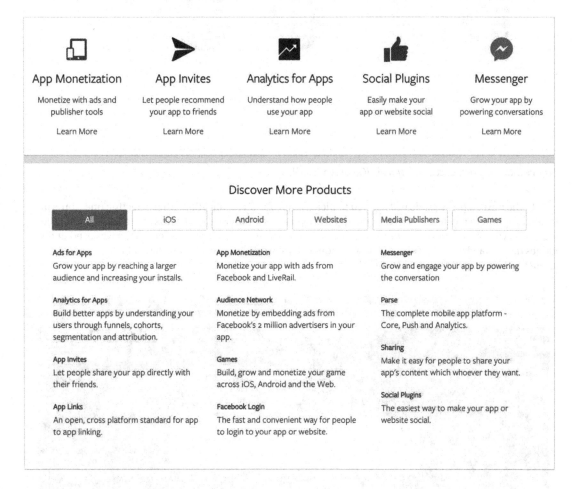

Figure 5-2. *The Facebook Developer web site*

Creating a Facebook Application Instance

After logging into Facebook Developer, you'll able to create a new application configuration. You can do this by clicking the My Apps menu item and selecting the Add a New App link. Alternatively, you can create a new application using the quickstart guide that you can find at https://developers.facebook.com/quickstarts/.

If you are starting out, it's recommended to use the latter. The first step of the quickstart guide will show a list of platforms (Figure 5-3). Select either iOS or Android. If you want to develop for both platforms, you can come back to the same step at a later point or add more platforms in the advanced application settings.

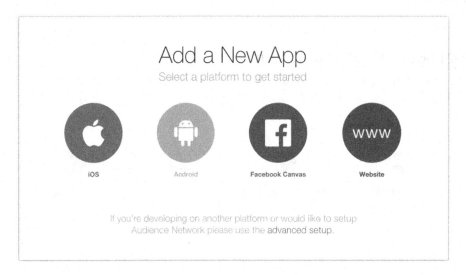

Figure 5-3. *To start, select a platform (iOS or Android)*

In the next step, the guide will ask you to pick a name for the application. After selecting one, you will have the option to create a new Facebook App ID (Figure 5-4). Choose *exactly* the same name (*not* bundle identifier) you picked for your PhoneGap application. In the example earlier, MySocialApp was used. If the names don't match exactly, Facebook integration will not work. You can change this value in the advanced application settings via the field Display Name.

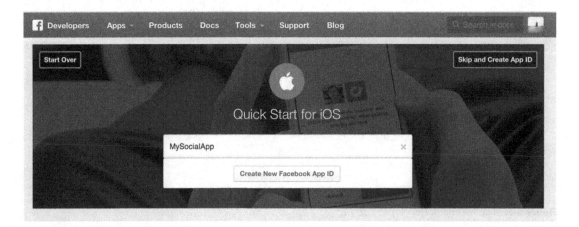

Figure 5-4. *Name the Facebook application*

Submitting this form will create a new Facebook application instance. This will be followed by Facebook asking you to download the iOS or Android Facebook SDK. You can skip this task because you'll be adding the SDKs using a PhoneGap plug-in.

iOS: Bundle Identifier

If you're creating an iOS application, scroll down to the section called Supply us with your Bundle Identifier. Paste the bundle identifier created earlier, com.apress.mySocialApp (see Figure 5-5).

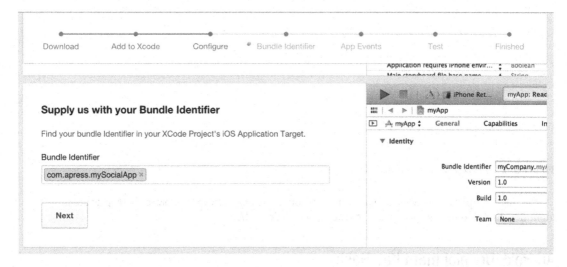

Figure 5-5. *Supply the bundle identifier of your PhoneGap application*

Android: Package Name

For Android setup, scroll down to the section called Tell us about your Android project. As shown in Figure 5-6, use the bundle identifier as value for the Package Name. Next, you need to provide the Default Activity Class Name. This value is a concatenation of your bundle identifier and application name.

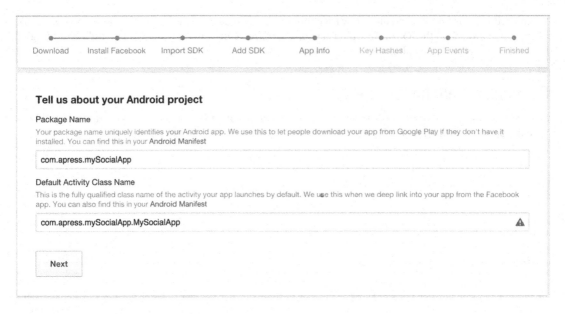

Figure 5-6. *Android package name settings*

In this example, using `MySocialApp` as application name and `com.apress.mySocialApp` as the bundle identifier, the value will be `com.apress.mySocialApp.MySocialApp`.

Android: Development Key Hash

Finishing the Facebook application setup for Android requires an additional task: you need to generate your development key hash, and optionally the release key hash if your app has already been published. These keys are needed to ensure the authenticity of the interactions between your app and Facebook.

To generate a development key hash on a Mac, run the command shown in Listing 5-3. On Windows, run the command shown in Listing 5-4.

Listing 5-3. Generating a Development Key Hash on a Mac, and Ubuntu

```
keytool -exportcert -alias androiddebugkey -keystore ~/.android/debug.keystore | openssl
sha1 -binary | openssl base64
```

Listing 5-4. Generating a Development Key Hash on Windows

```
keytool -exportcert -alias androiddebugkey -keystore %HOMEPATH%\.android\debug.keystore |
openssl sha1 -binary | openssl base64
```

The `keytool` and `openssl` will generate a 28-character key hash unique to your development environment. If you need a unique development key hash for each Android development environment, copy and paste it into the field called Development Key Hashes, shown in Figure 5-7. Repeat the step for every development environment.

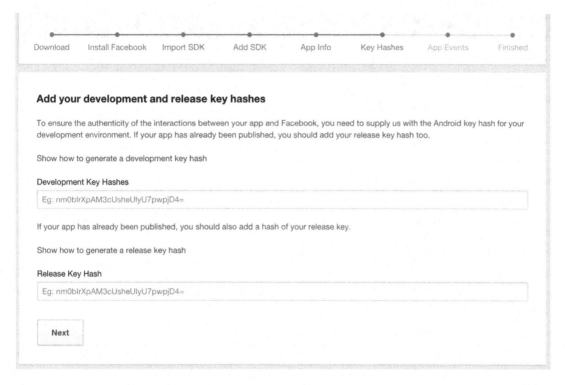

Figure 5-7. *Add development key hashes*

If you're developing in a team, your teammates need to provide their development hashes or add them on their own. You grant access to your Facebook application settings to teammates in the section Roles of the advanced application settings.

Facebook Application ID

Subsequent to finishing the Facebook application setup, head over to the advanced application settings. You can find a list of your applications by clicking the menu item Apps or by navigating to developers. facebook.com/apps/.

Verify your settings and save the Facebook application ID. You can find it in the form field App ID (see Figure 5-8). You'll need this value to configure the Facebook PhoneGap plug-in.

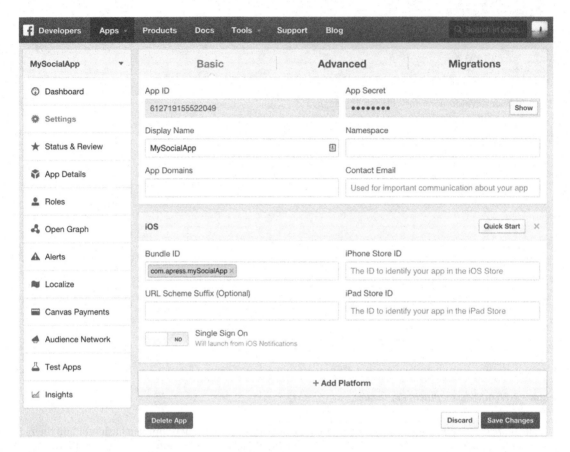

Figure 5-8. *Facebook application settings*

Installing the Facebook PhoneGap Plug-in

In the last step of the requirements, you will install the Facebook PhoneGap plug-in to your application. Open your terminal and navigate to your PhoneGap application directory.

Prior to installing the plug-in, add the platforms you want to work with (iOS and/or Android). For example, `phonegap build ios`.

Next, add the Facebook plug-in. In contrast to other plug-ins, it's not recommended to add the plug-in via a web request. Doing this will cause the plug-in installation to fail for iOS projects, as references to the Facebook SDK files will be broken. Instead, download the plug-in files from `github.com/Wizcorp/phonegap-facebook-plugin` or clone them to your local machine using the command shown in Listing 5-5.

Listing 5-5. Cloning the Facebook Plugin to Your Local Development Environment

```
git clone https://github.com/Wizcorp/phonegap-facebook-plugin.git
```

Next, add the plug-in via the command shown in Listing 5-6. Replace the values for {your-facebook-app-id} and {DisplayName} with your application's values, also adjust {/path-to-phonegap-facebook-plugin} to the local path where you saved the plug-in files.

Listing 5-6. Adding and Configuring the Facebook Plug-in to Your Project

```
phonegap plugin add {/path-to-phonegap-facebook-plugin} --variable APP_ID={your-facebook-
app-id} --variable APP_NAME={DisplayName}
```

■ **Note** The Wizcorp Phonegap Facebook plug-in is currently using an outdated version of the Facebook SDK for iOS and Android (3.x), but this version is still supported and working. The latest Facebook SDK version is 4.x. You can check for updates to the plug-in on its github page at https://github.com/Wizcorp/phonegap-facebook-plugin.

The plug-in installation variables APP_ID and APP_NAME will be added to the global plug-in configuration file. When you build your Android or iOS application, it will automatically add the needed configuration values to the Android and iOS application settings.

■ **Tip** If your display name contains spaces, you need to escape the spaces by adding quotes surrounding the variable and escaping every space character with a backslash (\). For example, if your display name is My App Name, you need to use the string APP_NAME="{My\ App\ Name}". The following code shows a full example of the correct syntax:

```
phonegap plugin add {/path-to-phonegap-facebook-plugin} --variable APP_ID={your-facebook-
app-id} --variable APP_NAME="{My\ App\ Name}"
```

Run the application on a test device (virtual or physical) to verify your installation. If the debugging tool doesn't report any errors, you're good to go.

Graph API Explorer

You can test the Graph API without your PhoneGap application by using the online tool *Graph API Explorer* from developers.facebook.com/tools/explorer/. With this tool you can test every API endpoint as well as the login or permission dialogs. Switch to your application and use the Get Access Token button to request a login dialog, as shown in Figure 5-9.

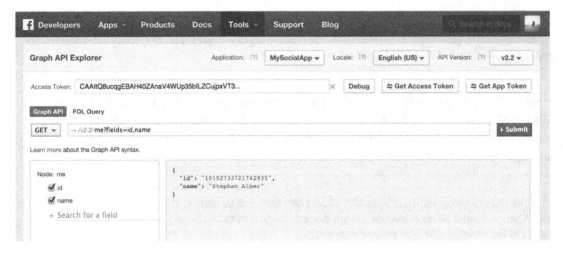

Figure 5-9. *Graph API Explorer*

Resetting Permissions

You may at one point need to test every login or permission dialog multiple times. To do this, you need to remove the app or single permissions. You can do this via the app settings page in your Facebook account settings (`www.facebook.com/settings?tab=applications`). Once you select an app, click Remove App, as shown in Figure 5-10 on the very bottom left.

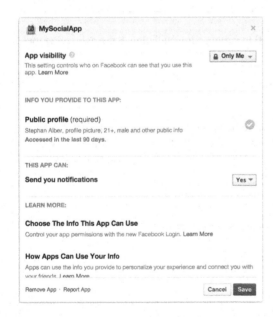

Figure 5-10. *Remove an application via the Facebook account settings (bottom left)*

Usage Examples

Once you finished the general Facebook application and plug-in setup, you can start using the Facebook Platform. You can use some features like the Facebook Share Dialog without asking the user to log in to your application. For this example, the user will have to log in using the dialog window. It's recommend to add any Facebook functionality *after* logging in the user. This can allow you to provide useful features or functionality using the user's information.

The following examples will cover logging in and out via Facebook, requesting permissions, reading and posting via the Graph API, and using the Share dialog.

Basic Setup

Use the sample application created by the phonegap create command as a bootstrap for your Facebook sample application. Clean up the HTML template (www/index.html) and remove all code that doesn't apply, like the sample styles and body elements, as shown in Listing 5-7.

First, you need to add your common development tools like jQuery, Twitter Bootstrap, and Handlebars.js, which can be found on the web sites of their respective projects. Download and reference the libraries in your project. An example is shown in Listing 5-7.

Create a new JavaScript file called www/js/**myFacebookApp.js** which will contain all Facebook-related functionality. Add a script reference to newly created file as well.

Listing 5-7. The Basic HTML Template (www/index.html)

```
<!DOCTYPE html>
<html>
  <head>
    <title>My Social App</title>
    <meta charset="utf-8" />
    <meta name="format-detection" content="telephone=no" />
    <meta name="msapplication-tap-highlight" content="no" />
    <meta name="viewport" content="user-scalable=no, initial-scale=1, maximum-scale=1,
minimum-scale=1, width=device-width, height=device-height, target-densitydpi=device-dpi" />
    <link rel="stylesheet"  href="https://maxcdn.bootstrapcdn.com/bootstrap/3.3.1/css/
bootstrap.min.css">
    <link rel="stylesheet"
href="https://maxcdn.bootstrapcdn.com/bootstrap/3.3.1/css/bootstrap-theme.min.css">
    <style type="text/css">
      body { padding-top: 40px; }
    </style>
  </head>
  <body>
    <div class="container"></div>
    <script type="text/javascript" src="js/jquery-2.1.3.min.js"></script>
    <script type="text/javascript" src="js/handlebars.min.js"></script>
    <script type="text/javascript" src="cordova.js"></script>
    <script type="text/javascript" src="js/index.js"></script>
    <script type="text/javascript" src="js/myFacebookApp.js"></script>
    <script type="text/javascript">
      app.initialize();
    </script>
  </body>
</html>
```

Login with Facebook

The first feature of your test application will be the *Facebook Login*. For this feature, you want to display a login button that, once clicked, will show a dialog offering to connect users to the application using their Facebook account. If users approve this login request, your application will receive a session that is unique for the user and your application.

Next, the users will authorize the application to access certain personal information. On a basic level this will be the information contained in their public profile. We'll come back to the matter of reading detailed profile information at a later point in time.

Figure 5-11 shows two versions of a login dialog.

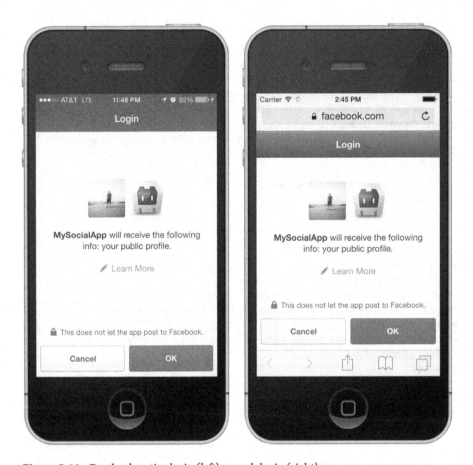

Figure 5-11. *Facebook native login (left) vs. web login (right)*

As you can see, there is a version using the iOS (or Android) Facebook application to request the user to log in (left screen) and a web version of the same (right screen). The latter is shown to users who did not install Facebook for iOS (or Android) on their phones.

As expected, the native version will be a little bit faster and visually more compelling. It may also seem smoother if the user is already logged into Facebook (if they have the Facebook application installed). In both instances, the same features will pass back the same data to your application.

Asking for Additional Permissions

When using the Facebook login, your application can optionally ask for additional permissions. Adding these permissions will allow your application to read a subset of data that person might have added to Facebook. For example, if you want to access to a person's primary email address, you ask for the permission email. Or if you want to access to the list of things a person likes, you ask for the permission user_likes.

A list of all permissions as well as additional information on this topic is available in the Facebook Developer documentation at developers.facebook.com/docs/facebook-login/permissions/.

Getting the User's Login Status

Next, implement the Facebook login. But before offering a login button, you want to know whether the user is already logged in or not. Depending on this information, the application should show a login or logout button. The next listing outlines what you'll be using to log a user in.

You begin with an object (myFacebookApp) that will contain the entire contents of your application. At this point, it will only contain some code to get you started (see Listing 5-8).

Listing 5-8. The JavaScript Skeleton of Your Facebook Test Application (www/js/myFacebookApp.js)

```
var myFacebookApp = {
    init: function() {
        facebookConnectPlugin.getLoginStatus(
            myFacebookApp.handleLoginResponse,
            myFacebookApp.debugResponse
        );
    },
    handleLoginResponse: function(response) {
        console.log('response', response);
        alert("Message: " + JSON.stringify(response));
    },
    debugResponse: function(response) {
        console.log('response', response);
        alert("Message: " + JSON.stringify(response));
    }
};
```

To get the login status information, use the plug-in function facebookConnectPlugin.**getLoginStatus()**. The function will read local session data if it's available, then verify whether the session is still valid. The response of this task will be passed to the success callback function myFacebookApp.**handleLoginResponse**, which is passed as first function argument. Next, you pass an error handler as second function argument, myFacebookApp.**debugResponse**. For the moment, the callbacks do not fulfill any tasks. For testing purposes, you just want to debug the Facebook API responses.

Next, you want to initialize the execution of the Facebook plug-in code. You do this by calling the myFacebookApp.init() function in the receivedEvent callback of the PhoneGap default application script in www/js/**index.js**, as shown in Listing 5-9. You may remove any other code executed in this place.

Listing 5-9. Initializing This Application When PhoneGap is Ready (www/js/index.js)

```
receivedEvent: function(id) {
    myFacebookApp.init();
}
```

At first, the user's status will be unknown. Once the user is logged in, you'll get more detailed session information, as shown in Figure 5-12.

Figure 5-12. *Facebook login status debugging of a logged-out (left) and logged-in (right) user*

Login and Logout Buttons

Next, you add the Facebook login and logout buttons to the HTML template. You start by placing the Twitter Bootstrap Panel element and the buttons inside the `<div class="container"></div>` element (see Listing 5-10).

Each button has a `click` event, which will either log the user in or out. Furthermore, you wrap the buttons in containers having the classes `loggedout` and `loggedin` so that it's easily possible to visually switch between a logged-out and logged-in view.

Each button has an inline `onclick` event. Assigning events inline with DOM may be considered bad practice, as assigning them via JavaScript would be more efficient since you can dynamically assign events. This is done in Listing 5-10 for simplicity and demonstration.

Listing 5-10. Login and Logout Button Template (www/index.html)

```
<div class="panel panel-default">
  <div class="panel-heading">
    <h3 class="panel-title">My Social App</h3>
  </div>
  <div class="panel-body">
    <div class="loggedout">
      <div class="btn-group-vertical" role="group">
        <button type="button" class="btn btn-primary btn-lg"
onclick="myFacebookApp.login();">
          Login with Facebook
        </button>
      </div>
    </div>
    <div class="loggedin">
      <div class="btn-group-vertical" role="group">
        <button type="button" class="btn btn-primary btn-lg"
onclick="myFacebookApp.logout();">
          Logout
        </button>
      </div>
    </div>
  </div>
</div>
```

Since you don't know the user's login status before calling the getLoginStatus() function, initially both buttons should be hidden. Let's add some simple styles to accommodate this instance, as shown in Listing 5-11.

Listing 5-11. CSS Styles for Hiding the Login and Logout Button on Page Load

```
<style type="text/css">
  body { padding-top: 40px; }
  .loggedin, .loggedout { display: none; }
</style>
```

At this point, you want the handleLoginResponse function to actively react to the Facebook API response. If the status value indicates that the user is **connected**, you hide the login button and show the logout button; if not, do the opposite (see Listing 5-12).

Add a new property to the application named switchToView. It contains two functions for the login and logout button callbacks. Figure 5-13 shows the buttons in a device UI based on the current session status.

Listing 5-12. JavaScript Code for Handling the Login Status Response (www/js/myFacebookApp.js)

```
handleLoginResponse: function(response) {
  if (response.status == 'connected') {
    myFacebookApp.switchToView.loggedin();
  } else {
    myFacebookApp.switchToView.loggedout();
  }
},
```

```
switchToView: {
    loggedin: function() {
        $('.loggedin').show();
        $('.loggedout').hide();
    },
    loggedout: function() {
        $('.loggedin').hide();
        $('.loggedout').show();
    }
}
```

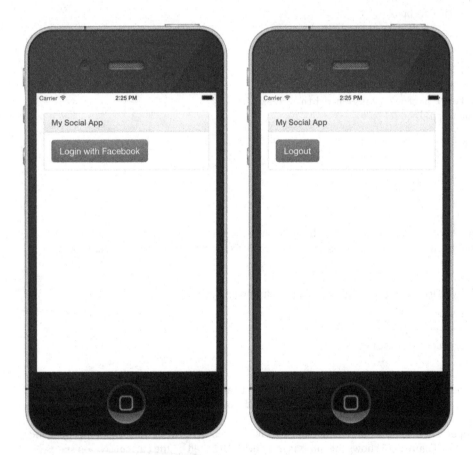

Figure 5-13. *The Facebook test application's logged-out state (left) vs. logged-in state (right)*

Login and Logout Events

To make the test application functional, you still need to add event handlers for the login and logout buttons. Let's start with the login button.

To request a login dialog, as described at the beginning of this section and shown in Figure 5-13, call the function `facebookConnectPlugin.login()`. The first argument of the function must be an array containing permission strings. You must request at least one permission to use the API. If you do not have any special requirements, just ask for the permission `public_profile`.

The response format of the login() method is identical to the response of the getLoginStatus() call. Knowing this, you can reuse the handleLoginResponse() method to handle the login response.

For the logout() function, just switch the view to the loggedout state if the logout process was successful; otherwise, keep the loggedin state, as demonstrated in Listing 5-13. Also, you add two new properties to the application, login and logout.

Listing 5-13. Login and Logout via the Facebook PhoneGap Plug-in (www/js/myFacebookApp.js)

```
login: function() {
    facebookConnectPlugin.login(["public_profile"],
        myFacebookApp.handleLoginResponse,
        myFacebookApp.debugResponse
    );
},
logout: function() {
    facebookConnectPlugin.logout(
        myFacebookApp.switchToView.loggedout,
        myFacebookApp.switchToView.loggedin
    );
}
```

■ **Note** Initially the login will be valid for about 60 days. However, if a user comes back to your application often, the session will never expire. It will be extended once a day when requests to Facebook's servers are executed (for example, by calling the getLoginStatus() method). If users do not use the application within 60 days and come back to the application, they need to log in again.

Requesting Permissions on Login

When asking for permissions during the login process, you can ask for multiple permissions at the same time. However, you can only ask for reading permissions, not for publishing permissions. Listing 5-14 demonstrates an example of retrieving multiple read-only values.

Listing 5-14. Logging a User In and Requesting More than One Permission

```
login: function() {
    facebookConnectPlugin.login(
    ["public_profile",
        "email",
        "user_photos",
        "user_tagged_places"],
        myFacebookApp.handleLoginResponse,
        myFacebookApp.debugResponse
    );
}
```

The result for this example request is shown in Figure 5-14. A summary of the requested permission is shown below the user's profile picture and application icon. By tapping the link "Edit the info you provide," the login dialog will switch to a view that offers users options to deselect permissions if they don't want to share the corresponding sections of their profiles.

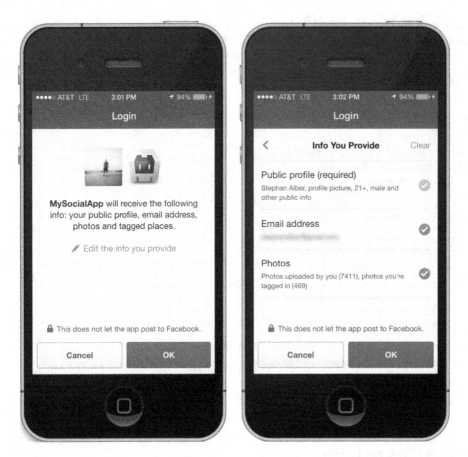

Figure 5-14. *A Facebook login dialog requesting multiple permissions (left) and a form to reject single permissions (right)*

Requesting Publishing Permissions

After a user logs in, you can ask for publishing permissions. As people are often very sensitive about granting publish permissions, you should only ask for them if you need them.

To request new permissions, simply call the login function again, this time passing a new permission array.

Add a new property to the app named getPublishingPermissions and use the publish_actions permission, as shown in Listing 5-15. Next, add a button to the loggedin section of your HTML template calling the permission request (Listing 5-16).

Listing 5-15. Requesting Permissions by Calling the Login Method Again (www/js/myFacebookApp.js)

```
getPublishingPermissions: function() {
    facebookConnectPlugin.login(["publish_actions"],
        myFacebookApp.handleLoginResponse,
        myFacebookApp.debugResponse
    );
}
```

Listing 5-16. Action Button for Requesting Publishing Permissions (www/index.html)

```
<button type="button" class="btn btn-default btn-lg"
  onclick="myFacebookApp.getPublishingPermissions();">
  Get Publishing Permissions
</button>
```

Hitting the button will show the dialog shown in Figure 5-15. In addition to accepting or rejecting the requests, users may change the privacy setting regarding the visibility of their potential posts.

Figure 5-15. *A permission request dialog for publishing posts on a user's timeline*

Getting a User's Email Address

After requesting permission to a user's profile information, read this data via the *Graph API*. You can read about all possible API endpoints in the Graph API reference documents at developers.facebook.com/docs/graph-api/reference/.

To access an API endpoint, call the function facebookConnectPlugin.api() (after logging in the user). The first argument is the path of the API endpoint, for example /me, which is a shortcut to the currently logged in user. You can specify your request by defining fields in the query string (e.g. fields=id,email).

You may pass a permission configuration array as second argument to ensure your application is in the possession of the required permissions, which is the email permission in your case.

Add a new property named getEmailAddress, as shown in Listing 5-17. This function gets the user's email address using the Graph API.

Listing 5-17. Getting the User's Email Address via the api() Method (www/js/myFacebookApp.js)

```
getEmailAddress: function() {
    facebookConnectPlugin.api("/me?fields=id,email", ["email"],
        // success callback
        myFacebookApp.debugResponse,
        // error callback
        myFacebookApp.debugResponse
    );
}
```

Verifying Permissions

There may be cases when you want to know whether the user granted permissions or not. Depending on the status, you could, for example, offer a button named "Enable Facebook sharing" or avoid such a button if the user already granted the publishing permission.

To get a status of all granted permissions, call the API endpoint /me/permissions. You can test the endpoint using the Graph API Explorer. Listing 5-18 shows an example response.

Listing 5-18. Response for Requesting a List of Granted Permissions

```
{
  "data":
   [
      {
        "permission": "public_profile",
        "status": "granted"
      },
      {
        "permission": "manage_pages",
        "status": "granted"
      },
      {
        "permission": "user_photos",
        "status": "granted"
      }
   ]
}
```

If you want to know about a specific permission, just add the permission name to the API request path, such as /me/permissions/email. If the user granted the email permission, the response will look like Listing 5-19. Otherwise, the response will contain an empty data array.

Listing 5-19. Response for Verifying a Single Permission

```
{
 "data": [{
    "permission": "email",
    "status": "granted"
  }]
}
```

Instead of using the Graph API Explorer, create a new function that will help verify a permission, as shown in Listing 5-20. In place of the variable scope, use the permission string you want to test, such as email.

Listing 5-20. Verifying a Single Permissions via the PhoneGap Facebook Plug-in

```
apiRequest: function(path, scope, callback) {
  facebookConnectPlugin.api("me/permissions/" + scope, null,
    // success callback permissions request
    function(response) {
      var missing_permissions = response.data.length > 0 && response.data[0].status ==
      "granted" ? null : [scope];
      facebookConnectPlugin.api(path, missing_permissions,
        // success callback for api request
        callback,
        // error callback for api request
        myFacebookApp.debugResponse
      );
    },
    // error callback for permissions request
    myFacebookApp.debugResponse
  );
}
```

Making API Requests

Let's build something more useful using a Graph API request. One example could be to get all photos in which a user is tagged. To do this, call the API endpoint me/photos, documented under "User Photos" at developers.facebook.com/docs/graph-api/reference/user/photos.

Test the API endpoint using the Graph API Explorer one more time. You will observe that the response key data contains an array of image objects. Use this to pass the response object to a Handlebars **compile()** call, as shown in Listing 5-21.

Listing 5-21. Getting Photos in Which the Current User Is Tagged (www/js/myFacebookApp.js)

```
getUserPhotos: function() {
  myFacebookApp.apiRequest("me/photos", "user_photos", function(response) {
    var source = $("#photos-template").html();
    var template = Handlebars.compile(source);
    var html = template({
      photos: response
    });
    $(".panel-body").html(html);
  });
}
```

An example template using Twitter Bootstrap to display a gallery is shown in Listing 5-22. Invoke the API request using another button in your `loggedin` state container (see Listing 5-23).

Listing 5-22. Gallery Template (www/index.html)

```
<script id="photos-template" type="text/x-handlebars-template">
  <div class="row">
    {{#each photos.data}}
    <div class="col-xs-6 col-md-3">
      <div class="thumbnail">
        <img src="{{images.3.source}}" alt="" />
      </div>
    </div>
    {{/each}}
  </div>
</script>
```

Listing 5-23. Action Button to Invoke the Photo Load Request (www/index.html)

```
<button type="button" class="btn btn-default btn-lg" onclick="myFacebookApp.getUserPhotos();">
  Get User Photos
</button>
```

The result of the compact script should be a gallery like in Figure 5-16. If you don't get a result, verify that your Facebook account actually contains tagged photos.

Figure 5-16. *Photo gallery based on a Facebook API request*

POST to Facebook via Graph API

There is one little limitation in the current version of the facebookConnectPlugin.api() method: you cannot execute POST or DELETE requests, which are required to publish a message or delete an element via the Graph API. However, for your application, you need to send a POST request to publish data on Facebook, for example to publish a message on a user's timeline (see developers.facebook.com/docs/graph-api/reference/user/feed).

Fortunately, the Facebook Graph API can be accessed via any system supporting HTTP requests. Using jQuery, this can be handled by simply using the $.ajax method to access any API endpoint, for example https://graph.facebook.com/me/feed, to get a user's feed. To post to their feed, switch the request type to POST and define the message and link to share in the key data. Next, use the access_token obtained from the Facebook login to identify them.

To have something to post, add a button to the HTML template to call a new postToFeed() function (Listing 5-24) that you add to the application. The UI element that triggers this call is shown in Listing 5-25. You can see the result of the test in Figure 5-17. You can use the same system to execute any POST or DELETE request using the Graph API.

Listing 5-24. Posting to the Facebook Graph API Using a jQuery XHTTP Request

```
postToFeed: function() {
  facebookConnectPlugin.login(["publish_actions"], function(response) {
      if (response.status != "connected") {
        return false;
      }
      $.ajax({
        type: "POST",
        url: "https://graph.facebook.com/me/feed",
        data: {
          access_token: response.authResponse.accessToken,
          message: "Hello World!",
          link: "http://blog.parse.com/"
        },
        success: function(response) {
          console.log(response);
        },
        dataType: "json"
      });
    },
    myFacebookApp.debugResponse
  );
}
```

Listing 5-25. A Custom "Share on Facebook" Button

```
<button type="button" class="btn btn-default btn-lg" onclick="myFacebookApp.postToFeed();">
  Share on Facebook (API)
</button>
```

Figure 5-17. *The post result of sharing a link via the Facebook Graph API*

Uploading a Picture

The same challenge as for posting links and messages via the Facebook PhoneGap plug-in applies to the matter of uploading photos or videos: the plug-in does not offer this kind of functionality. However, there is a similar solution for this.

In this case, you can't use the jQuery xHTTP approach to upload files directly from the PhoneGap application. Instead, you'll use the Cordova File Transfer plug-in (github.com/apache/cordova-plugin-file-transfer).

The File Transfer plug-in provides a way to upload files using an HTTP multi-part POST request. You can use it for downloading files as well. To install the plug-in, execute the terminal command shown in Listing 5-26.

Listing 5-26. Adding the Cordova File Transfer Plug-in to Your Project

```
phonegap plugin add org.apache.cordova.file-transfer
```

Next, you need a photo to be uploaded to Facebook. In Chapter 11, you will learn how to access photos from a device, or take new photos using the device's camera. To keep things simple, you'll use a static image for now.

Place a photo of your choice in /www/img. Next, add a new button to invoke the upload process in the loggedin section (see Listing 5-27).

Listing 5-27. Upload Button (www/index.html)

```
<button type="button" class="btn btn-default btn-lg" onclick="myFacebookApp.uploadFile();">
  Upload File
</button>
```

To publish photos, you can use the endpoint /{user-id}/photos or the shortcut /me/photos. The image data will be sent encoded as multipart form data using the key source. You can additionally provide a photo caption via the key message.

You configuring these parameters using the FileUploadOptions object. The property fileKey is set to source. This defines the name of the form data element. Using the property params, you can define a set of key/value pairs to pass in the HTTP request. In this place, you pass the photo caption in the key message as well as an access_token obtained by the login response object.

Let's add some new properties to the main application object for uploading photos. Add three new methods for uploading files: the main function, and a success and error method. This is demonstrated in Listing 5-28.

After successfully posting an image using the upload feature, go on facebook.com and see your work. Figure 5-18 illustrates a working demo.

Listing 5-28. Uploading a Static Photo to Facebook

```
uploadFile: function() {
  facebookConnectPlugin.login(["publish_actions"], function(response) {
    var options = new FileUploadOptions();
    options.fileKey = "source";
    options.chunkedMode = false;
    options.httpMethod = "POST";

    var params = {};
    params.access_token = response.authResponse.accessToken;
    params.message = "Hello World!";

    options.params = params;

    var filePath = cordova.file.applicationDirectory + "/www/img/my_photo.jpg";
    var ft = new FileTransfer();
    ft.upload(filePath, encodeURI("https://graph.facebook.com/me/photos"),
    myFacebookApp.onUploadSuccess, myFacebookApp.onUploadFail, options);
    },
    myFacebookApp.debugResponse
  );
},
onUploadSuccess: function(uploadResponse) {
  console.log(uploadResponse);
  var response = JSON.parse(uploadResponse.response);
  console.log(response);
},
onUploadFail: function(response) {
  myFacebookApp.debugResponse(response);
}
```

Figure 5-18. *An example of a static image shared using your sample application*

■ **Tip** Read about additional parameters in the Facebook Developer documentation at developers.facebook.com/docs/graph-api/reference/user/photos/.

Share Dialog

You have already seen how to post directly to a person's feed using the Graph API. Next, you'll do the same, except this time using the Share dialog. This method doesn't require a Facebook login or need any special permissions. The implementation is a bit more straightforward since you don't have to deal with making an XHTTP request.

Start by adding a new button to the view (see Listing 5-29). As this is a test example, you will hard-code the link you would like to share. In your example, it's www.parse.com (see Listing 5-30). An example of how this would look like once the link is posted to your feed is shown in Figure 5-19.

Listing 5-29. Share Dialog Button

```
<button type="button" class="btn btn-default btn-lg" onclick="myFacebookApp.showDialog();">
  Share on Facebook (Dialog)
</button>
```

Listing 5-30. Functionality for Share Dialog Button

```
showDialog: function() {
  facebookConnectPlugin.showDialog({
    method: "feed",
    link: "https://www.parse.com/",
    caption: "Add a message ..."
  },
```

```
   // success callback
   myFacebookApp.debugResponse,
   // error callback
   myFacebookApp.debugResponse
   );
}
```

Figure 5-19. *An example post using the Share dialog*

Summary

This chapter focused on integrating a PhoneGap application with the Facebook API. The Facebook Platform offers a range of tools and services such as sharing features and monetization opportunities.

Syncing a Facebook-enabled PhoneGap application requires precise naming configuration. When creating a new PhoneGap application with the CLI, you specified the bundle identifier that will be associated with a Facebook application.

After logging into Facebook, you were given the opportunity to create a new application and configure it for an existing PhoneGap application. iOS and Android integration varies.

Using the Facebook Graph Explorer, you were able to request user data to use for your application. Permissions vary widely and are based on how you want to use a user's information. Users must accept the permission(s) you are requesting in order to use your application, so be mindful.

We approached two different ways for users to log into Facebook: native and web. Each usage was triggered based on many factors, including if the user has the Facebook app installed natively and is logged in. Using the login and logged out functionality that Facebook provides, you were able to show a unique view based on the users session state.

The Graph API allowed you to post content on behalf of your users. You created a way to post images and other media to a user's feed.

CHAPTER 6

The Messenger Application

Laying the Foundation to Build a Messaging Application

The best way to appreciate the marriage between Parse and PhoneGap is to create an application from scratch. In this chapter, we will establish the basic coding pattern that will be used as the application grows.

This chapter will lay the foundation for a fully functional real-world application that you will build over the remaining chapters. Using what you have learned from previous chapters, you will set up this application's namespace structure, test the app using an emulator, and add the app's first feature namespace for storing the core functionality of the app.

Your goal for the rest of this book is to build a robust app that is purposely designed to demonstrate some of the capabilities that Parse and PhoneGap together have to offer. You will soon discover that what you learn from this application can be used to build that other amazing app idea you have in your head.

The Messenger App will have modern features such as social sharing, location detection, and user management. Some other key features that this application will demonstrate include the following:

- Signing up new users

- Logging in and session management

- Camera access

The Messenger App

This jack-of-all-trades application uses some great extendable features that we encourage you to expand on to make your own app. Together, we'll introduce key concepts in both Parse and PhoneGap, step-by-step.

When building an application, it's always good to know whom you are building it for. If you have experience using instant messaging, text messaging, online chatting, and sharing content with your social network, then *you* are the target audience this application is looking to serve. However, this time instead of being the app consumer, you will be building it from the ground up.

We drew the inspiration for our Messenger application that you will be building from the Facebook Messenger app. We felt the Facebook Messenger app has just the right amount of features that you would find in any modern instant messaging application. Figure 6-1 shows how the application appears on Google Play.

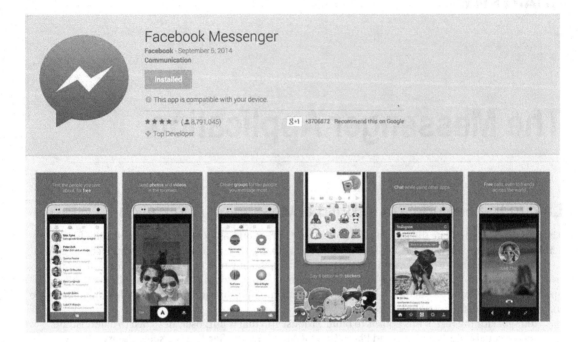

Figure 6-1. *The Facebook Messenger application as it looks on Google play*

Goals for the Messenger App

Our goal is not to replicate this application. We are taking some of the features and recreating them with Parse and PhoneGap to illustrate the power that they have when used together.

The application you will begin to build in this chapter will demonstrate some of the most common features of most instant messaging apps. Once users sign up through the user registration page via e-mail or Facebook, they will be able to do things such as the following:

- Send and receive messages

- Attach media and location information with messages

- Make content shareable using the Facebook SDK

We will explore core features in Parse and PhoneGap that will give you a grasp on how to add them to your next application. These skills will assist you in building the foundation for creating advanced database-driven applications. Using PhoneGap, you will learn to access native mobile features programmatically that we will use to sync with Parse.

Application Views

You already know that this application will be used to share and send messages between users, but how exactly will each section of the application work?

When it comes to software development, the term *view* is used to describe a graphical user interface (GUI) that is used to interact with a particular section of an application. The most fundamental view of this application will be the *login* view. This page will have a form where users can sign into the application using the credentials they supplied in the *registration* view. As you progress through the development of this application, we will introduce different states that the user will experience while using it.

110

Thinking about the views of an application will help you to mentally reserve logical data that will be associated with each view. Breaking it up in this manner will help you focus on one section of the application at a time. There may come a time when two different views of an application require the same functionality. Because of this, it is imperative to think ahead and plan out how you intend on adding your desired features.

Choosing Third-Party Libraries

There are *many* ways to build a JavaScript application. Entire frameworks and libraries are dedicated to providing code structure and reusable patterns to assist you in creating a maintainable application.

Of course, we recommend using a powerful JavaScript framework for building your application. Yet, in our examples, we passed on using such a framework to avoid strong dependencies. We'll merely lean on simple libraries like jQuery, which may easily be replaced by your favorite framework. This way we are able to focus on demonstrating the concept of combining Parse with PhoneGap and giving you great flexibility to follow your personal approach to organize your code.

It's all JavaScript. What this means is that because JavaScript is such an extendable and popular language, the approaches to developing an application can be virtually endless. Knowing this, we decided to go without the aid of any fancy third-party scripts and use a simple system that allows for demonstration of complex ideas in an intuitive way.

Let's dig into some code and start building this application!

Project Setup

Before jumping directly into your code editor, it is important to plan things out to get an overall perspective of what you'll be building. The following exercise will help you customize a default PhoneGap application so that extending upon it is done in a clear and obvious way.

YOUR PROJECT SETUP

We begin the Messenger App by creating a new PhoneGap application. You'll add some dependencies and slightly modify the JavaScript file that PhoneGap produces when creating a new project.

In your terminal, navigate to the location where you intend on saving this project.

1. Create a new project by executing. `phonegap create TheMessenger`. Change the current directory to the new folder using `cd TheMessenger`.

2. To be able to debug the application, add the console plug-in using the following terminal command: `phonegap plugin add org.apache.cordova.console`.

3. Open the `config.xml`, located in the root folder in your editor, and adjust the widget `id` for this application. Update the `<name>` to `TheMessenger` (case sensitive). You can optionally edit the `<description>`.

4. In the `www/js` directory, rename the `index.js` file to **app.js**. The purpose of renaming this file is to aid in organizing our code semantically. The file will be our starting point of the application; hence, we want its name to represent this task.

Next, download vendor libraries used for this project. You will be adding more for later parts of the application:

1. Create a new folder in www/js named vendor. This will be used for third-party JavaScript files.

2. Download Twitter Bootstrap at http://getbootstrap.com/. After unzipping the files, complete the following steps:

    •   Copy the CSS files bootstrap.min.css and bootstrap-theme.min.css to www/css/.

    •   Copy the fonts directory to the www folder.

    •   Copy js/boostrap.min.js to www/js/vendor/.

3. Download the Production (Minified) Parse JavaScript library at https://parse.com/docs/downloads. Save parse-1.4.2.min.js to www/js/vendor/.

4. Download the compressed production of jQuery at http://jquery.com/download/. (We are using jquery-2.1.4.min.js.) Copy the jQuery library to www/js/vendor/.

5. Download Handlebarsjs at http://handlebarsjs.com/ and save it in www/js/vendor.

Figure 6-2 shows our project's file structure up to this point.

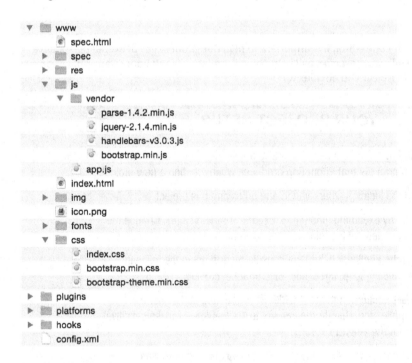

Figure 6-2. The file structure of the project up to this point

Adding all of our vendor files to our new PhoneGap application allows us to begin adding custom code that will make use of them.

Application File Setup

Now it's time to add some *custom* JavaScript code. This application will have many JavaScript files, so it's important to start things off right.

We begin by extending the app namespace that PhoneGap gives us when creating a new application. This is where we define the main sections of our application, beginning with the definition of the application itself. You will then alter the app.js file with some test code, as well as create the core file of this application. Once that's all set up, you'll add some sample HTML to the index page and preview the application using an emulator.

SET UP APPLICATION AND CORE FILES

You will first create the core of the app—a file that stores functionality that will be used throughout the application. You'll then edit the default JavaScript file that PhoneGap provides when creating a new application.

1. Create a new file in the www/js directory named core.js.

2. Populate it with the following code snippet:

```
app.core = {
  initialize: function() {
    alert('Initialize application');
  }
};
```

3. Open the app.js file and empty the contents of the receivedEvent function with exception to console.log(). Then add a call to the initialize function from the core namespace:

```
receivedEvent: function(id) {
  console.log('Received Event: ' + id);
  app.core.initialize();
}
```

This demonstrates how we will be using the object literal pattern for developing our application by calling the initialize function of core.js from app.js.

Testing Your Application

If you were to run your application right now, it wouldn't work as you expected. The index.html file is still referencing the index.js file that you renamed to app.js earlier.

As you learned in Chapter 2, there are a few ways to test a PhoneGap application. After a few more updates, we will be using the cordova emulator to test out the early stages of this application.

To get started, open up the index.html file located in the www directory of your project. You will see the following code right before the closing of the body tag:

```
<script type="text/javascript" src="js/index.js"></script>
<script type="text/javascript">
    app.initialize();
</script>
```

First, apply the name change from index.js to app.js in the script reference. Then add a new script reference to core.js:

```
<script type="text/javascript" src="js/app.js"></script>
<script type="text/javascript" src="js/core.js"></script>
<script type="text/javascript">
    app.initialize();
</script>
```

BUILD AND TEST THE APPLICATION

In this exercise, you'll add a new PhoneGap platform to test out the application.

1. Install the platform you intend on testing with. Navigate to the root directory of your project in your terminal and run phonegap build <platform>. For example, to install and build the iOS platform, run phonegap build ios. For Android, run phonegap build android.

2. Emulate the current build to test it out. As the phonegap command doesn't support calling an emulator, we'll fall back to the cordova command. Your application will still work using the cordova instead of the phonegap command. To run the emulator, execute cordova emulate <platform>, for example, cordova emulate ios. Running the emulate command will execute a build before launching the emulator.

This should open the emulator with your custom application code (see Figure 6-3).

Figure 6-3. *A screenshot of the alert message that is executed from the call in the receivedEvent function defined in www/js/app.js*

After building the desired platform and launching the iOS or Android emulator, an alert message lets us know that our application has loaded successfully.

Loading Application Scripts

Web developers have many tools in our arsenal. As this application grows, you will be adding more and more JavaScript files. Some will be third-party vendor scripts, while others may be custom code that will be used for a feature in the app.

There are many ways to deal with adding new scripts to a development workflow. In an effort to keep things simple and concise, you will be adding a new vendor, *LABjs*, to help us deal with loading scripts in an organized way.

We will be storing references to our scripts in a variable called `scripts`. This object variable will have properties that we will assign paths to JavaScript files in our application. This will help organize the scripts in a purposeful way. Later on in the application, you will add other properties to `scripts` to aid in organization.

115

The order in which the script references are defined *do* matter; the first script defined in the common array is the first script to load from the collection. The following exercise will put our script loader into action.

ADDING A SCRIPT LOADER AND EXTENDING THE CORE OF THE APPLICATION

Here you will add LABjs and customize `app.core` so that we can organize the way to load scripts. You will be using the technique you learn here throughout the application.

1. Download the latest version of LABjs at `http://labjs.com/`, unpack the ZIP file, and copy `LAB.min.js` to the `www/js/vendor` directory.

2. Edit the `index.html` file by adding the new dependency above the `app.js` script reference. The final script references will look as follows:

```
<script type="text/javascript" src="cordova.js"></script>
<script type="text/javascript" src="js/vendor/LAB.min.js"></script>
<script type="text/javascript" src="js/app.js"></script>
<script type="text/javascript" src="js/core.js"></script>
<script>
    app.initialize();
</script>
```

3. Next, you will add a new variable to the core file for storing references to JavaScript files. We will use these files in `app.core.initialize()` to call a new function, `app.core.afterLoad()`,once all the of scripts have loaded. Note that the order of the scripts is important.

4. Edit `core.js` like so:

```
var scripts = {
    common: [
        // Vendors
        './js/vendor/parse-1.4.2.min.js',
        './js/vendor/jquery-2.1.4.min.js',
        './js/vendor/bootstrap.min.js',
        './js/vendor/handlebars-v3.0.3.js'
    ]
};
app.core = {
    initialize: function() {
        $LAB.script(scripts.common).wait(app.core.afterLoad);
    },
    afterLoad: function() {
        // Initialize this Parse application
        Parse.initialize('your-app-id', 'your-javascript-key');
        alert('Initialize application');
    }
};
```

5. As you did with the previous exercise, test the build out and make sure the script loader is working correctly. Rebuild the application by running `phonegap build <platform>`. To run the emulator, execute `cordova emulate <platform>`.

In this exercise, you implemented the LABjs JavaScript loader by adding it to the `index.html` page. You then extended the `app.core` namespace by adding a new `afterLoad()` function that is called *after* the scripts load. In order to make sure it all worked correctly, you were asked you to run the emulator again to ensure the alert message was called properly, thus proving that all of our scripts loaded successfully.

Now that we have a simple script loading process set up, it will be easy to add new features and vendor files to our application. This is extremely useful when you are knee deep in development and want to add new features to this application.

Because this application will have multiple views (or HTML pages), each one will require the same CSS and JavaScript files. We will be using this new `index.html` page, the application's home page view, as a base template for the rest of the views we add. The next section will discuss further preparing our home page to use as a base for other views.

The Home Page View

The home page, or index page, of any web site is typically the first page that users see when visiting the site— or in our case, our application. At this point in our application, the home page isn't that exciting. There is an alert message that doesn't provide anything useful for prospective users, and the layout is still the same one that is generated once a new PhoneGap application is created. Let's change that.

In an effort to simplify the aesthetics of this application, we choose Twitter Bootstrap to do the heavy lifting. Of course, you could always customize it when you complete the application, but for simplicity and rapid prototyping, it is nice to have some out-of-the-box features that we know already work.

In an earlier exercise, you added some dependencies that we are using in the application to make our development a bit easier. In order to make use of them, we need to reference them in our pages. The next exercise will do just that for the home page.

SETUP APP AND CORE FILES

Here, you'll add the references to CSS files that come with Twitter Bootstrap. Using the newly added styles, you'll create a basic layout for the home page view.

1. Delete the file `www/css/index.css` and remove the link tag reference from `index.html` template to get rid of the style rules provided by the PhoneGap default application. Add a new file called `style.css` to collect your custom style rules.

2. Open the `index.html` file in your text editor. Insert the following snippet above the `title` tag to reference the style sheet:

    ```
    <link rel="stylesheet" type="text/css" href="css/bootstrap.min.css">

    <link rel="stylesheet" type="text/css" href="css/bootstrap-theme.min.css">

    <link rel="stylesheet" type="text/css" href="css/style.css">
    ```

3.   Now that we have access to the styles provided by Bootstrap, populate the `<body>` of index.html with the following snippet:

```
<div class="container">
 <br>
 <div class="jumbotron">
   <h1>The Messenger</h1>
     <p>
        Welcome to The Messenger! With this app you
        will be able to send messages to your friends.
        Use it as a starting point to create something
        more unique.
     </p>
     <p>
       <a href="login.html" class="btn btn-primary btn-lg" role="button">
         Login &raquo;
       </a>
     </p>
     <p>
       <a href="registration.html" class="btn btn-primary btn-lg" role="button">
         Registration &raquo;
       </a>
     </p>
   </div>
</div>
```

4.   Edit core.js by removing the alert test message we added earlier.

5.   Preview the app by running `cordova emulate <platform>`. You should see its home page as shown in Figure 6-4.

Figure 6-4. *The home page of our application using the styles from Twitter Bootstrap*

Here we added the main CSS files that we'll be using throughout the app. You created a simple home page using some of the styles as defined by the Twitter Bootstrap library.

You'll notice that there are two links that point to pages that don't yet exist. Clicking these links will result in an error, which is expected. In the next chapter, you will dig into Parse and learn how to register a new user.

Summary

This chapter marked the beginning of the Messenger application. After creating a new PhoneGap project, we downloaded and added references to dependencies that are used by the app.

Because all applications have *states*, commonly grouped into *views*, creating the core script is the first step in this app's functionality. New PhoneGap applications come with a default view and script. We extended the app namespace and ran the first emulated test to make sure the app initialized.

As you learned in Chapter 4, script loading can be a challenging task. We used the LABjs library to help organize the loading of all of our JavaScript files. By loading LABjs first, followed by the app.js and core.js file, we are able to sequentially load files based on the order that was set in the scripts variable in core.js. Using a new afterLoad() function on the app.core namespace, we were able to test out the way scripts load by confirming the call to afterLoad(), which currently alerts the message "Initialize Application".

Using Twitter Bootstrap we styled the home page view of our application. The two links in the index.html page point to views that we will create in the next chapters. The first of these two views will be the registration page.

CHAPTER 7

■ ■ ■

User Registration with Parse

If you Build it, *Hopefully* they will Come

This chapter focuses on registering a new user with Parse, and having them log in using their credentials. We'll also cover related topics like a password reset feature and registration via Facebook.

To unlock all of the awesome features you'll be building for the Messenger App, a user of this application first needs to be a registered user. At this point in your digital life, you may already have a few online accounts that you need to provide some credentials to be able to use. Similarly, the Messenger App will need to know who is using it.

Like most dynamic web sites and applications that involve user accounts, there is likely some database table that is responsible for storing a user's information. There are many other attributes that could be tied to a user, such as a profile image or birthday–pretty much anything that your application can use to customize the experience of your application on a personal level.

Parse User Registration

Parse has a special way of handling and creating users. Unlike normal classes that you create manually, you will be using the `Parse.User` object, a subclass of `Parse.Object`, to handle the users of the Messenger App. Later in this section, you'll make use of the console plug-in to help you debug. Let's begin by registering new users to your growing application.

The `Parse.User` object has fields and methods that are unique to the `User` class. There are two fields that are required when registering a new user. As you may have already imagined, they are the *username* and *password* fields. The class reserves the following user-specific fields:

- username
- password
- authData
- emailVerified
- email

As with other Parse classes, the following fields also come standard by default:

- objectId
- createdAt
- updatedAt
- ACL

You will be using the fields username, password, and email as you progress through the development of the registration process. You'll also learn about the authData and emailVerified fields in this chapter.

Preparation: Adding View Initialization

In Chapter 6 you defined the method app.core.afterLoad() in the JavaScript file www/js/core.js. The method is called when all of the scripts, which you defined in the variable scripts, are loaded. This is the perfect moment to initialize a view because you know that all of your libraries, like jQuery or Parse, are ready to be used.

In your case, this view will be the registration view, using the namespace app.registration. If you want to make your application work for just this view, you would initialize the view using a static call:

```
app.registration.initialize();
```

Naturally, this cannot be the goal. Instead, you use a variable named config.view as placeholder for the view you want to initialize. As shown in Listing 7-1, you'll define this value for each view in its HTML template individually.

Listing 7-1. An Example of How to Configure Views

```
<script>
    var config = {
        view: 'name-of-view'
    };
    app.initialize();
</script>
```

To be able to use this system, update the method app.core.afterLoad() to the code of Listing 7-2. You will verify that the view name actually exists in the namespace app. If that's the case, you call the initialize function to execute the view's specific JavaScript code. Each view script must contain a function named initialize to be initialized.

Listing 7-2. Script Loader Configuration (www/js/core.js)

```
app.core = {
    initialize: function() {
        $LAB.script(scripts.common).wait()
            .script(scripts.models).wait(app.core.afterLoad);
    },
    afterLoad: function() {
        // Initialize this Parse application
        Parse.initialize('your-app-id', 'your-javascript-key');
        // Initialize View
        if (config.view in app) {
            app[config.view].initialize();
        }
    }
};
```

Registration View

Next, you'll add the registration view for this application. After adding the presentation layer (HTML/CSS), you will add and reference a new JavaScript file specifically used for this view. You will keep all JavaScript files in the directory called www/js/views.

Duplicate the index.html file and name the new file registration.html. Remove the content between the <body> tag as well as the content *before* the first script tags. Don't remove the script tag references; you need them to run the application! Add a registration form containing fields for first name, last name, email, and password, as shown in Listing 7-3. If you build out your registration form correctly, it will look like Figure 7-1.

Listing 7-3. The HTML Code for the Registration View

```
<div class="panel panel-default">
  <div class="panel-heading">
    <h3 class="panel-title">Create Account</h3>
  </div>
  <div class="panel-body">
    <form role="form">
      <div class="form-group">
        <input type="text" name="first_name" class="form-control input-lg"
            placeholder="First Name" required autofocus>
      </div>
      <div class="form-group">
        <input type="text" name="last_name" class="form-control input-lg"
            placeholder="Last Name" required>
      </div>
      <div class="form-group">
        <input type="email" name="email" class="form-control input-lg"
            placeholder="Email Address" required>
      </div>
      <div class="form-group">
        <input type="password" name="password" class="form-control input-lg"
            placeholder="Password" required>
      </div>
      <div class="form-group">
        <button class="btn btn-lg btn-primary btn-block" type="submit"
            id="login-submit">Register</button>
      </div>
      <div class="form-group">
        <a href="index.html" class="btn btn-default">< back</a>
      </div>
    </form>
  </div>
</div>
```

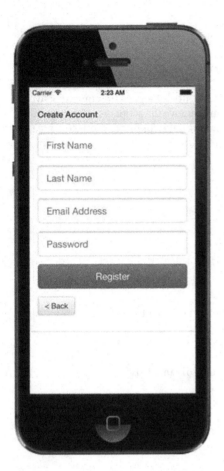

Figure 7-1. *The registration view of the Messenger App*

Registration Task

Next, you'll need a script to handle the form and send the registration data to Parse. Add a new file called registration.js in the folder www/js/views. Add a new property to app named registration. The object will have two functions, initialize and submit. When the form responds to the submit event, it will make a call to the submit function on the registration namespace. This behavior is shown in Listing 7-4.

Listing 7-4. Registration JavaScript Code (www/js/views/registration.js)

```
app.registration = {
    initialize: function() {
        $('form').on('submit', function(event) {
            event.preventDefault();
            app.registration.submit();
        });
    },
    submit: function() {}
};
```

You do not want to execute code that belongs to other views in the registration form. For this reason, you call the script by checking against the variable `config.view` (Listing 7-5) to execute the appropriate function.

Listing 7-5. Registration View Configuration (www/registration.html)

```
<script>
    var config = {
        view: 'registration'
    };
    app.initialize();
</script>
```

To make the script accessible for your application, add the new `registration.js` file to the `scripts` object in `core.js`, as shown in Listing 7-6.

Listing 7-6. Script Loader Configuration (www/js/core.js)

```
var scripts = {
    common: [
        // Vendors
        './js/vendor/parse-1.4.2.min.js',
        './js/vendor/jquery-2.1.4.js',
        './js/vendor/bootstrap.min.js',

        // Views
        './js/views/registration.js'
    ]
};
```

Preparing User Data

You will now write the functionality used to read the data submitted on the registration view. This data will populate a `Parse.User` object. Your actions ultimately derive from the `Parse.Object`. You will use the `set()` function to set values to the object, *then* save them to Parse.

To avoid duplicate submissions while the script is still working, all form buttons and inputs will be disabled. Add the function body of Listing 7-7 to the `submit()` function in `www/js/views/registration.js` and test the form submission using the `console.log()` function.

Listing 7-7. Registration Form Submit (www/js/views/registration.js)

```
submit: function() {

    $('button, input').attr('disabled', 'disabled');

    var first_name = $('input[name=first_name]').val();
    var last_name = $('input[name=last_name]').val();
    var email = $('input[name=email]').val();
    var password = $('input[name=password]').val();
```

```
var user = new Parse.User();
user.set("first_name", first_name);
user.set("last_name", last_name);
user.set("username", email);
user.set("email", email);
user.set("password", password);

// View the details of the user variable a Parse.User object
console.log(user.attributes);

}
```

Rebuild the application by executing phonegap build <platform>. You can test the form by running cordova emulate <platform>.

■ **Tip** Debug using the cordova console plug-in! Add some sample data to the form and submit it. After submitting the form, you might anticipate seeing the contents of user.attributes. The data will not sync to Parse just yet. Before you get there, explore the console and see what is inside the user object. Testing the output of variables while you are developing is helpful for debugging and exploring your application.

Sending User Data to Parse

Being the special User class that this is, Parse has some magic behind the signUp method. It not only ensures that the username and email are unique database entries, it also encrypts the password field to securely send its value in the cloud.

Technically speaking, the signUp method is an extension of Parse.Object, by way of Parse.User. You can either provide attributes using the set() function before calling the signUp function as in

```
user.set("key", value);
user.signUp(null, ...);
```

or by passing a simple data object as first parameter to the signUp function like

```
user.signUp({
    key: value
}, ...)
```

And just as in the Parse.Object.save() function, the second parameter is an object that has success and error callback methods. These methods can help you react to invalid inputs or take the user to the next step.

Updating Your Application Code

In `www/js/views/registration.js` add the snippet of Listing 7-8 to the `submit()` function. Rebuild your application and submit the form to Parse using some sample data. Keep the values simple for quick testing.

Listing 7-8. Parse signUp Function

```
user.signUp(null, {
    success: function(user) {
        alert("Success!");
    },
    error: function(user, error) {
        alert("Error: " + error.code + " " + error.message);
        $('button, input').attr('disabled', 'disabled');
    }
});
```

View the test input data submitted to Parse using the Data Browser, as shown in Figure 7-2. Do so by selecting the current application at `https://www.parse.com/apps/`, and then click Core. The Data Browser is the first item to open.

Figure 7-2. *The Parse Data Browser showing submissions of the registration form*

Figure 7-3 shows the `Parse.User` object in action. Parse will throw an error if a duplicate username is found. This is the result of the `error` callback function of the `Parse.User.signUp` method.

Figure 7-3. *Parse.User error handling*

User Registration Recap

What good is an application if there aren't any users? This section covered using the `Parse.User` object to create a new user for your application. The `Parse.User` class is a special class that encrypts data and lets you use the `signUp` method to add new users.

Debugging is part of the computer programming process. You used the PhoneGap console plug-in to enable you to get insight into the code. First, you created a view for the registration form. This is the presentation layer where users register. After adding a custom script under the main app namespace, you used the initialize function of `app.registration` to bind an event to the submission form.

After experimenting with the console log, you sent the data to Parse for storage. This is available for viewing in the data browser upon a successful response from Parse during registration.

Login and Logout Using Parse

After registering for the application using `Parse.User.signUp()`, the user is automatically logged in to Parse. The session is cached and available until the user logs out. So far, you have not yet detected whether the user is logged in or out. At this point in your application, users who are logged in are still able to use the registration form again. Simply restarting the application will show the registration view, even though they are already logged in.

We will cover the matter of detection and existing session later in this chapter. For now, let's focus on building the logout and login views. The latter will provide a simple form with username, which is the user's email address in this case, and password. After submitting the form, you will add a JavaScript call that will communicate with Parse and verify whether the provided user credentials are valid.

Let's start things off by building the login view. In the second part of the exercise we'll come back to logging a user out. Figure 7-4 shows the completed login form.

Figure 7-4. *The view of the login page*

Login: Setting Up the Template

You start by creating a new HTML page for the login view. Use the index.html page as a starting point. After customizing the view, you add the code to log in a user.

Duplicate the index.html file and rename it to login.html. Empty out the body content without removing the script references. Add the HTML code of Listing 7-9 to create the view. In the same file, update the config.view value to login (Listing 7-10).

Listing 7-9. Login Template (www/login.html)

```html
<div class="panel panel-default">
    <div class="panel-heading">
        <h3 class="panel-title">Login</h3>
    </div>
    <div class="panel-body">
        <form role="form">
            <p>
                <input type="email" name="email" class="form-control input-lg"
                    placeholder="Email Address" autofocus>
            </p>
            <p>
                <input type="password" name="password" class="form-control input-lg"
                    placeholder="Password">
            </p>
            <p>
                <button class="btn btn-lg btn-primary btn-block" type="submit"
                    id="login-submit">Log in</button>
            </p>
            <p>
                <a href="registration.html" class="btn btn-lg btn-default btn-block">
                    Sign Up
                </a>
            </p>
        </form>
    </div>
</div>
```

Listing 7-10. Login View Configuration (www/login.html)

```html
<script>
    var config = {
        view: 'login'
    };
    app.initialize();
</script>
```

Add a new JavaScript file to www/js/views/login.js for this view. Attach a submit event handler to the form (Listing 7-11). The submission of the form will call a submit function, which you'll populate shortly. Next, add a script reference to the new file (Listing 7-12).

Listing 7-11. Login Template (www/js/login.js)

```javascript
app.login = {
    initialize: function() {
        $('form').on('submit', function(event) {
            event.preventDefault();
            app.login.submit();
        });
    },
    submit: function() {}
};
```

130

Listing 7-12. Updated Script Loader (www/js/core.js)

```
var scripts = {
    common: [
        // Vendors
        './js/vendor/parse-1.3.0.min.js',
        './js/vendor/jquery-2.1.1.js',
        './js/vendor/bootstrap.min.js',

        // Views
        './js/views/registration.js',
        './js/views/login.js'
    ]
};
```

Now that the HTML is set up, you can get the inputs from the login form when it is submitted. This view only gets initialized because of the value in `config.view` set in `login.html`.

To log in a user with Parse, you use the `logIn` method of the `Parse.User` object. The `logIn` function takes three parameters. The first two are the username and password of the user. The last parameter is an object that has two functions, `success` and `error`.

When the login form is submitted, the form input values are sent to Parse for processing. If the login was successful, Parse creates a user session so the app knows who's currently using it.

Login: Verifying Credentials

In this section, you will add functionality to the `submit` function of `login.js` to send the user data to Parse. In the `submit()` function from Listing 7-11, you will next call the `Parse.User.logIn()` function and provide an email address and password as function arguments, as shown in Listing 7-13.

Listing 7-13. Parse Login Handler (www/js/views/login.js)

```
submit: function() {
  $('button, input').attr('disabled', 'disabled');
  var email = $('input[name=email]').val();
  var password = $('input[name=password]').val();
}
```

Logging data to the console is always helpful. However, this time instead of calling `console.log` in the success function, you redirect the user to a welcome page. Replace the console.log message with a redirect, as shown in Listing 7-14. Once the user has a successful login, they will be redirected to a new view, the Welcome page. You will create this page next. If the user login fails, the form inputs will be re-enabled for the user to try again.

Listing 7-14. Redirecting the User After a Successful Login

```
Parse.User.logIn(email, password, {
    success: function(user) {
        window.location.href = 'logout.html';
    },
    // ...
}
```

Logout: Template and Functionality

Users can now log in to the application. This next view, the welcome page (see Figure 7-6), will show the user their name and provide a logout button. Duplicate the index.html file and rename it to logout.html. Without removing the JavaScript references, replace the <body> contents with the snippet of Listing 7-15. Update the config variable in logout.html to use the logout view (Listing 7-16).

Listing 7-15. Welcome and Logout Template (www/logout.html)

```
<div class="container">
    <br>
    <div class="jumbotron">
        <h1>
            Hello <span id="username"></span>
        </h1>
        <p>
            You are logged in!
        </p>
        <p>
            <a href="#" class="btn btn-primary btn-lg btn-block"
                role="button" id="logout-button">
                <i class="glyphicon glyphicon-log-out pull-right"></i>
                Logout
            </a>
        </p>
    </div>
</div>
```

Listing 7-16. Logout View Configuration (www/logout.html)

```
<script>
    var config = {
        view: 'logout'
    };
    app.initialize();
</script>
```

When the user is directed to logout.html, the initialize function of app.logout will be called. Use the current() method of the Parse.User object and get their *first name* to display it on the page. The current method retrieves the *currently* logged in Parse.User.

Create a new file called www/js/logout.js and populate it with the code of Listing 7-17. The logout.html view serves as an example of how you can get information from a user who is *currently* logged into your application. Using the Parse.User.logOut method lets you end the current user session. You redirect the user to the home page after logging out.

Listing 7-17. Logout Code (www/js/views/logout.js)

```
app.logout = {
    initialize: function() {
        $('#username').text(Parse.User.current().get('first_name'));
        $('#logout-button').on('click', function(event) {
            event.preventDefault();
            Parse.User.logOut();
            window.location.href = 'index.html';
        });
    }
};
```

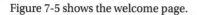 **Tip** The Parse user session is stored in the local storage of the application. It is valid until the user actively logs out.

Figure 7-5 shows the welcome page.

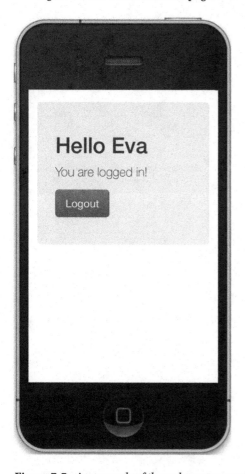

Figure 7-5. An example of the welcome page with a logged-in user named Eva

Protecting Views for Logged-in Users

Now, let's use what you just learned about logging users in and out. By detecting a user's session status, you will be able to direct them in and out of views that you deem public or private.

Besides protecting private data, you can use session data to provide different experiences for users who are logged in versus out. In your application, if the user session is invalid or expired, you redirect them to the login view to continue.

Each feature you have created so far requires a new HTML file. You will be adding the main navigation for users who are logged in. More than one page will require this navigation.

This means that *each* of your views requires the *same* HTML snippet for the navigation. If there were 10 views in this application, maintenance would be a pain. Happily, there *is* a better way.

You will be using templates to populate data dynamically. You learned about the Handlebars library in Chapter 4. Now it's time to see it in action.

By adding a new function to the app.core namespace, you will be able to render a template with dynamic script data. This allows you to create one HTML file that represents the main navigation. The logout button will fit perfectly in the nav menu. Once the initialize function of the view is called, you will load the navigation bar template when you call the new render function, which you'll be writing later.

Figure 7-6 illustrates how your main new main navigation will look when added to the application. You'll be leveraging styles and functionality that Twitter Bootstrap provides.

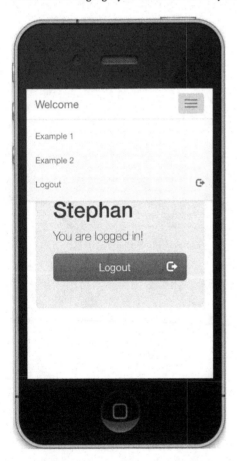

Figure 7-6. *The welcome view with dynamically loaded navigation*

There are two main states for this application. Each state is represented by the session state of the current user. Using the `config` property that is defined in each HTML file, you will add a new property named `public_access`, which can only be `true` or `false`. If a page is set as private (`public_access = false`), then only users who are logged in will be able to see it. To make a views available to everyone (logged in or out), set `public_access = true`.

Configuring Access Control

In the following exercise, you will learn how to configure your views to be public or private. You will extend the `app.core` namespace with new functions, which will be used to control access to your views.

You want to collect all functions related to the `Parse.User` object in one class. In this example, you will name this class `MyParseUser`. You'll also add some preliminary steps for controlling the experience for the user based on their current session status.

Create a new file called `MyParseUser.js` and place it in the folder `www/js/models`. You'll use the file to extend the `Parse.User` class, as shown in Listing 7-18. At the beginning of development this file will be more or less empty. You'll add functionality over time as you add features to this application.

Also, add the file `www/js/models/MyParseUser.js` to your JavaScript file loader `config` in `core.js`. The models need to be loaded *after* the Parse SDK. To ensure this behavior, create a new key named `models` in the `script` configuration object (Listing 7-19).

Adjust the LAB loader script in `app.core.initialize()` to load all models after the common scripts are loaded (Listing 7-20).

Listing 7-18. Custom Extension of the Parse.User Class (www/js/models/MyParseUser.js)

```
window.MyParseUser = Parse.User.extend({
    // Instance Methods
    }, {
    // Class Methods
});
```

Listing 7-19. Adjusted Script Loader for Custom Models

```
var scripts = {
    common: [],
    models: [
        // models
        './js/models/MyParseUser.js'
    ],
    web: []
};
```

Listing 7-20. Adjusted Script Loader for Custom Models

```
$LAB.script(scripts.common).wait()
    .script(scripts.models).wait(app.core.afterLoad);
```

Now you want to define access rules for each view. For each HTML file, add the property `public_access` to the `config` variable. For views that are public, set the value to `true`. For views requiring a login, set `public_access` to `false`. Your updated configuration object may look like Listing 7-21.

Listing 7-21. View Configuration Example

```
var config = {
    view: 'login',
    public_access: true
};
```

Update the views index.html, registration.html, and login.html to use the value true for public_access. Use the value false for the view logout.html.

Next, add the business logic to your application to respond to these new properties. As the access verification needs to be executed every time a user is accessing a view, you'll add this code part to your application core in the app.core object.

You will be adding two new functions named accessControl and globalEvents. Use accessControl to handle the access rules, and globalEvents to collect event handlers for cases like a global logout button. Add both functions calls in the afterLoad() function, as shown in Listing 7-22.

Listing 7-22. Updated afterLoad() Function (www/js/core.js)

```
app.core = {
    initialize: function() {
        // ...
    },
    afterLoad: function() {
        // ...
        // Protect Access
        app.core.accessControl();

        // Init Global Events
        app.core.globalEvents();

        // Initialize View
        if (config.view in app) {
            app[config.view].initialize();
        }
    },
    accessControl: function() {},
    globalEvents: function() {}
}
```

Finally, you'll add some access control rules. If a user is logged in, they will be redirected to the welcome view for logged-in users. In the current state of your application, logout.html is the welcome view. At a later state, you'll replace this view with another, such as a list of conversations.

If a user is logged out and is trying to access a private view, redirect them to the login view. Populate the accessControl() function with the code of Listing 7-23.

Listing 7-23. Updated accessControl() Function (www/js/core.js)

```
accessControl: function(){
    // user is logged in and accessing a public view
    if (MyParseUser.current() && config.public_access) {
        window.location.href = 'logout.html';
        return;
    }
}
```

```
    // user is not logged in and trying to access protected view
    if (!MyParseUser.current() && !config.public_access) {
        window.location.href = 'login.html';
        return;
    }
}
```

In this exercise you prepared a new Parse model that you'll use later. You extended the `app.core` namespace for access control management for forwarding users who aren't logged in.

There will be some new views coming up that will need to render dynamic content. In order to do this, you will add a new application script dependency to the `scripts` variable in `core.js` for Handlebars. Once this is set up, you will create a template for the main navigation.

Navigation Bar for Logged-in Users

You will use the Twitter Bootstrap navigation CSS styles. The link examples you're using are nonfunctional and are only used to demonstrate the structure. You'll replace them later with valid links. Furthermore, you'll add the variable `{{title}}`, which will be replaced by the current view's title.

Create a new file named www/navbar.html and populate it with the snippet shown in Listing 7-24. In this example, you use a Bootstrap component navbar. You can read more about the navigation bar in the Bootstrap documentation at `http://getbootstrap.com/components/#navbar`.

In the following step, extend the `accessControl` function by adding the navigation template rendering shown in Listing 7-25. Using jQuery's `ajax` method, load the `navbar.html` file. Adding the option `async: false` will make the script load synchronously, which means that the script execution will pause until the file is loaded. In a web application, you wouldn't use this approach because that environment depends on a server providing this file. In PhoneGap, the file is loaded from the application's local file system. To guarantee that the file is loaded instantly, use the synchronous load method demonstrated in Listing 7-25.

Once it's done loading, use Handlebars to compile the template and dynamically prepend its contents to the body.

Listing 7-24. Navigation Bar Template (www/navbar.html)

```
<nav class="navbar navbar-default navbar-fixed-top" role="navigation">
  <div class="container-fluid">
    <div class="navbar-header">
      <button type="button" class="navbar-toggle collapsed"
        data-toggle="collapse" data-target="#navigation">
        <span class="icon-bar"></span>
        <span class="icon-bar"></span>
        <span class="icon-bar"></span>
      </button>
      <a class="navbar-brand" href="#">{{title}}</a>
    </div>
    <div class="collapse navbar-collapse" id="navigation">
      <ul class="nav navbar-nav">
        <li><a href="example-1.html">Example 1</a></li>
        <li><a href="example-2.html">Example 2</a></li>
```

```
      <li>
        <a href="#" id="logout">
          <i class="glyphicon glyphicon-log-out pull-right"></i>
          Logout
        </a>
      </li>
    </ul>
  </div>
 </div>
</nav>
```

Listing 7-25. Template Loader and Render Methods (www/js/core.js)

```
accessControl: function() {
    // user is logged in and accessing a public view
    if (MyParseUser.current() && config.public_access) {
        window.location.href = 'logout.html';
        return;
    }
    // user is not logged in and trying to access protected view
    if (!MyParseUser.current() && !config.public_access) {
        window.location.href = 'login.html';
        return;
    }
    // Do not add navbar for logged out users
    if (!MyParseUser.current()) {
        return;
    }
    // Add Navbar
    $.ajax({
        url: "navbar.html",
        async: false
    }).done(function(source) {
        var template = Handlebars.compile(source);
        $('body').prepend(template(config)).addClass('has-navbar');
    });
}
```

Nothing is perfect. Preview the snippet you just added. You are adding a class to the body named has-navbar. This is how you can customize the appearance of views that use the navigation template. By default, the navbar is 50px high. Open the www/css/style.css and add the class body.has-navbar, as proposed in Listing 7-26.

Listing 7-26. Navbar CSS Rule (www/css/style.css)

```
body.has-navbar {
    padding-top: 70px;
}
```

Navigation Bar Title

Now let's add a title to the view configuration. In the Handlebars template navbar.html you added the variable {{title}} as a placeholder for the view title. Each view should have an individual title. For this purpose, add another property named title to the global config variable. Since there won't be a navigation bar for public views, you only need to set a value for all views requiring a login.

As an example, edit your logout view and add the title "Welcome" (see Listing 7-27). In the logout view, when the navigation bar loads, the {{title}} will be populated using the config.title value.

Listing 7-27. Navbar CSS Rule (www/logout.html)

```
var config = {
    view: 'logout',
    public_access: false,
    title: 'Welcome'
};
```

You created a new HTML file that represents the navigation bar. In the accessControl function, you added some new code to **render** the navigation bar if the user was in an active Parse session. After adding some custom CSS, you populated the {{title}} text using a property from the config variable.

Common Render Method

You used Handlebars to dynamically load the navigation bar. There will be other instances where you need to load dynamic content. For this reason, you'll add a new utility method to the core namespace so it can be used throughout the application. Open core.js and add the method shown in Listing 7-28.

This simple yet powerful extension of the core namespace provides you the ability to render a dynamic template in one line. See Listing 7-29 for an example of the method.

Listing 7-28. Handlebars Render Method (www/js/core.js)

```
//...
},
render: function(target, template_name, data) {
        var source = $("#" + template_name + "-template").html();
        var template = Handlebars.compile(source);
        $(target).html(template(data));
 },
// ...
```

In this case, you are populating a DOM element with an id of content-container. The name of your template is "content," which has a reserved section where the {{body}} is populated by the data object passed into it. You will use the render method later in this chapter. Listing 7-29 shows how to use the method.

Listing 7-29. Render Method Example

```
app.core.render('#content-container', 'content', {
    body: 'Content loaded by an external template!'
});
```

Resetting a Password Using Parse

Now that users can register, and log in and out of this application, there is a crucial feature that you need to add: the ability to reset a user's password.

We have all been there before. You're asked to enter your password and your mind goes blank! Where is the Forgot Password link?! People these days need to store many passwords in their minds, and it's easy to forget one or two. For this reason, you will add a feature that allows them to reset their password for this application.

As with other new features added to this application, you need to add views associated with users resetting their passwords. The first will be an update to the login page; you'll add a link that will go to a page that allows them to reset their password. Next, you'll add the view that will allow users to do so by entering the email address associated with their account. Figure 7-7 illustrates these updates.

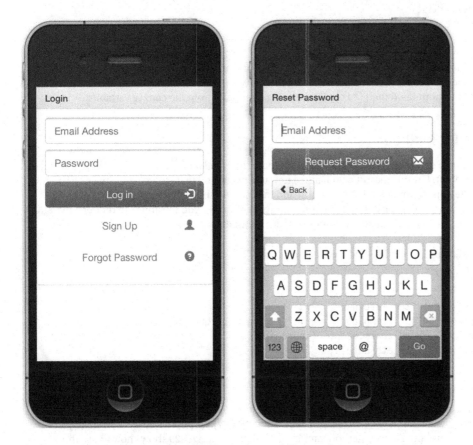

Figure 7-7. *The updated version of the login view and the new forgot password view*

The Forgot Password Template

Now that you have a few more views for the application, you can populate some links on the login page. You'll use the Twitter Bootstrap icons to give the user interface some flare.

Update the login view by adding a Forgot Password link to www/login.html (Listing 7-30). Next, create a new HTML template named www/reset.html. You can duplicate an existing view as a starting point. Without removing the script tags, populate the <body> tag with a form providing an input field for the user's email address and a button to submit the request (Listing 7-31).

Listing 7-30. Forgot Password Link (www/login.html)

```html
<p>
    <a href="reset.html" class="btn btn-lg btn-block">
        <i class="glyphicon glyphicon-question-sign pull-right"></i>
        Forgot Password
    </a>
</p>
```

Listing 7-31. Forgot Password Template (www/reset.html)

```html
<div class="panel panel-default">
    <div class="panel-heading">
        <h3 class="panel-title">Forgot Password</h3>
    </div>
    <div class="panel-body">
        <form role="form">
            <p>
                <input type="email" name="email" class="form-control input-lg"
                    placeholder="Email Address" autofocus>
            </p>
            <p>
                <button class="btn btn-lg btn-primary btn-block" type="submit"
                    id="login-submit">
                    <i class="glyphicon glyphicon-envelope pull-right"></i>
                    Request Password
                </button>
            </p>
            <p>
                <a href="login.html" class="btn btn-default">
                    <i class="glyphicon glyphicon-chevron-left"></i>
                    Back
                </a>
            </p>
        </form>
    </div>
</div>
```

As with the rest of your views, you need to configure the config.view property to **reset** (Listing 7-32). Now that the view is set up, you want to add a namespace to the app that encapsulates the logic for these features. Create a new JavaScript file called www/js/views/**reset.js** and populate it with the code from Listing 7-33.

After creating and configuring this new view, attach an event handler to the form. When the *forgot password* form is submitted, the app.reset.submit function will be called. You will populate this function in the following section.

Listing 7-32. Forgot Password View Configuration (www/login.html)

```
<script>
    var config = {
        view: 'reset',
        public_access: true
    };
    app.initialize();
</script>
```

Listing 7-33. Forgot Password Handler (www/js/views/reset.js)

```
app.reset = {
    initialize: function() {
        $('form').on('submit', function(event) {
            event.preventDefault();
            app.reset.submit();
        });
    },
    submit: function() {}
};
```

Parse's Forgot Password Feature

Parse does it again. The Parse.User object has a function called... wait for it... requestPasswordReset()!
It saves you hours of work by supplying a simple way to safely and securely reset a user's password.

Once the forget password form is submitted, the email address is sent to Parse for processing. If the address was successfully found, Parse will send an email to that address along with a unique URL that allows the user to type in a new password. When the user submits their new password, their account is updated!

The requestPasswordReset() function takes two parameters. The first is the email you want to look up, and the next (like most Parse objects) is an object with a success and error method.

In reset.js, update the submit function with the code of Listing 7-34.

Listing 7-34. Forgot Password Handler (www/js/views/reset.js)

```
submit: function() {
    $('button, input').attr('disabled', 'disabled');
    var email = $('input[name=email]').val();
    Parse.User.requestPasswordReset(email, {
        success: function() {
            window.location.href = 'reset-success.html';
        },
        error: function(error) {
            alert("Error: " + error.message);
            $('button, input').removeAttr('disabled');
        }
    });
  }
}
```

After successfully executing the password reset procedure in the cloud, the callback function should show a view to inform the user about the next actions they must take. In this example, you are doing this by redirecting the user to the view reset-success.html.

Since this view doesn't exist yet, it's time to create this file. Name the new file reset-success.html and transfer the basic HTML structure, as you have done in the past, from existing examples. Populate the body with a success message, as shown in Listing 7-35.

Listing 7-35. Forgot Password Success Message Template (www/reset-success.html)

```
<div class="container">
    <br>
    <div class="jumbotron">
        <h1>Forgot Password</h1>
        <p>
            Check your Emails!
        </p>
        <p><a href="login.html" class="btn btn-primary btn-lg" role="button">Login >></a></p>
    </div>
</div>
```

Figure 7-8 shows the result.

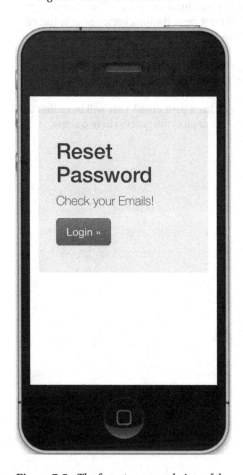

Figure 7-8. *The forgot password view of the application when a user is logged out*

143

Testing the New Feature!

After submitting the Forgot Password form, Parse will validate the request. If the email address doesn't exist, the application will present an error message using an `alert()` message. Otherwise, you will receive an email from Parse within a few seconds or minutes (times may vary depending on your email provider and if the Parse server status is operational).

■ **Tip** Are your requests to Parse slower than usual? Check the server status at `https://status.parse.com/` to see a log of past and possible service interruptions.

The email will contain a message with reset instructions and a custom link, which will lead the user to a form where they will be able to change their password. The password form is a micro web site hosted by Parse. There is no need to set up anything and it works right out of the box! Parse offers the opportunity for developers to customize the reset form, which we will explain later in this chapter.

As mentioned previously, the form will be an external web site, *not* a view in the application, so it will be displayed using the default web browser on the user's device. Having this open in a web browser is a great thing. Although it is possible to create an in-application password reset view, it would unnecessarily increase the complexity of the build and decrease the stability of the feature. The user is already in a tough spot, so why make things more complicated?

After submitting the Forgot Password form, the user can use their new password instantly. If a new password request is sent *before* bringing a previous request to an end, the previous request will expire in favor of the most recent one.

For your application, when a user clicks the reset password link from their email, they will be redirected to the reset password view that you created in Listing 7-31. Figure 7-9 depicts the process in two steps.

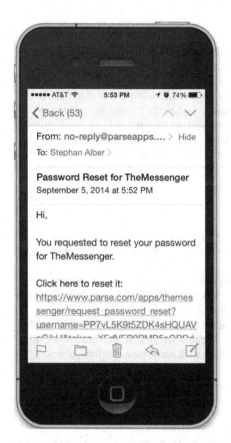

Figure 7-9. *View of the email that Parse sends to a user who requests a password change. On the right is the reset password view, provided by Parse*

Registration and Login via Facebook

We covered the Facebook API extensively in Chapter 5. Now we'll show you how to register a new user to this application with Parse and Facebook together. Signing up a new user with Facebook is an optional and powerful feature that you can add to your *next* app.

Facebook offers developers the ability to extend their applications by using Facebook's SDK. This is a great feature since it provides most users who sign up for a new service, like the Messenger App we're building, the convenience of creating an account for your application using their existing Facebook credentials.

The exercises you have completed so far in this chapter have given you what you need in order to register a new user to the application. Using the username and password a user provided during registration, you were able to log users in and out of the application while providing minimal security configurations.

This section will focus on the same task, except that this time you'll be using a user's Facebook account to create a new user for the Messenger App.

How Parse Integrates with Facebook

One of the reasons we choose Parse is because of their incredible API. So far, we've been registering users using the `Parse.User` object. This also comes with features like password reset and session management. Parse has another trick up its sleeve, `Parse.FacebookUtils`.

The goal for this chapter is to not only utilize a user's Facebook credentials to log in and sign up, but to use a *native* Facebook login session to do it. This means that if someone has the Facebook application installed on their phone (and they're logged in), they can log in or register an account with the application.

If the user is not using the Facebook app, they can still log in with Facebook using the web view. Either way, they can still use your application with their Facebook account. Going with the assumption that they *do* have it installed, using the native app feels quicker.

How to Log In with Facebook

To log in to Parse via Facebook, use `Parse.FacebookUtils.logIn()`. This function integrates with the Facebook JavaScript SDK, calls the `FB.login()` function, then turns the Facebook session into a *Parse session* (*and* User account if one doesn't exist!).

You are facing one challenge here: this route is solely based on JavaScript. And since you are not building a web application, this just doesn't work. Instead, you will follow a different approach, which will merge native and JavaScript elements into a seamless user experience.

Usually in a web app you load the Facebook JavaScript SDK and initialize it via `Parse.FacebookUtils.init()`. This function will initialize the Facebook SDK and connect to the Parse JavaScript SDK. At a later point you call the `logIn()` function and pass a Facebook permission string along with some other options, like so:

```
Parse.FacebookUtils.logIn(permissions, options)
```

You can and will still use this approach for your application to make it work in a web browser. This way you'll be able to test and debug the Parse-Facebook login *outside* of PhoneGap.

For the native version of your application you'll do things differently. You'll use the PhoneGap Facebook plug-in, which was introduced in Chapter 5, to offer a native login experience to the user. After logging in, the plug-in will provide a Facebook session object. This session object contains information like an access token and Facebook user ID.

You will convert this session information into a Parse-compatible format and use it as authentication data for the `Parse.FacebookUtils.logIn()` function. We will refer to this Parse-compatible authentication data as `FacebookAuthData`.

Long story short: instead of asking for a login using a Facebook permissions string, you will use the `FacebookAuthData` object when calling the `logIn()` function, like so:

```
Parse.FacebookUtils.logIn(FacebookAuthData, options)
```

This will log in the user to Parse based on their Facebook session information. This is the same as if you followed the web approach using the Facebook JavaScript SDK. If you have any troubles related to the Facebook application and plug-in setup, take a look at Chapter 5, where we explained the Facebook API ecosystem in detail.

The sample code in this section is written for the Messenger App that you've been building. This code *will* work in an isolated environment, too. Every application you write that borrows from pre-existing code will need some tailoring (project structure, custom functionality, etc.).

CHECKLIST: BEFORE YOU START

The following is a checklist that is required for you to continue the rest of this chapter. After completing this short list of tasks, you will learn how to connect users to an application with their Facebook account.

1. Sign in to Facebook and visit the developer website at `https://developers.facebook.com/apps`.

2. Create a new Facebook Application and fill out the basic application information.

3. Add the platform web for testing your app in the browser. Set the hostname of your web server (e.g. `http://localhost/`).

4. Add your mobile platform. If you are using Android, provide the **Package Name**; for iOS, fill out the **Bundle ID**. Both values should be identical to your PhoneGap application ID, which you can set in the file called `www/config.xml`. In our case, we used `com.fernandezalber.themessenger`.

The project configurations you use locally will need to match the values you set in the Facebook application settings page (Figure 7-10). There are other options in this section that you can explore; however, all you need at this point are the items listed above.

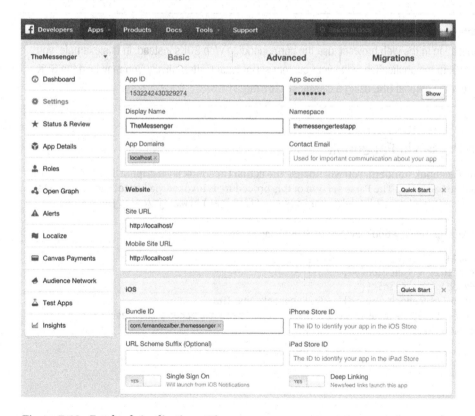

Figure 7-10. *Facebook Application settings*

Facebook JavaScript SDK Setup

To be able to test the FB login with a web browser, you need to use the Facebook Web SDK. This SDK should *not* be loaded in the native app, so this next configuration entry (Listing 7-36) is just for the web app.

The Parse JavaScript SDK provides an easy way to integrate Facebook with your application. We will use version 2.3 of the Facebook JavaScript SDK. Download the Facebook JavaScript SDK at the Facebook Quick Start Guide to get the required JavaScript file (https://developers.facebook.com/docs/javascript/quickstart/v2.3) or directly download it at http://connect.facebook.net/en_US/all.js.

Your current JavaScript loader defined in core.js has a property named common. This is where you're keeping application scripts. Create a new property named web and add the Facebook library, as shown in Listing 7-36. This section of the scripts configuration object will be used for files that should only be loaded in the web application for testing, but not in the native version of your application!

Listing 7-36. Updated Scripts Configuration in www/js/core.js

```
common: [
    // ...
],
web: [
    './js/vendor/facebook/all.js'
]
```

■ **Tip**   You cannot use the Facebook iOS or Android SDK in your web environment. To still be able to test and debug the application in the web browser, use the corresponding Web SDKs instead. In this example, you add the Facebook SDK to the application using your custom script loader. Alternatively, you may load the SDK directly via HTTP from the original URL using a classic `script` tag.

Logging In to Parse via Facebook

Deviating from the Facebook standard, you will not use the actual Facebook JavaScript SDK but instead the Parse SDK to initialize Facebook. The Parse version of this procedure is invoked via Parse.FacebookUtils.init(). Execute the code in Listing 7-37 right after Parse.initialize() in www/js/core.js.

Listing 7-37. Initializing the Facebook JavaScript SDK Using Parse

```
if (!window.cordova) {
    window.fbAsyncInit = function() {
        Parse.FacebookUtils.init({
            appId: '{facebook-app-id}', // Facebook App ID
            cookie: true, // enable cookies to allow Parse to access the session
            version: '1.0'
        });
    };
}
```

Facebook PhoneGap Plug-in

You'll be using the Facebook iOS or Android SDK for logging the user in to Facebook. For this purpose, use the Facebook Connect plug-in created by Wizcorp (https://github.com/Wizcorp/phonegap-facebook-plugin). Add the plug-in as shown in Listing 7-38.

Listing 7-38. Facebook PhoneGap Plug-in Installation

```
phonegap -d plugin add https://github.com/Wizcorp/phonegap-facebook-plugin.git --variable
APP_ID="{facebook-app-id}" --variable APP_NAME="{facebook-display-name}"
```

Replace {facebook-app-id} with the **ID** of your Facebook Application, and use the Display Name of your Facebook Application for {facebook-display-name}. You can find both values in your Facebook Application settings form (see Figure 7-12). The value for APP_NAME must be the same as your Facebook Display Name, otherwise the Facebook Login won't work. Note that the value APP_NAME may be different from your PhoneGap application name defined in config.xml.

In this case, the Display Name is TheMessenger, hence the value for APP_NAME **must** be TheMessenger. After adding the PhoneGap plug-in, you need to rebuild the platform via cordova build ios or cordova build android.

Your settings page should look similar to Figure 7-11.

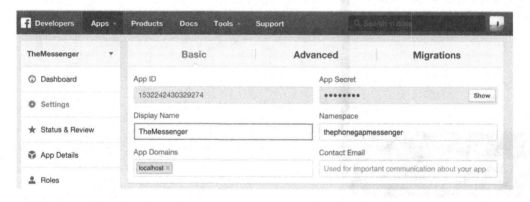

Figure 7-11. *The Facebook Application settings with Display Name highlighted*

Logging with Facebook View

In the next step, you'll add a Login with Facebook button to the login view (www/login/html). Before this, you should apply a minor adjustment to the existing form. Currently there is an autofocus attribute assigned to the email address input field. Remove this attribute. The reason you do this is because once the page loads, autofocus will open the users keyboard and hide the Facebook login button.

Add the Login with Facebook button to your login form as shown in Listing 7-39.

Listing 7-39. The Login with Facebook Button (login.html)

```
<p>
    <a href="#" class="btn btn-lg btn-primary btn-block" id="facebook-login">
        <i class="glyphicon glyphicon-new-window pull-right"></i>
        Log in with Facebook</a>
</p>
```

You add the icon **glyphicon-new-window** to indicate that the Facebook login dialog (Figure 7-12) will be opened a new window. The dialog will either be provided by the native Facebook Application (if installed) or as a fallback to the Facebook mobile web site.

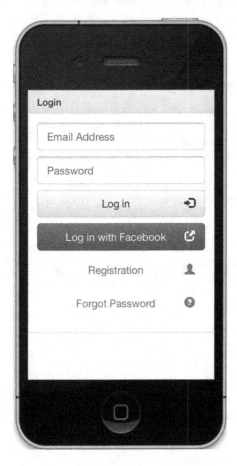

Figure 7-12. *The updated view of the login page with the added Facebook login button*

Next, you'll add an event handler to the login button, calling the function app.login.facebookLogin(), which you will build in the following steps (Listing 7-40).

Listing 7-40. Login Button Handler (www/js/views/login.js)

```
$('#facebook-login').on('click', function(event) {
    event.preventDefault();
    app.login.facebookLogin();
});
```

Logging In to Facebook

Parts of this application can be used without PhoneGap. Here, you'll add a flag to determine if the user is using a native or web version. You'll check if the `cordova` namespace is on the `window` object. If it is, that means it's a native app.

In the web version, the method `FB.login` is used. For the native application, you will call the method `facebookConnectPlugin.login()`, which will call the corresponding login script in the Facebook iOS or Android SDK. The first parameter of the `facebookConnectPlugin.login` method is the variable `scope`, which is an array of Facebook permissions. The callback function will be executed after the login request is either accepted or rejected.

Be careful! The Facebook Connect plug-in uses the arguments in an inversed order (Listing 7-41). Next, the permissions scope is passed using an array, instead of a comma-separated string as in the Facebook JavaScript SDK.

Both SDKs, the web and the native (respectively, iOS and Android), provide the same response format. You will use the same callback function for both login methods. Name this function `parseFacebookLogin()`; we'll come back to it in the next section.

Listing 7-41. Function facebookLogin in www/js/views/login.js

```
facebookLogin: function() {
    var scope = ['email'];
    if (!window.cordova) {
        return FB.login(app.login.parseFacebookLogin, { scope: scope.join(',') });
    }
    facebookConnectPlugin.login(scope, app.login.parseFacebookLogin);
}
```

Using Facebook Authentication Data for Login

The method `parseFacebookLogin()` will receive the FB login response, which may look like Listing 7-42.

Listing 7-42. Facebook Graph API: Login Response

```
{
    "authResponse": {
        "accessToken": "{accessToken}",
        "userID": "10152483215327935",
        "expiresIn": 4163,
        "signedRequest": "{signedRequest}"
    },
    "status": "connected"
}
```

As previously stated, the Facebook JavaScript SDK, iOS, and Android SDK use the same format for the response. Now you need to transform the response into a new structure. It will contain the Facebook user ID, access token, and when the token will expire.

Parse expects the expiration date to be provided in the ISO format (ISO 8601 Extended Format), which can be constructed as `YYYY-MM-DDTHH:mm:ss.sssZ`. The time zone is always UTC, as denoted by the suffix "Z". Listing 7-43 shows an example.

Listing 7-43. Parse FacebookAuth Data Format

```
{
    "id": "10152483215327935",
    "access_token": "{access_token}",
    "expiration_date": "2014-09-03T16:59:59.999Z"
}
```

To create this date, you use the variable expireIn to store the current date and time (which is provided in seconds) to the current date and create the ISO string using the function toISOString(). You then pass this newly created authentication data to the Parse.FacebookUtils.logIn() function (see Listing 7-44).

Listing 7-44. Convert Facebook API Response into Parse-Compatible Format

```
parseFacebookLogin: function(response) {
    var expiresIn = new Date();
    expiresIn.setSeconds(expiresIn.getSeconds() + response.authResponse.expiresIn);
    var facebookAuthData = {
        "id": response.authResponse.userID,
        "access_token": response.authResponse.accessToken,
        "expiration_date": expiresIn.toISOString()
    };
    Parse.FacebookUtils.logIn(facebookAuthData).then(app.login.updateUserData);
}
```

As a callback, you execute the function app.login.updateUserData().

___

■ **Tip** There might be a case in which a user is still logged in to Facebook but not to Parse. You may use the method facebookConnectPlugin.getLoginStatus() together with Parse.User.current() to identify this state and offer the user a different Facebook login button (for example, "Welcome Back [username], continue with Facebook").

___

Validation Recommended

In this example, you assume that the user will accept the Facebook login request. This is sufficient enough for a prototype, but in a real-world case you would verify your assumption. You can do this by checking for the key authRepsonse in the response object, as shown in Listing 7-45.

Listing 7-45. Validate Login Response

```
if (response.authResponse) {
    // Continue script execution
} else {
    alert("User cancelled login or did not fully authorize.");
}
```

If you don't get a value for authResponse, the user either canceled the login or did not fully authorize.

Updating User Profile Based on Facebook Graph API Data

In comparison to the registration via email and password, the Facebook version of your registration feature does not require the user to fill out the form that asks for their first and last name. This is not an issue, but is certainly very convenient for the user. You will instead get this data via the Facebook Graph API by calling the API endpoint /me.

"Me" is an alias for the current user's Facebook user ID. You can adjust the fields that are being queried using the parameter fields. In your case, you want to know the user's email address, and both first and last name. You'll also grab the user's profile picture. The full API path is provided in Listing 7-46. An API response could look like the example in Listing 7-47.

Listing 7-46. Full Path of the API Endpoint

```
/me?fields=email,first_name,last_name,picture
```

Listing 7-47. API Response Example

```
{
  "email": "name@domain.com",
  "first_name": "Stephan",
  "last_name": "Alber",
  "picture": {
    "data": {
      "is_silhouette": false,
      "url": "https://fbcdn-profile-a.akamaihd.net/..."
    }
  },
  "id": "123456789"
}
```

You integrate the user data from Facebook and save it to Parse using a new method named updateUserData() as part of the app.login object. For PhoneGap requests, the PhoneGap Facebook plug-in method facebookConnectPlugin.api() is used. For web requests, the application will fall back to the Facebook JavaScript SDK and call the method FB.api().

As a callback of the API request, you apply the response values to the Parse.User object User. This is passed over from the Parse.FacebookUtils.logIn() to the updateUserData() function. Afterwards, you save the obtained information to the Parse database (Listing 7-48).

Listing 7-48. Updating User Data via Facebook API Data (www/js/views/login.js)

```
updateUserData: function(User) {

    var requestPath = '/me?fields=email,first_name,last_name,picture';

    var callback = function(response) {
        User.set('email', response.email);
        User.set('first_name', response.first_name);
        User.set('last_name', response.last_name);
        User.set('picture', response.picture.data.url);
        User.save().then(function() {
            window.location.href = 'logout.html';
        });
    };
```

```
    if (!window.cordova) {
        FB.api(requestPath, callback);
    } else {
        facebookConnectPlugin.api(requestPath, null, callback, alert);
    }

}
```

Once that's done, you redirect the user to the home view of the application. Right now this is the logout view. At a later time, you may want to change this to the contacts or conversations view, which you'll build in the following chapters.

Avoiding Repeated Updates

If you do not want to update user data on every login, but only the very first time, you may use the function User.existed(). It is used to determine whether to execute this script part or not (Listing 7-49).

Listing 7-49. Test Whether User Existed Before

```
updateUserData: function(User) {
    if (User.existed()) {
        window.location.href = 'logout.html';
        return;
    }
}
```

■ **Tip** To log out a Facebook user, you still use the Parse.User.logOut() method. Do not use the facebookConnectPlugin.logout(). This might cause the Parse.User and Facebook session to fall out of synchronization.

You add new methods to the app.login namespace. Listing 7-50 presents the code in full.

Listing 7-50. Full Code for js/views/login.js

```
app.login = {

    initialize: function() {

        $('form').on('submit', function(event) {
            event.preventDefault();
            app.login.submit();
        });

        $('#facebook-login').on('click', function(event) {
            event.preventDefault();
            app.login.facebookLogin();
        });

    },
```

```
submit: function() {

    $('button, input').attr('disabled', 'disabled');

    var email = $('input[name=email]').val();
    var password = $('input[name=password]').val();

    Parse.User.logIn(email, password, {
        success: function(user) {
            window.location.href = 'contacts.html';
        },
        error: function(user, error) {
            app.core.message(error.message);
            $('button, input').removeAttr('disabled');
        }
    });

},
facebookLogin: function() {

    var scope = ['email'];

    if (!window.cordova) {
        return FB.login(app.login.parseFacebookLogin, scope.join(','));
    }

    console.log(facebookConnectPlugin);

    facebookConnectPlugin.login(scope, app.login.parseFacebookLogin);

},

parseFacebookLogin: function(response) {

    var expiresIn = new Date();
    expiresIn.setSeconds(expiresIn.getSeconds() + response.authResponse.expiresIn);

    var facebookAuthData = {
        "id": response.authResponse.userID,
        "access_token": response.authResponse.accessToken,
        "expiration_date": expiresIn.toISOString()
    };

    Parse.FacebookUtils.logIn(facebookAuthData).then(app.login.updateUserData);

},
```

155

```
    updateUserData: function() {

        var requestPath = '/me?fields=id,email,first_name,last_name,picture';

        var callback = function(response) {
            var User = Parse.User.current();
            User.set('email', response.email);
            User.set('first_name', response.first_name);
            User.set('last_name', response.last_name);
            User.set('picture', response.picture.data.url);
            User.save().then(function() {
                window.location.href = 'contacts.html';
            });
        };

        if (!window.cordova) {
            FB.api(requestPath, callback);
        } else {
            facebookConnectPlugin.api(requestPath, null, callback, alert);
        }

    }

};
```

Logging In with Facebook Screen

After building out this complex and yet very important feature, let's test it! The PhoneGap plug-in will use Facebook for iOS or Android application, if installed. Otherwise, it will fall back to the web login view (Figure 7-13).

Figure 7-13. *Log in with Facebook dialog: the native version (left) versus the web view (right)*

Parse + Facebook = Simplicity

This is great, isn't it?! Using a simple data transform you were able to build a bridge between the native Facebook SDK and the Parse JavaScript SDK. As Leonardo da Vinci said, "Simplicity is the ultimate sophistication." The user will be able to register for your application via two simple taps.

Furthermore, after signing in via Facebook, you are able to use all of Facebook functionality we described in Chapter 5. In the next section, we will create a list of the user accounts created during these exercises.

Listing Users

As a preparation for Chapter 8, which covers the topic of messages, let's build a list of users in your application. You will use this list to select the user you want to write a message to. In a real-world example, you would probably start with an empty contacts list and add contacts via a request-accept system. For learning purposes, you'll skip this part and just make all the users that sign up for the application your contacts. However, you could extend this part of the application by adding a feature like adding and removing contacts. Figure 7-14 illustrates how the contacts list appears in this application.

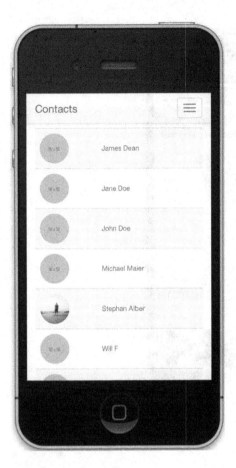

Figure 7-14. A list of users

Preparation

Before coming to the actual contacts view, you will add a navigation item to link to the contacts view and create a helper to display a user profile picture.

Contacts Navigation Item

To make the contacts list accessible, you add a corresponding link in the navigation bar. As a little eye-catcher, you add a user icon to the navigation item. For the navigation bar, replace the existing <ul> with the code in Listing 7-51.

Listing 7-51. Contacts Link (www/navbar.html)

```
<ul class="nav navbar-nav">
  <li><a href="contacts.html">
       <i class="glyphicon glyphicon-user pull-right"></i>
       Contacts
     </a>
  </li>
```

```
<li>
  <a href="#" id="logout">
    <i class="glyphicon glyphicon-log-out pull-right"></i>
    Logout
  </a>
</li>
</ul>
```

Displaying a User Profile Picture

"You eat with your eyes (first)!" While you're building the next view, we also want to introduce ways to easily improve the visual appearance of your views. In this example, it would be nice to display a picture right next to each user, instead of just showing the user's first and last name.

Actually, you already prepared this feature in the section "Registration and Login via Facebook". You added a picture for each account using the Facebook Graph API. Now you will use this value in the contacts template and show a placeholder image for users who don't have a picture.

While doing this, you avoid cluttering templates with unattractive if and else constructions. Instead, you make use of the instance methods system offered by the Parse.Object class. In this case, you will add a new instance method to the Parse.User class (see Listing 7-52).

To make use of all the small algorithms you'll be adding to the Parse.User, you previously created the file MyParseUser.js in www/js/models. In this example, you add the method getPicture to the MyParseUser class. The method will check the field picture for a value and return a URL to the picture, if there is one. If not, you return a placeholder picture using the service http://placehold.it/.

Listing 7-52. Custom Parse.User Class (www/js/models/MyParseUser.js)

```
window.MyParseUser = Parse.User.extend({
    getPicture: function() {
        return this.get('picture') ?
            this.get('picture') : 'http://placehold.it/50x50';
    }
});
```

As mentioned before, doing this will improve the structure of your templates on a pivotal level: you simply need to call the function getPicture() to populate the source value of an image tag. In addition, you can use this function in *other* views like the conversations list view. You only have to code this function once and you can use it in multiple places.

Contacts Template

You now have everything set up for adding the contacts view. Using a templating engine like Handlebarsjs allows you to render dynamic data coming from an external source, like Parse. The Bootstrap table style lets you quickly create a placeholder container for your data.

There will likely be more than one user in your application. Because of this, you need to loop through *each* of them to show them in the view. You do this by using a #each keyword provided by Handlebarsjs. #each is one of what Handlebarsjs refers to as *block helpers*.

Create a new view named contacts.html, based on a previous example. Populate the body with an empty div container, which you'll use as placeholder element for the user list, as well as the handlebars template contacts-template, as shown in Listing 7-53.

Listing 7-53. Contacts Template (www/contacts.html)

```
<div class="container"></div>

<script id="contacts-template" type="text/x-handlebars-template">
  <table class="table table-striped">
    {{#each users}}
      <tr>
        <td>
          <a href="conversation.html?id={{ id }}">
              <img src="{{ getPicture }}" class="img-circle pull-left">
          </a>
        </td>
        <td class="small" style="vertical-align: middle">
          <a href="conversation.html?id={{ id }}">
            {{attributes.username}}
          </a>
        </td>
      </tr>
    {{/each}}
  </table>
</script>
```

■ **Tip**   Handlebars can call functions or use variables inside templates. In this case, it's calling the instance method `getPicture()` of the `MyParseUser` class.

You are using the recently created `MyParseUser.getPicture()` function directly in the template, by solely using `{{ getPicture }}`. The magic behind this is that instead of running a query on the `Parse.User` class, you'll use your custom class `MyParseUser`. Thus all results of the query will possess the `getPicture()` method.

Also, for each expression, Handlebars can either print a simple string value or the return value of a function. As there is no simple string key for `MyParseUser.getPicture`, Handlebars will call the function `getPicture()`.

You may use this same technique to further extend the app. It's even thinkable to render Handlebars templates within a `Parse.Object` instance method. This might be helpful to create little widgets like a user-connected popover.

View Configuration

Update the view configuration at the bottom of the `contacts.html` template. You want to keep this view private. In a real-world example, you would also verify the access for each listed contact (Listing 7-54).

Listing 7-54. Contacts View Configuration (www/contacts.html)

```
<script>
    var config = {
        view: "contacts",
        title: "Contacts",
        public_access: false
    };
    app.initialize();
</script>
```

Query Users

Let's bring this home and populate the template with users. You will add this functionality in the `initialize` function. Execute a query on your custom class `MyParseUser`. If you base your query on the `Parse.User` class, you won't be able to use the `getPicture()` instance method in the Handlebars template. To get a certain set of results, do not apply any filters to the query. If your user base becomes too big, you may want to limit the amount of search results.

As you are displaying the first and last name in the contacts template, you bring the results in a corresponding order by using the `query.ascending()` method. The key to order by may be a string of comma-separated values, an array of keys, or multiple keys, which you will use in your example.

After the results are loaded, you use the response array as variable for the Handlebars template and place the compiled results inside the `<div>` element having the class `.container`, as shown in Listing 7-55.

Listing 7-55. Contacts Script (www/js/views/contacts.js)

```
app.contacts = {
    initialize: function() {
        var query = new Parse.Query(MyParseUser);
        // Sort results in ascending order
        // by first and last name
        query.ascending("first_name", "last_name");
        query.find().then(function(users) {
            app.core.render('.container', 'contacts', {
                users: users
            });
        });
    }
};
```

E-Mail Verification

During the registration process you collect the user's email address. However, you don't know whether this email address actually exists. To verify a potential user's email address, you can use a classic account activation system: after the user signs up, an email is sent to the provided email address so they can verify it. Within this email is a link containing an activation code (Figure 7-15). The user activates their account by clicking the link.

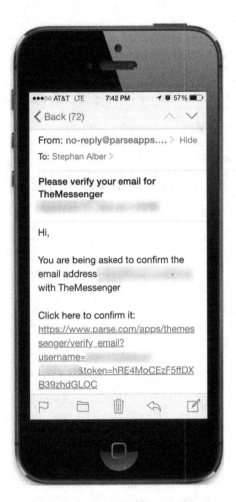

Figure 7-15. *Verification email example*

The status of each account is tracked in the field emailVerified. After clicking the link, this value will turn from false to true. Every time a user's email address is modified, emailVerified will be set to false again. At the same time Parse will send another verification email to the user.

You can enable this feature by simply requesting it in the Parse application settings in the Email section (Figure 7-16). All prospective registrations will receive an email to verify their email address. Although you can assume that all Facebook email addresses had been verified before, you can either enable this feature for all registrations or none of them.

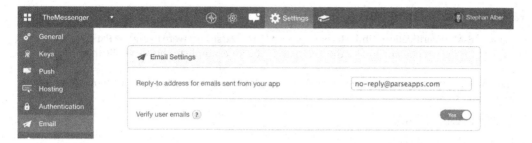

Figure 7-16. *Enabling email verification via Parse application settings*

Avoiding Automatic Login

After registering using the `Parse.User.signUp()` method, the user automatically gets logged in. This behavior doesn't change by enabling the email verification feature. If you want to change this behavior, you need to log out the user instantly after registering for your application.

It seems like a bewildering task to log the user in and then promptly log them out again, yet there is no other option to create this behavior right now. See Listing 7-56 for an example implementation.

Listing 7-56. Optionally Disabling Auto-Login After User Registration (www/js/views/registration.js)

```
user.signUp(null, {
    success: function(user) {
        Parse.User.logOut();
        window.location.href = 'verification_pending.html';
    },
    error: function(user, error) {
        $('button, input').removeAttr('disabled');
    }
});
```

Next, you need to do a similar adjustment for the Login view. If the user's email address is not yet verified, by default a session will still be created. Add a condition to destroy the session using `Parse.User.logOut()`: if the value for `emailVerified` is not true, display an error message with information to the user about the email verification requirement, as shown in Listing 7-57.

Listing 7-57. Disabled Login for Non-Verified Users (www/js/views/login.js)

```
Parse.User.logIn(email, password, {
    success: function(user) {
        if(user.get('emailVerified') == true) {
            window.location.href = 'contacts.html';
        } else {
            Parse.User.logOut();
            $('button, input').removeAttr('disabled');
            alert("Please verify your e-mail address");
        }
    },
    error: function(user, error) {
        $('button, input').removeAttr('disabled');
    }
});
```

163

E-Mail and Web Templates

In the sections "E-Mail Verification" and "Reset Password Using Parse" we were using the Parse default templates, both for the emails sent and for the web pages used for example to show a verification success message.

It is possible, but not required, to customize these templates. You can customize the following templates via the application settings:

- Email Verification Mail
- Password Reset Mail
- Choose a new Password Page
- Password Changed Page
- Email Verified Page
- Invalid link Page

Mail Templates

For each mail template, Parse will provide a form to customize the mail text (Figure 7-17). You can use the variables shown in Table 7-1 within each mail template.

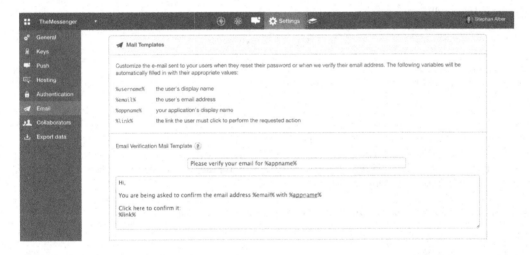

Figure 7-17. *Parse Mail Templates Form*

Table 7-1. *E-Mail Template Variables*

Variable Name	Description
%username%	The user's display name
%email%	The user's email address
%appname%	Your application's display name
%link%	The link the user must click to perform the requested action

Page Template

In the Email Settings section Parse offers an example template for each page template. You need to download this example file and upload it to a publicly accessible web server. After uploading your custom templates, you need to provide a URL to the template files using the Customize User-Facing Pages form shown in Figure 7-18.

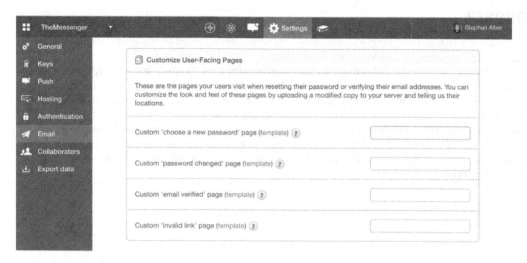

Figure 7-18. *Custom Page Template Settings*

You may use HTML, CSS, and images to change the look and feel. But be careful not to break the functionality of pages containing a form. An extract of the choose_password.html template is shown in Listing 7-58. The Parse examples are using JavaScript to read the URL arguments. Those could be username, request ID, or the application. You could also use a backend language like PHP to read the arguments and customize the template.

Listing 7-58. Choosing a New Password Page Template (choose_password.html)

```
<h1>Reset Your Password<span id='app'></span></h1>
<noscript>
    We apologize, but resetting your password requires javascript
</noscript>
<div class='error' id='error'></div>
<form id='form' action='#' method='POST'>
    <label>New Password for <span id='username_label'></span></label>
    <input name="new_password" type="password"/>
    <input name='utf-8' type='hidden' value='âœ"'/>
    <input name="username" id="username" type="hidden"/>
    <input name="token" id="token" type="hidden"/>
    <button>Change Password</button>
</form>
```

■ **Tip** You can use the Parse Cloud Hosting service to publish page template files. We explain how to use this service in the section "Parse Cloud Hosting" in Chapter 3.

Summary

User registration is HUGE. For creating a customized user experience as well as enabling communication between users, the registration and login views are essential.

In this chapter, you designed additional features like resetting a user's password or verifying their email address. One of the most powerful features you added is registration via Facebook. As of the first quarter of 2015,[1] there are more than one billion Facebook users active monthly. Integrating Facebook with your applications' registration process will likely increase conversation rates.

In Chapter 8, you will use the user base to use a basic form of communication: sending text messages. Yet your application doesn't need to be limited to messages only. Communication could be a friend request, an invitation to a group, liking content, or writing a comment about it. You'll learn more about sending data between registered users next.

---

[1]http://www.statista.com/statistics/264810/number-of-monthly-active-facebook-users-worldwide/

CHAPTER 8

Messages

Did you get my message?

Now that you have a way for users to register with your app, it's time to give them what they came for: the ability to send messages!

You will be creating a conversation between two people. Other users won't be able to see or interact with another private conversation (group chat, for example). There are several pieces of functionality that combine to create the definition of a conversation for this application. This chapter describes how each section will play a role in the bigger picture—a conversation.

Conversation vs. ConversationList

You will be creating two similarly named views. The first is called conversation and it displays a message input form as well as the messages of a conversation. The second one is called conversationList and it lists the names of people participating in the conversation. Please be careful not to confuse these terms.

A conversation shows all of the messages sent and received between two people in a conversation. Beneath this is an input form for composing a message. You will extend this to be able to attach images and other media to a message.

Parse Classes and Their Roles

In this chapter, you'll create two new custom Parse classes: **Conversation** and **Message**. A conversation is composed of many messages. Table 8-1 describes how each class is used to create a conversation.

Table 8-1. *Basic Classes: Conversation and Message*

Class	Occurrence per Conversation	Description
Conversation	2	Each Conversation has two User objects participating. Both User objects have their own perspective on the Conversation. Hence, there are two Conversation objects for each Conversation.
Message	1 - *infinite*	A Conversation can have an infinite amount of Message objects, but it needs at *least* one. It also needs one Sender and one Receiver, as well as the message_body that defines a Message.

Senders and Receivers

To construct a conversation, we use messages. The user *sends* a message to another user—the *receiver*. The differences between them are described in Table 8-2. You use the Message class to handle messages for both the sender and receiver of each message.

There are always two sides to every story, right? The same can be applied to saving a conversation with Parse. You use the Conversation class to manage how each participant sees a conversation: as an owner (first person perspective) or partner (other party's perspective).

Table 8-2 describes how to use the Conversation and Message classes to create a conversation.

Table 8-2. *Roles: Sender, Receiver, Owner, and Partner*

User Roles	Related Class	Description
Sender	Message	Each Message has one Sender. The moment you send a Message, you are always the Sender. Speaking in code, Parse.User.current() is the Sender.
Receiver	Message	As well as a Sender, there is a Receiver for each Message.
Owner	Conversation	If you are talking about the Owner of a Conversation object, you take a subjective perspective on the Conversation. Personal information, which the Partner shouldn't know about, is saved in this object. This could be a setting to block a Conversation Partner who shouldn't have access to or influence on personal information.
Partner	Conversation	On the other end of the line is the Conversation Partner. You need to know who you are talking to, so a reference to the other Parse.User is part of each Conversation object.

Writing Messages

Before displaying any messages, you need to create some. You'll start with the act of writing messages. Writing a message requires an input textarea and a submit button (see Figure 8-1).

Figure 8-1. *The view for writing messages*

Creating the Conversation View Template

As with the previous views, you want to use an existing view as a template to quickly implement your new feature. Create a new HTML file based on an existing view and name the file `conversation.html`. Listing 8-1 shows the markup for this template.

Listing 8-1. The HTML Markup for the Body of the Conversation View (www/conversation.html)

```
<div class="container">
  <form role="form">
    <div class="form-group">
      <textarea class="form-control" rows="3" placeholder="Your Message"></textarea>
    </div>
    <div class="btn-toolbar" role="toolbar">
      <div class="btn-group">
        <a href="#" id="submit" class="btn btn-primary">
          <i class="glyphicon glyphicon-send"></i>
```

```
        Send Message
      </a>
    </div>
  </div>
</form>
</div>
```

Prepping for a Conversation

Along with the view, create a new JavaScript view file named `conversation.js` to store the functionality. As with other scripts, add this new one to your loader in `core.js`. The basic object structure of the file is shown in Listing 8-2. For the moment, it will just contain a basic skeleton, which you'll bring to life in a subsequent section.

Listing 8-2. The Skeleton for the Conversation Script (www/js/views/conversation.js)

```
app.conversation = {
    Receiver: null,
    initialize: function() {},
    getReceiverName : function() {},
    renderMessages: function() {},
    setReceiver: function() {},
    messageHandler: function() {},
    sendMessage: function() {}
};
```

Besides the well-known `initialize()` function, you add a `renderMessages ()` function that will be responsible for loading the conversation using the Parse classes described in Table 8-1.

The `setReceiver()` method determines which person you intend to send a message to, and the `getReceiverName()` method loads the `Receiver` object and sets their name to the header bar. You use `messageHandler()` to manage interactions like pressing a Send button. Eventually, the method `sendMessage()` will be used to save a message to the Parse database. The key `Receiver` will be used to store a `Parse.User` user instance that represents the person *receiving* the message.

Reading URL Query Parameters

In Listing 7-53 from Chapter 7, the links had a query string parameter named `id` added to the URL of the page, such as `conversation.html?id=XYZ123`.

Before you can use the variable `id`, you need a way of reading parameters from the query string. *Neither PhoneGap nor jQuery offer a method for this out of the box*, so you need to create a *custom* function to do this job.

With a typical web site, you can access the current URL using `window.location.href`. This will return the full path, including the domain name. A URL path in a PhoneGap application, unless it explicitly has a full domain name, will request the file relative to the local path.

With this function, you won't have to worry about parsing the `href`. You'll be using a *regular expression* to select the query string parameters from a URL. Regular expressions are complex configurations to examine strings and look for patterns. We won't explain them here, so just follow the code provided in Listing 8-3 and you'll be able to access all query parameters from a URL.

Add the script to the *core* of your application. Open the file www/js/core.js and add the function named `getParameterByName()` as part of the object `app.core` (Listing 8-3).

When calling the function, you pass the name of the key you are looking for as argument. For example, the call of getParameterByName('example') will return the string y for the URL page.html?example=y.

Listing 8-3. Reading Query Parameters (www/js/core.js)

```
getParameterByName: function(name) {
    var results = new RegExp('[\\\?&]' +name+ '=([^&#]*)').exec(window.location.href);
    if (!results) {
        return 0;
    }
    return results[1] || 0;
}
```

Initializing the View

When the view is rendered in the initialize() method, you want to load the receiver's information and assign events to handle the message form submission. You start by adding call references to two placeholder functions, getReceiver() and messageHandler() (Listing 8-4).

Listing 8-4. The Outline of the Initialize Method (www/js/views/conversation.js)

```
initialize: function() {
    app.conversation.setReceiver();

    // With whom are we talking?
    app.conversation.getReceiverName();

    // Load Messages in parallel
    app.conversation.renderMessages();

    // handle media attachements
    app.conversation.messageHandler(); }
```

Add a file reference for conversation.js to the scripts variable in www/js/core.js (Listing 8-5).

Listing 8-5. The config Variable Customized for the Conversation View (www/conversation.html)

```
<script>
    var config = {
        view: "conversation",
        title: "Conversation",
        public_access: false
    };
    app.initialize();
</script>
```

The Loading Icon

We've all mindlessly looked at a loading icon, waiting for our content to appear. Its purpose is to provide the user feedback as to the status of the content that's loading. You will be doing the same while users wait for a response from Parse. Using an animated gif, you start the conversation view with a loading icon. After you get a response, you remove it and render the content to the view.

You can find loading icons at a site like http://ajaxload.info. The image should be small in file size. The purpose here is to create a pleasant experience for the user as they wait for the awesome. After picking your favorite loader image, save it to the folder www/img. Create a new CSS class for the loading image in style.css. If there is content in the loading container, hide it by using a star (*) selector and the display: none rule, as shown in Listing 8-6.

Listing 8-6. Adding a New Class to style.css for the Loading Image (www/css/style.css)

```
.loading {
    background:transparent url(../img/ajax-loader.gif) no-repeat center;
    padding:50px;
}
.loading * {
    display:none;
}
```

In order to use this icon, you add a new <div> tag to your content holding the new class loading. Additionally, you use the CSS class placeholder. This class does not contain any styles and is used as a JavaScript element selector only (see Listing 8-7). You will use this snippet later in this chapter and throughout the application.

Listing 8-7. An Example of the Loading Placeholder

```
<div class="placeholder loading"></div>
```

Conversations will likely have many messages. While these are loading to the view from the initialize function, add the loading class on a designated placeholder (Listing 8-8).

Listing 8-8. Adding the Loading Placeholder to the Existing initialize Function (www/js/views/conversation.js)

```
initialize: function() {

    // Keep existing code
    $(".placeholder").addClass('loading');
}
```

Creating a Receiver Object

In the very first moments this view loads, you don't need to possess every piece of information about the Receiver. Instead, you can just create a local instance of the MyParseUser object and set the object's id to the value you are getting via the query string method getParameterByName(), as shown in Listing 8-9.

Listing 8-9. Creating a Receiver Object (www/js/views/conversation.js)

```
setReceiver: function() {
    app.conversation.Receiver = new MyParseUser();
    app.conversation.Receiver.id = app.core.getParameterByName('id');
}
```

Loading the Actual Receiver Object

While the setReceiver method made sure that the view is in possession of a Receiver object, you load the *actual* Receiver object from the Parse database in the background. Following this approach will enable you to have a *send message* form ready, no matter whether you already loaded the Receiver data or not.

Next, you populate the getReceiverName (Listing 8-10) with a new Parse query that requests a conversation, and then updates the UI with the user's first name.

Listing 8-10. Loading the Actual Receiver Object (www/js/views/conversation.js)

```
getReceiverName: function() {
    var query = new Parse.Query(MyParseUser);
    return query.get(app.conversation.Receiver.id).then(function(Receiver) {
        app.conversation.Receiver = Receiver;
        $('.navbar-brand').text('Conversation with '
            + Receiver.get('first_name'));
    });
}
```

Message Form Handler

Next, you add an event handler to the message form. Your main concern is that when a user submits the form, it should send a message.

To create a better user experience, you want to keep the keyboard open after the user sends a message. One method can be to instantly focus the textarea immediately after the user hits the submit button. This will either, depending on the system, keep the keyboard open *or* reopen it after a few milliseconds. There are better approaches, yet for the moment this will be sufficient. Add an event handler for the submit button, as shown in Listing 8-11.

Then you call the sendMessage() function, which handles the details of sending a message and will be populated at a later point of this chapter.

Listing 8-11. Loading the Receiver Object (www/js/views/conversation.js)

```
messageHandler: function() {
    $('#submit').on('tap click', function(e) {
        e.preventDefault();
        $("textarea").focus();
        app.conversation.sendMessage();
    });
}
```

The Message Class

To save and read messages, you add a new class named Message to the Parse Database. The Message class has three properties: Sender, Receiver, and message_body. Messages are saved as strings. The Sender and Receiver objects represent users. Next, you make use of the Parse.Object default property createdAt to show when a message was sent.

You'll use the Message object in many different places and situations, and you want to avoid writing certain behavior again and again, so you will collect all "business logic" related to the Message object in one class, the MyParseMessage class, and its respective file, MyParseMessage.js. As a reminder, you already know this model system from the MyParseUser class of Chapter 7.

The first instance method of the new class is a method to save messages to the database, the send() method. The method does the following:

- Sets the Receiver
- Sets the Parse.User.current() as Sender
- Sets the message_body
- Returns a Parse.Promise object, which will pass the saved Message object as an argument to potentially call then() functions

---

■ **Tip**   There are two ways to define new classes and their structures. The first way is to create them manually using the Parse data browser, as explained in Chapter 3. The second way is to create and update class structures on the client side. Once you create a new class or set a new property, the class structure in the cloud is updated automatically. To enable this feature, check the option "Allow client class creation" in the General section of the App Permission settings on parse.com. Use this mode in your development phase only. Disable it once you publish your app.

Furthermore, you add the class method afterSave(), which is called directly after saving the Message. This function executes tasks like adding a location.

All attributes are passed in the form of an object named options. Each key should correspond its appropriate value, such as options.Receiver for the Receiver. The full implementation of the MyParseMessage class is shown in Listing 8-12. Also, don't forget to add the new file MyParseMessage.js your JavaScript loader, as shown in Listing 8-13.

Listing 8-12. The MyParseMessage Class (www/js/models/MyParseMessage.js)

```
var MyParseMessage = Parse.Object.extend('Message', {
    // Instance Methods
    send: function(options) {

        // Set the Receiver
        this.set('Receiver', options.Receiver);

        // Set the Sender
        this.set('Sender', MyParseUser.current());

        // Set the Message Body
        this.set('message_body', options.message_body);

        // Save the Message to Parse
        return this.save().then(MyParseMessage.afterSave);
    }
}, {
    // Class Methods
    afterSave: function(Message) {
        return Message;
    }
});
```

■ **Tip** All methods passed to `Parse.Object.extend()` as a second argument, after providing the name `Message` in the first one, are *instance methods*, and all methods passed in the third argument are *class methods*.

Listing 8-13. Updating the JavaScript Loader Configuration (www/js/core.js)

```
var scripts = {
    common: [
        // Keep existing configuration
    ],
    models: [
        // models
        './js/models/MyParseUser.js',
        './js/models/MyParseMessage.js'
    ],
```

Sending a Message

After preparing the event and database handling, you need to connect both parts so that the user can eventually send their message. This happens in the `sendMessage` method of the `app.conversation` object. You added this earlier when you created a placeholder for this method (Listing 8-2).

Next, create a new object named `options` and set the values for the keys `Receiver` and `message_body`, as they are expected in the `send()` method of the `MyParseMessage` class. The `options` object is passed to the `send()` method, as shown in Listing 8-14.

The call `Message.send()` returns a promise object. The attached `then()` method is called once the process of saving the message is completed successfully. In this moment, you want to clear the message textarea because the user doesn't want to send the same message twice.

For debugging purposes, you call an `alert()` method to inform the user that the message was sent. If the message cannot be sent for any reason, the `fail()` method will be called.

Listing 8-14. A Message Is Saved to Parse, and an Alert is Sent (www/js/views/conversation.js)

```
sendMessage: function() {
    var Message = new MyParseMessage();
    Message.send({
        Receiver: app.conversation.Receiver,
        message_body: $('textarea').val()
    }).then(function(Message) {
        $('textarea').val('');
        console.log(Message);
        alert('Message was sent!');
    }).fail(function(error) {
        console.log(error);
        alert('Message was not sent!');
    });
}
```

Sending a Test Message and Review

Send some test messages between the same two users, then head over to the Parse data browser (https://parse.com/apps/) and review the messages you sent. You can see an example dataset in Figure 8-2.

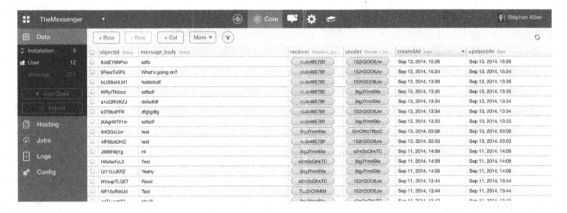

Figure 8-2. *A view of the data browser with example messages between different users*

■ **Tip**   Clicking the User objects in the receiver and sender fields takes you to a detailed view of that user.

Improving Dialog Styles (Optional)

Plug-ins! Cordova has some great core and third-party plug-ins that can be used to add extra functionality to your application.

Up until this point, you have been using the alert JavaScript function to display messages to the user. This displays an alert message using the web browser's native style. If the platform supports it, this plug-in will use the native device styles and also extend the functionality. The Cordova Dialogs plug-in currently (version 0.2.10) supports the following platforms:

- Amazon Fire OS

- Android

- BlackBerry 10

- Firefox OS

- iOS

- Tizen

- Windows Phone 7 and 8

- Windows 8

Plug-ins offer a great way to improve the experience of the application you are building with little effort. As you have done before, install the plug-in using the command line. Make sure you are in the root of your project and run

```
cordova plugin add org.apache.cordova.dialogs
```

Next, update the usage of the `alert` functions. Use the function `navigator.notification.alert` to invoke the plug-in functionality.

Continue to use the alert() function for non-PhoneGap requests. Otherwise, testing your application in the browser will fail. To do this, see if `cordova` is in the `window` object, as shown in Listing 8-15. You can see a result of the plug-in in Figure 8-3. Instead of showing an unaesthetic title like `conversation.html`, you are using the application name as dialog title.

Listing 8-15. Choose Either Native or Browser Implementation

```
if(window.cordova) {
    navigator.notification.alert('Message was sent!', function() {}, 'TheMessenger', 'OK!');
} else {
    alert('Message was sent!');
}
```

Figure 8-3. *Cordova Dialog plug-in example*

Features Offered by the Dialogs Plug-in

The Dialogs plug-in is capable of doing a lot more than just sending alerts. Other functions include

- `navigator.notification.confirm`
- `navigator.notification.prompt`
- `navigator.notification.beep`

You will use the `alert()` part of this plug-in these application examples. To get familiar with the other parts, try it on your own. Be creative and test ways to use this plug-in in your applications.

Reading Messages

Just as it's crucial that your messages get sent between users, it is equally so that users are able to *read* them. This section will populate the conversation history using the messages sent between the authorized users.

Bootstrap provides an excellent set of user interface styles that are a great fit for your conversation view (see Figure 8-4). After adding the functionality to populate the template you'll be creating, you'll provide some optional user interface optimization tips using a new PhoneGap plug-in.

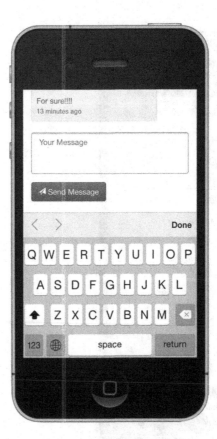

Figure 8-4. *The layout of the conversation view*

Querying Conversation Messages

The body of a conversation should only include messages by the parties involved. This application is designed for only one Sender and one Receiver to participate in a conversation. However, you can extend the app to be able to send messages to multiple users in a group chat where there is one Sender and many Receivers. Yet be aware, it's a complex topic!

To populate the conversation view, you need to get all the messages *sent* from the current user to their intended Receiver. This is shown in Listing 8-16. And of course you need the messages *received* by the current user (Listing 8-17).

Listing 8-16. Querying for Sent Messages. Notice that the Sender is the Current User

```
var senderQuery = new Parse.Query(MyParseMessage);
senderQuery.equalTo("Receiver", Receiver);
senderQuery.equalTo("Sender", MyParseUser.current());
```

Listing 8-17. Querying for Received Messages. Here, the Receiver Is the Current User

```
var receiverQuery = new Parse.Query(MyParseMessage);
receiverQuery.equalTo("Receiver", MyParseUser.current());
receiverQuery.equalTo("Sender", Receiver);
```

Compound Queries

Naturally, you want to merge these two results into one. One approach would be to execute both queries–in parallel or in series–and merge the results after both are finished. However, this is not a good approach. Can you imagine why?

Instead, you will compound those queries into one query using the `Parse.Query.or()` method. This approach will enable you to keep all messages in order and your code clean and simple.

In Listing 8-18, you can see an example of a compound query combining three different queries. If a record matches at least one criterion of these three queries, it will be part of the result set.

Listing 8-18. Abstract Compound Query Example

```
var query1 = new Parse.Query(MyClass);
query1.equalTo('key', value1);

var query2 = new Parse.Query(MyClass);
query2.equalTo('key', value2);

var query3 = new Parse.Query(MyClass);
query3.equalTo('key', value3);

var compoundQuery = Parse.Query.or(query1, query2, query3);
compoundQuery.find();
```

For this example, you simply pass the previously created `senderQuery` and `receiverQuery` to the `Parse.Query.or()` method to get all messages between the two conversation participants (Listing 8-19).

Listing 8-19. Compound Query for Sent and Received Messages

```
var messageQuery = Parse.Query.or(senderQuery, receiverQuery);
```

Managing Conversations

To keep all business logic related to conversations in one place, use a custom Parse.Object named MyParseConversation. Name the corresponding class in the Parse database as Conversation. So far, your MyParseConversation class will just contain class methods. We'll come back to the actual object structure and instance methods at a later point in this chapter.

Create a new file called www/js/models/MyParseConversation.js. Add a method called getMessage to execute the just-discussed compound query (Listing 8-20).

Listing 8-20. Compound Query in the Custom Parse.Object MyParseConversation (www/js/models/MyParseConversation.js)

```
var MyParseConversation = Parse.Object.extend('Conversation', {
    // Instance Methods (currently empty)
}, {
    getMessages: function(Receiver, limit) {

        // Query messages sent by current user
        var senderQuery = new Parse.Query(MyParseMessage);
        senderQuery.equalTo("Receiver", Receiver);
        senderQuery.equalTo("Sender", MyParseUser.current());

        // Query messages sent by other user
        var receiverQuery = new Parse.Query(MyParseMessage);
        receiverQuery.equalTo("Receiver", MyParseUser.current());
        receiverQuery.equalTo("Sender", Receiver);

        // Combined Query with OR condition
        var messageQuery = Parse.Query.or(senderQuery, receiverQuery);

        // Limit the result
        messageQuery.limit(limit);

        // Show newer messages first
        messageQuery.descending('createdAt');

        // Pass result to render function
        return messageQuery.find();

    }
});
```

■ **Tip** Parse.Query.or takes multiple Parse.Query objects as arguments, allowing you to combine more than two queries at a time.

Rendering the Conversation View

Rendering the conversation view consists of three tasks: loading the messages, rendering them in a human-friendly way, and then removing the loading indicator.

To load the messages, use the just-created MyParseConversation.getMessages() method. It returns a promise object, and once the promise is resolved, it calls the then function, which holds the results of your compound query as function argument. Name this argument Messages.

However, before rendering the messages, invert their order. The newest messages should be at the bottom of the view, right next to the input and keyboard area. Older messages are at the top of the view. The user will be able to reach them by scrolling up. To invert the order of the Messages, simply call the Array method reverse().

After rendering the view using app.core.render, remove the class loading from the placeholder <div>. All steps are summarized in Listing 8-21.

Listing 8-21. The renderMessages Method Renders a List of Messages (www/js/views/conversation.js).

```
renderMessages: function() {
    var limit = 5;
    MyParseConversation.getMessages(
        app.conversation.Receiver, limit
    ).then(function(Messages) {
        app.core.render('.placeholder', 'conversation', {
            // Use reverse() to place old messages on the top
            messages: Messages.reverse()
        });
        $('.placeholder').removeClass('loading');
    });
}
```

■ **Tip** In this example, you see the last five messages. To display older messages, you can skip the first results by applying the method skip() to the Parse.Query object. For example, use query.skip(10) to skip the first 10 results.

Preparing Message Data for Rendering

Before working on the actual message template, let's think about what information you want to display. Besides the proper message text, you want the time when a message was sent and the identity of the sender (your conversation partner or you).

Yet you don't want to do this in the Handlebars template, as you might have expected. By experience, you know this will lead to messy templates, which are hard to maintain. Instead, you will handle all data formatting and visualization rules in the MyParseMessage class.

Formatting Dates with Moment.js

The most important part of this exercise is formatting the message time. As you know, all Parse.Object classes automatically track the information about their creation in the field createdAt. A value of this field could look like 2014-09-21T23:52:50.310Z, which is not a very user-friendly format.

To fix this issue, use the library Moment.js. It provides a set of methods to display such complex timestamps in better formats like September 9th 2014, 11:52:50 pm or 31 minutes ago.

Download the library from http://momentjs.com/. Save the file moment.min.js in the directory www/js/vendors and add a reference to your JavaScript loader in the scripts variable in core.js:

```
var scripts = {
    common: [
        './js/vendor/moment.min.js',
    }
};
```

To format the timestamp of a message directly in the class MyParseMessage, add a new instance method named getFromNow, as shown in Listing 8-22. Use the moment.js function fromNow() to format the timestamp. It will return the relative time that has passed since the message was sent (e.g. "4 hours ago").

As you learned in previous chapters, inside instance methods you can access the current object using this. For example, a new moment.js object can be created by using moment(this.createdAt). To convert the field to a relative time, apply the function fromNow() to the moment.js object.

Listing 8-22. Adding getFromNow to the MyParseMessage Object (www/js/models/MyParseMessage.js).

```
var MyParseMessage = Parse.Object.extend('Message', {
    getFromNow: function() {
        return moment(this.createdAt).fromNow();
    },
    send: function() {
        // Send Code
    },
    protectMessage: function() {
        // Protect Message Code
    }
});
```

Alternating Styling for Sent and Received Messages

To differentiate styles between sent and received message, add some Bootstrap magic to each message based on the user who sent it. First, detect whether the sender ID equals the current user's ID. Message sent by the current user are the message *owner*.

You reflect this inquiry in the function isOwner() in Listing 8-23. Based on the message owner, chose a different color using the Twitter Bootstrap alert-* classes. Messages sent by the current user are aligned to the right, which is a common standard when displaying messages in a chat history style. You can get the corresponding CSS class for each message by calling getCssClass in the template.

Listing 8-23. Determining Styles in the Parse.Object Message (www/js/models/MyParseMessage.js).

```
isOwner: function() {
    return this.get('sender').id == MyParseUser.current().id;
},
getCssClass: function() {
    return this.isOwner() ? 'alert-info pull-right' : 'alert-warning';
}
```

Using Instance Methods in Handlebars Templates

From previous tutorials you already know that you can access Parse.Object attributes in Handlebars templates using the syntax objectname.attributes.key.

Handlebars not only gives you access to object keys; you can also call methods from the object. As long as the function returns a string, Handlebars will render it to the DOM.

Subsequently, all instance methods you define for your Parse objects are accessible by Handlebars. For example, to access the function getFromNow() on the first record returned from a collection named messages, you use the syntax shown in Listing 8-24. When calling the same function in a loop, the syntax in Listing 8-25 will come into play. As you see, this will keep your templates clean and easy to read. You'll use the construction of Listing 8-25 in the conversation template, which you'll create in the following section.

Listing 8-24. Calling an Parse.Object Instance Method in Handlebars

```
{{ messages.0.getFromNow }}
```

Listing 8-25. Calling an Instance Method Inside a Loop

```
{{#each messages}}
    {{ getFromNow }}
{{/each}}
```

Creating the Conversation Template

After taking all of the preparatory steps, you've finally come to the conversation template. As stated earlier, the goal is to display a conversation that is composed of a single or multiple messages between two users, also known as monologue and dialog.

Because loading a conversation's data from a remote server usually takes some time, you need a way for users to know that their content is loading behind the scenes. For this, you'll use the CSS class loading, which was created earlier in this chapter. See Listing 8-26 for an example of how to use the class. Once the messages are loaded and processed, the conversation template of Listing 8-27 will replace this placeholder.

Listing 8-26. The Addition of a Placeholder div to the Existing Conversation View (conversation.html)

```
<div class="container">
    <div class="placeholder loading"></div>
    <!-- Existing submit form for new messages -->
</div>
```

That said, there will be a time when there are no conversations to list. This will happen once a user starts a new conversation with someone. So inside your Handlebars template you want to display a custom message if there are no messages to display. If there are, you then loop through all of the records and populate the conversation view (Listing 8-27).

Listing 8-27. The Handlebars Template Used for Displaying Messages of a Conversation (www/conversation.html)

```
<script id="conversation-template" type="text/x-handlebars-template">
    <div id="messages">
    {{#if messages}}
        {{#each messages}}
            <div class="clearfix">
                <div style="width: 80%" class="alert well-sm {{ getCssClass }}">
                    {{ attributes.message_body }}
                    <div class="small">
                        {{ getFromNow }}
                    </div>
                </div>
            </div>
        {{/each}}
        {{else}}
            <div class="well">Write a message!</div>
    {{/if}}
    </div>
</script>
```

Besides displaying the message_body, you format each message's <div> container by an alternating CSS class attribute, served by the instance method getCssClass(). Next, you use the instance method getFromNow() to display the time when the message was sent.

■ **Note**   The task of managing these HTML elements is managed in the renderMessages() method in Listing 8-21.

User Interface Optimizations (Optional)

Admittedly, the current implementation works as a proof of concept, but it isn't perfect. You can keep the current code samples and move on to the next section, but if you want to polish your application, you can add the following tweaks.

Removing the Keyboard Toolbar

An easy but big win is to remove the keyboard toolbar via the Ionic Keyboard plug-in. It will increase the available screen size while the user is typing their message. In your terminal, navigate to the root of the project and install the plug-in using

```
cordova plugin add com.ionic.keyboard
```

To remove the toolbar, call the following method when rendering the view:

```
cordova.plugins.Keyboard.hideKeyboardAccessoryBar(true);
```

You can see the result of the keyboard removal in Figure 8-5. Even though you win just a few pixels, it increases the space available for messages by about 20% (depending on the device size).

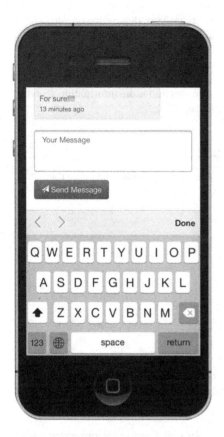

Figure 8-5. *Comparison: Message input with and without keyboard toolbar*

Removing the Keyboard When the Body Is Tapped

When the user is interacting with the body, for example by tapping it, you can assume the user doesn't want to enter a message. So let's hide the keyboard when the user is doing this. You combine this task with hiding the toolbar in the function `toggleKeyboardAccessoryBar()` in Listing 8-28.

In order to use the `tap` event, and other cool gestures like swiping, you will need to add an external library. Download `http://quojs.tapquo.com/` and add it to your project. Using $$ denotes the usage of *tapquo* (versus jQuery's single $ symbol).

Listing 8-28. Removing Keyboard on Tap

```
toggleKeyboardAccessoryBar: function() {
    cordova.plugins.Keyboard.hideKeyboardAccessoryBar(true);
    $$('body').tap(function(e) {
        if (!$(e.target).is("input,textarea")) {
            cordova.plugins.Keyboard.close();
        }
    });
}
```

Important! You are excluding all events happening within the textarea. Next, depending on your app design, you may want to apply this function to all your views by adding it to the app.core object and executing it on every view load.

The plug-in offers other methods, among which is the opportunity to close the keyboard via cordova.plugins.Keyboard.close() or disable the native scrolling via cordova.plugins.Keyboard.disableScroll(). Availability may depend on the operating system. You can find more information about the plug-in at https://github.com/driftyco/ionic-plugins-keyboard.

Hiding the Navigation Bar When Textarea Is Focused

The fixed navigation bar at the top might be in conflict with the textarea. To avoid this issue, hide the bar when the textarea is focused and bring it back when the focus is lost:

```
$("textarea").on('blur', function() {
    $('nav').show();
});

$("textarea").on('focus', function() {
    $('nav').hide();
});
```

Scrolling to Textarea and Focusing on Load

If it is a longer conversation and the user still wants to be able to enter a message quickly, you can enable a scroll to the textarea on page load. Execute the code after loading the message so that the script knows how far to scroll (Listing 8-29).

Listing 8-29. Scrolling to the textarea Element When Initializing the View (www/js/views/conversation.js)

```
window.setTimeout(function() {
    $(window).scrollTop($("textarea").offset().top -
        ($(window).height() - $("textarea").height()));
    window.setTimeout(function() {
        $("textarea").focus();
    }, 300);
}, 150);
```

Listing Conversations

In the last part of this chapter, you'll populate a view that lists conversations of the current user. The task sounds simple. Nevertheless, it is a challenge. Prior to listing conversations, you need to prepare the conversation data, which will include building a message *index*.

All intermediate steps will lead to building the conversation list view shown in Figure 8-6. For each conversation, the view will show the user's profile picture, name, time when the last message was sent.

Figure 8-6. This view lists all conversations a user started, with the newest on top

Gathering Metadata for Messages

Before rendering a conversation list, you need to take a moment to think about how to gather this information. The conversations you want to list are the messages users send to each other.

The ordering of the list items will be determined by the last message of the conversation, no matter whether it was the current user sending this message or receiving it. In an abstract way, the query should do something like this: *"Select all messages, order them by the sent date, but only return one message per sender-receiver combination."*

In other systems like SQL, this can be done via the SELECT DISTINCT statement. This statement will return only distinct (different) values. Parse currently doesn't offer such a query method, thus we need to think differently.

Creating a Message Index

Instead of running a query on all messages, you will create a structured message index, which will help you to create a conversation list view. Database indexes are a complex topic, yet we can describe the system in short as follows:

> *A database index is a data structure that improves the speed of data retrieval operations on a database table at the cost of additional writes and storage space to maintain the index data structure.*
>
> —http://en.wikipedia.org/wiki/Database_index

As you can see by the quote, creating database indexes is not a Parse-specific topic. It's used in other database systems as well. An example you use every day is Google. It doesn't search the Web for you in the moment you search. Its software prepared an index of what you might want to know in advance.

You will do something similar, yet on a way smaller scale. For your messages, each index entry will contain information about a most recent Message and the two participating users. Yet you will save this information twice per conversation, one entry for each participant's perspective. Next, once there is a new "most recent" Message, you will update the existing index entry to reflect this information.

As you'll be using this index solely for listing conversations, call this index Conversation.

One last question to be answered before completing the concept: When and where is this index being created? The solution is pretty simple. You will update the Conversation index each time a Message is sent. This way the conversation view will always be up to date and you don't need to "batch index" messages.

Tracking Conversations

Earlier in this chapter, within the section "Managing Conversations," you created the custom Parse.Object MyParseConversation. Using some foresight, you named the Parse class Conversation, the name of your conversation index.

As just discussed, the Conversation object will contain a reference to the most recent Message and the two participating users. The references to the participating users are static. The most recent Message will be updated every time a new message is sent.

Add the code for updating the Conversation object as a class method to the MyParseConversation class. Name this method update and call it after saving a Message using the latter as argument, as shown in Listing 8-29.

Listing 8-29. Calling the Conversation Update Method After Saving a Message (www/js/models/MyParseMessage.js)

```
afterSave: function(Message) {
    var Receiver = Message.get('Receiver');
    MyParseConversation.update(Message);
    return Message;
}
```

Setting Up the MyParseConversation Class

It's time to extend the MyParseConversation class. Add the placeholder methods shown in Listing 8-30 to the class while keeping the existing instance and class methods. We will discuss both functions, getOrCreate and update, in this section.

Listing 8-30. The Updates for the Conversation Object MyParseConversation

```
var MyParseConversation = Parse.Object.extend('Conversation', {

}, {
    getOrCreate: function() {},
    update: function() {}
});
```

In the beginning of the "Tracking Conversations" section, you already added the task invoking the process of updating a conversation, namely using the method `MyParseConversation.update()`. But before updating a `Conversation` object, you need one to work with. This means you either create a new `Conversation` object or use an existing one. This requirement leads you to think about the principle of having a unique entry in your database for a singular object.

For messages, guaranteeing this singularity is simple. You create a new `Message`, save it to the database, get a unique ID, then after that you (more or less) don't touch this message again. You can repeat this process again and again; your database integrity will be fine.

For the `Conversation` class, the scenario is somewhat different. There should be only one `Conversation` object per conversation perspective. As there are exactly two conversation participants in your application design, there must be two `Conversation` objects per conversation.

At the very first time–when the user starts a new conversation–saving those two `Conversation` objects is straightforward: create a new instance for each perspective, save it to the database, done. For the second, and all following situations, it's more complicated. If you stick to the same pattern of carelessly saving `Conversation` objects to the database, you will end up having a large amount of `Conversation` objects in the database for a single conversation.

What you must do instead is, if there is a database entry for the corresponding conversation, return the existing entry; if not, you create a new one. A *unique* entry is defined by a *unique* combination of `Owner` and `Partner` of a `Conversation` object.

■ **Note**   The roles of the conversation `Owner` and `Partner` were explained in the beginning of this chapter. If these terms are unclear, please take a look at Table 8-2.

If you translate this process into code, it will look like Listing 8-31. A query searches for a `Conversation` object using two user objects, the conversation participants, as filter. If a `Conversation` object is found, it will be returned. If not, a new instance will be created, saved to the database, and returned–as a `Parse.Promise` object. The fact that the process of creating a new `Conversation` instance will return a `Parse.Promise` object instead of a `Conversation` object won't make a difference, as you will treat the whole `getOrCreate` process as a promise anyway.

Listing 8-31. Getting or Creating a New Conversation Object (www/js/models/MyParseConversation.js)

```
getOrCreate: function(Owner, Partner) {
    var query = new Parse.Query(MyParseConversation);
    query.equalTo('Owner', Owner);
    query.equalTo('Partner', Partner);
    return query.first().then(function(Conversation) {
        if (Conversation) {
            return Conversation;
        }
```

```
        Conversation = new MyParseConversation();
        Conversation.set('Owner', Owner);
        Conversation.set('Partner', Partner);
        return Conversation.save();
    });
}
```

Updating Conversation Meta Information

After assuring the singularity of each Conversation object, you can eventually add meta information to
it. The only information you'll add in this example is the most recent Message reference. However, you
may extend the Conversation object to handle more information, such as how many messages were sent,
whether the conversation has unread messages, and so forth.

As previously described, each conversation holds two Conversation objects, so you'll update *both*
objects once a new message is sent. As shown in Listing 8-32, the Conversation object for each conversation
participant is requested using the method getOrCreate. Subsequently, the reference to the last Message is
set and saved to the Parse database.

Listing 8-32. The update Function That Updates Both Perspectives of a Conversation
(www/js/models/MyParseConversation.js)

```
update: function(Message) {
    var Receiver = Message.get('Receiver');
    // Update the Conversation for the current User
    this.getOrCreate(MyParseUser.current(), Receiver)
        .then(function(Conversation) {
            Conversation.set('last_message', Message);
            Conversation.save();
        });
    // Update the Conversation for the Receiver
    this.getOrCreate(Receiver, MyParseUser.current())
        .then(function(Conversation) {
            Conversation.set('last_message', Message);
            Conversation.save();
        });
}
```

Querying Latest Conversations

Creating a conversation index was the base functionality you needed for listing a user's conversations.
Reading this information is straightforward. You just need to query all Conversation objects that are owned
by the current user.

Add a new JavaScript js/views/conversationList.js. As with any new script you add to this project,
add the file references to the scripts.common variable in core.js.

The initialize function executes a simple Parse.Query using MyParseUser.current() as filter for the
Conversation object field Owner. Since you need the Partner and the last_message object in the template
to display the conversation partner's name and a preview of the text of the last message, you include both
objects using the method Parse.Query.include().

When the promise of the query is resolved, you pass the result to the Handlebars render. The Handlebars templates used in this case, conversationList, will be created in the upcoming "Conversation List Template" section. Listing 8-33 summarizes the process of loading the conversations and rendering them.

Listing 8-33. The Conversation List View Script (www/js/views/conversationList.js)

```
app.conversationList = {
    initialize: function() {
        var query = new Parse.Query(MyParseConversation);
        query.include('last_message');
        query.include('Partner');
        query.equalTo('Owner', MyParseUser.current());
        query.limit(10);
        query.descending('updatedAt');
        return query.find().then(function(Conversations) {
            app.core.render('.placeholder', 'conversationList', {
                conversations: Conversations
            });
            $('.placeholder').removeClass('loading');
        });
    }
};
```

Preparing Conversation Data for Rendering

Analog to the MyParseMessage class, you will add a few instance methods to the MyParseConversation class to keep the handlebars templates clean and readable (Listing 8-34).

The first two of these functions are getPartnerId and getPartnerName. They simply expose the ID and first_name and last_name values of the conversation Partner. Doing the same inside a Handlebars template is more complex.

The getPicture function serves as an intermediary function calling the MyParseUser.getPicture() function and returning the user's picture saved when creating a new account via Facebook. You'll only display profile pictures for Facebook users; for other users, you will show a placeholder image. In Chapter 10, we will add the ability to add a profile image for all accounts.

The getMessagePreview() function serves as an intermediary function as well. It gets the value for last_message, which is actually a Message object, and applies the function getPreview() of the MyParseMessage class on it. The function getPreview() is defined in Listing 8-35. It shortens the message_body if it's too long.

Next, you reuse the previously created getFromNow() method of the Message object, applied to the last_message instance as well.

Listing 8-34. Adding Methods to the Existing MyParseConversation Object

```
var MyParseConversation = Parse.Object.extend('Conversation', {
    // The user ID of the conversation partner
    getPartnerId: function() {
        return this.get('Partner').id;
    },
    // Name of the conversation partner
    getPartnerName: function() {
        return this.get('Partner').get('first_name') + ' ' +
            this.get('Partner').get('last_name');
    },
    // Profile picture of the conversation partner
    getPicture: function() {
        return this.get('Partner').getPicture();
    },
    // A preview of the last message
    getMessagePreview: function() {
        return this.get('last_message').getPreview();
    },
    // The time elapsed since the last message was sent
    getFromNow: function() {
        return this.get('last_message').getFromNow();
    }
}, {
    // Keep existing code
});
```

Listing 8-35. The getPreview Method Returns a Short Preview of the Message Body
(www/js/models/MyParseMessage.js)

```
var MyParseMessage = Parse.Object.extend('Message', {
    getPreview: function() {
        return this.get('message_body').length > 40 ?
                this.get('message_body').substring(0, 40) + '..' :
                this.get('message_body');
    }
}, {
    // Keep existing code
});
```

Conversation List Template

Now that there is data to populate the view, you create the Handlbarsjs template that will render a
conversation's messages. Start by creating a new conversationsList.html file (Listing 8-36). Each row in
the list links to the existing conversation.html view. Apply the method getPartnerId to set the value for id
in the URL parameters.

Listing 8-36. The conversationsList.html Template That Lists Separate Conversations Between Different Individuals

```html
<div class="container">
    <div class="placeholder loading"></div>
</div>

<script id="conversationList-template" type="text/x-handlebars-template">
    <table class="table table-striped">
        {{#each conversations}}
            <tr>
                <td>
                    <a href="conversation.html?id={{ getPartnerId }}">
                        <img src="{{ getPicture }}" class="img-circle pull-left">
                    </a>
                </td>
                <td class="small" style="vertical-align: middle">
                    <a href="conversation.html?id={{ getPartnerId }}">
                        {{ getPartnerName }}  <br>
                        <small>
                            {{ getFromNow }}<br>
                            <em>{{ getMessagePreview }}</em>
                        </small>
                    </a>
                </td>
            </tr>
        {{/each}}
    </table>
</script>
```

Listing 8-37. The config Variable Customized for the Conversation List View (www/conversationsList.html)

```html
<script>
    var config = {
        view: "conversationList",
        title: "Conversations",
        public_access: false
    };
    app.initialize();
</script>
```

■ **Tip**   After a user logs in, you currently redirect them to the view `contacts.html`, so that he can select another user to send message to. Clicking the contact name takes them to the conversation view, which you will build in Chapter 9. After building this new view, you should change your default view to be `conversationsList.html`. If the user didn't start any conversations yet, redirect them to the view `contacts.html`.

Summary

This chapter covered the heart of your application: sending and receiving messages to display in a conversation. Using the Parse.User object, you are able to send messages between users. Each Message that is sent is perceived uniquely based on the person sending or receiving it. You used the names Sender and Receiver to differentiate which role a user plays in relation to a single Message, while using the same object type, Parse.User.

Sending messages happens in the conversation view. This is also where you load messages two users sent to each other in the past. Besides Sender and Receiver, you use the property message_body in your Message class to save the actual message text. Using the built-in createdAt property allows you to order the messages by time. Using the Cordova Dialogs plug-in you were able to add native styles for alerts.

Populating a conversation is composed of two separate queries that are combined to make a *compound query*. You use the Parse.Query.or method to select all messages sent between two users. The returned result is displayed in the conversation view. Using moment.js, you are able to format the time each message was created in a user-friendly way.

You added some optional user interface optimizations with the Ionic Keyboard plug-in. Further, you improved the user experience by adding scroll, blur, and focus event handlers to the conversation view. We use the terms Owner and Partner to distinguish the relationship of conversation participants in the new custom class MyParseConversation. It stores all of the functionality needed to manage a conversation and its messages. Using instance methods in the MyParseMessage and MyParseConversation classes, you were able to keep your templates clean and simple.

CHAPTER 9

■ ■ ■

Location Services

Life isn't only about where you're going. It's also about where you're at.

There are three things you need to know about real estate:

1. Location

2. Location

3. Location

For mobile, it's not all about location, but it sure counts. Terms like SoLoMo (Social-Local-Mobile) have been formative for the app industry in the last few years. It's not the Holy Grail, but a part of it. And after adding the **SO**cial part into your **MO**bile application, we'll show how to implement the **LO**cation part.

The geolocation plug-in is the perfect example for PhoneGap's goal, or let's call it "theory;" using or pioneering open web standards. It follows the Geolocation API Specification, created by the World Wide Web Consortium (W3C, `http://dev.w3.org/geo/api/spec-source.html`). If you already know the `navigator.geolocation` API, you don't need to learn anything new. You can use the same methods and data formats you already know.

A wide range of browsers (`http://caniuse.com/#feat=geolocation`) supports this specification. The hope is that other plug-ins find their way into future browser software releases. A potential example for this is the PhoneGap camera plug-in (`navigator.camera`), which we'll cover in Chapter 10. If these kinds of features become a part of every browser someday, it'll be possible to create much richer user experiences without using a hybrid tool like PhoneGap or an actual native application.

Coming back to the PhoneGap GeoLocation plug-in, as mentioned you can use the `navigator.geolocation` object. If the browser (or web view) of the appropriate system supports this API, your application will use it. If not, PhoneGap will fall back to the native implementation and serve the information back to the application via the Cordova plug-in API.

In doing so, the plug-in will use different sources to detect the device location, including the Global Positioning System (GPS) and location inferred from network signals such as IP address, RFID, WiFi, Bluetooth MAC addresses, and GSM/CDMA cell IDs. Yet there is no guarantee that the API will return the device's *actual* location. To explain the usage of the geolocation plug-in, we'll build upon the previous tutorials of the Messenger application. You'll be able to execute all code using your own application and data examples.

For this example, the goal is to add location information to each message, as you know from services like the Facebook Messenger. In the second step, we'll show you how to track a user's location using a background service. Then you'll convert location information into a city name. As a triumphant finale, you'll show locations on a map inside the application.

■ **Tip** Collecting a device's, or user's, location is not just a technical feat. Whenever you track a user's location you should give them options to control this: tell them how you use the data, how you save it, and provide an opportunity for them to delete it. Another factor is the precision of the collected data. If you just save country or region information once, it's less critical than if you constantly track the exact position of the user and create a geo-profile.

Geolocation Plug-in

It all starts with installing the geolocation plug-in. Even though the browser's implementation of the standard might be good enough for most cases, some features, like watching a user's location over time and using the method navigator.geolocation.watchPosition(), will only work as long as the application is *active*.

Running such a service in the background will require another plug-in. We'll come back to the implementation of this feature at a later point in this chapter. To install the plug-in, run the command shown in Listing 9-1.

Listing 9-1. Geolocation Plug-in Installation

```
cordova plugin add org.apache.cordova.geolocation
```

In the first part, you'll use the method navigator.geolocation.getCurrentPosition(). This method has three parameters, geolocationSuccess, geolocationError, and geolocationOptions.

geolocationSuccess

This callback function is called when a user location is being detected. It will pass the current position as argument to the function. The format of the response will look like Listing 9-2.

Listing 9-2. Geolocation Response Format

```
{
    "timestamp": 1234567895231,
    "coords": {
        "speed": null,
        "heading": null,
        "altitudeAccuracy": null,
        "accuracy": 54,
        "altitude": null,
        "longitude": -73.863131,
        "latitude": 41.756271
    }
}
```

geolocationError

An error callback is executed if an error occurs. You do not need to define an error callback. Yet your application will just not work in some cases without informing the user of this fact. For your case, this would be acceptable; if you cannot track the location of the user, the message will still be sent. So the essentials are fulfilled.

The error object contains an error code and message. You explored some debugging techniques in the "PhoneGap Testing Tools" section from Chapter 4. You may also debug errors as demonstrated in Listing 9-3. Although using an alert is admittedly not the best debugging technique, it does what it says on the box and alerts the user of an error.

Listing 9-3. Geolocation Response Format

```
function onError(error) {
    alert('code: ' + error.code + '\n' + 'message: ' + error.message + '\n');
}
```

geolocationOptions

Use the options enableHighAccuracy, timeout, and maximumAge to customize your request (Listing 9-4). If you set the value enableHighAccuracy to true, the plug-in will request a more accurate position, such as GPS. Enabling a higher accuracy might cause a bigger delay for the response and more battery consumption.

The option timeout (in milliseconds) will define the maximum time that is allowed to serve a response. The option maximumAge will define how "old" location information is allowed to be (also in milliseconds). By using this option in a smart way you'll get faster response times and save the user's battery.

Listing 9-4. Geolocation Options

```
{
    enableHighAccuracy: true,   // enabled
    timeout: 10000,             // 10 seconds
    maximumAge: 300000          // 5 minutes
}
```

Adding Location Information to a Message

Just debugging numbers is no fun. Eventually you want to use and see this service in action. To do this, take your Messenger application and extend the MyParseMessage class. Add a new class method called addLocation() to the class, as shown in Listing 9-5. Call the method every time a message has been sent, which means in the afterSave() method, which you created in Chapter 8.

Within the addLocation() method make use of the previously introduced navigator.geolocation. getCurrentPosition() method. The first time a user invokes this method, the application will ask the user to grant access to this information (iOS), as shown in Figure 9-1. Debug the response via the console plug-in. You can perform the same test using your desktop web browser.

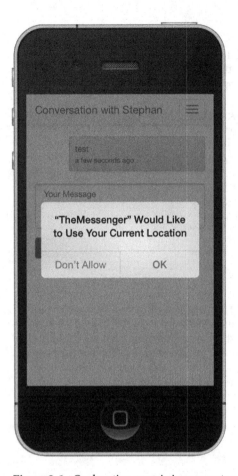

Figure 9-1. Geolocation permission request on iOS

Listing 9-5. Using the getCurrentPosition() Method (www/js/models/MyParseMessage.js)

```
afterSave: function(Message) {
    MyParseMessage.addLocation(Message);
    return Message;
},
addLocation: function(Message) {
    navigator.geolocation.getCurrentPosition(function(location) {
        console.log(location);
    }, function(error) {
        alert('ERROR(' + error.code + '): ' + error.message);
    });
}
```

___

■ **Tip** If you base your example on the previous tutorial, make sure to remove the alert('Message was sent!'); call. Calling an alert will interrupt the execution of navigator.geolocation.getCurrentPosition(), and the location won't get tracked.

___

■ **Tip** If you are using the iOS simulator, make sure that you provide a location to the simulator. You can do this by selecting Debug ➤ Location in the menu bar. Use either a preset or a custom location. The pre-filled values of the custom location are based on your current location.

Geolocation Permission Settings

If a user declines the first geolocation permission request, the response of this request and everything following it will fail. You cannot ask for this permission again within the application. If this issue occurs, you need to inform the user that he manually has to grant this permission in his phone's privacy settings (iOS).

To make the adjustment, switch to Settings ➤ Privacy ➤ Location and enable the location services, both for your phone and your application, as shown in Figure 9-2.

Figure 9-2. *Geolocation permission settings on iOS*

Geolocation in Parse

Of course Parse offers a special data type for the location matter, and of course Parse uses geographic coordinates to describe a location. Thus, you can seamlessly move the plug-in location data to Parse. The data type is called `Parse.GeoPoint`. It is simply defined by a `latitude` and `longitude` value.

Besides saving geolocation information, you can use this data type to run queries to find nearby points via `Parse.Query.near()` or to calculate the distance to a point via `Parse.GeoPoint.milesTo()`. We'll discuss these methods as well as other location queries later in this chapter.

To create a new `Parse.GeoPoint`, pass the values `latitude` and `longitude` in the form of an object to the instance call, as shown in Listing 9-6.

Listing 9-6. Creating a new Parse.GeoPoint Instance

```
var point = new Parse.GeoPoint({
    latitude: location.coords.latitude,
    longitude: location.coords.longitude
});
```

The `Parse.GeoPoint` can be used as a field in `Parse.Object`. To assign a `Parse.GeoPoint` value to a class, you simply use the `Parse.Object.set()` method. In your example, you set the value of the field `location` to the just-created GeoPoint (Listing 9-7). After assigning the value, you save the `Message` object. That's it! Listing 9-8 demonstrates combining the steps of getting and saving the location.

Listing 9-7. Assigning a GeoPoint to a Parse.Object

```
Message.set('location', point);
Message.save();
```

Listing 9-8. Getting the Device's Location and Saving It to Parse (www/js/models/MyParseMessage.js)

```
addLocation: function(Message) {
    navigator.geolocation.getCurrentPosition(function(location) {
        var point = new Parse.GeoPoint({
            latitude: location.coords.latitude,
            longitude: location.coords.longitude
        });
        Message.set('location', point);
        Message.save();
    }, function(error) {
        alert('ERROR(' + error.code + '): ' + error.message);
    });
}
```

Location Setting Interface

As previously discussed, location is not just about technology but also about privacy. In your current implementation, you add the location straight to the message without giving the user the opportunity to enable or disable the service.

Your goal is to offer a setting per conversation. So add a location service toggle button right next to the Send Message button, as shown in Figure 9-3.

Figure 9-3. *Geolocation permission settings on iOS*

LocalStorage for Device-Related Information

Before updating the user interface, you need to think about saving the setting so that the user doesn't have to change it again and again. An important criterion is that this setting is a local one. You do not want to overwrite another device's settings when using the application on multiple devices. For this purpose, you will use the LocalStorage API.

The usage of localStorage does not require a plug-in because it is part of all modern browsers (http://caniuse.com/#search=localstorage). The LocalStorage API works similar to browser cookies, yet you can save large amounts of data. It is also known as web storage, simple storage, or by its alternate session storage interface. The API provides synchronous key/value pair storage, which also offers the advantage that the data is available instantly, without waiting for an answer from Parse.

Call the method's getItem() to read a value and setItem() to save a value to the local storage of your phone (Listing 9-9).

Listing 9-9. Reading and Saving Values Using the Local Storage

```
// Get a value
var foo = localStorage.getItem("bar");
// Set a value
localStorage.setItem("bar", foo);
```

The next requirement is that this property is not essentially view related; it has a global role. Hence you'll outsource this code part into a "module." Create a new directory called modules in www/js to collect this and other modules. Add the methods isEnabled() and toggle() to the object app.modules.location (Listing 9-10).

Listing 9-10. Location Module (www/js/modules/location.js)

```
app.modules.location = {
    isEnabled: function(receiver_id) {
        var key = 'location_' + receiver_id;
        return localStorage.getItem(key);
    },
    toggle: function(receiver_id) {
        var key = 'location_' + receiver_id;
        localStorage.setItem(key, !localStorage.getItem(key));
        return localStorage.getItem(key);
    }
};
```

Use isEnabled() to ask whether the location service is enabled and toggle() to invert the current value. Use the prefix location_ in combination with the receiver_id as identifier. As it's a local storage and the user ID of the conversation partner is unique, this formula is adequate. Add the module to the JavaScript loader, as shown in Listing 9-11.

Listing 9-11. Script Loader Configuration (www/js/core.js)

```
var scripts = {
    common: [
        // vendors
        // ...

        // modules
        './js/modules/location.js',

        // views
        // ...
    ]
};
```

Location Setting Button

Let's get this module working! Add a location toggle button to the conversation view (Listing 9-12). Your updated message input area should look like Figure 9-3.

Listing 9-12. Enable/Disable Location Button Template (www/conversation.html)

```
<div class="btn-toolbar" role="toolbar">
    <div class="btn-group">
        <a href="#" id="location" class="btn btn-default">
          <i class="glyphicon glyphicon-map-marker"></i>
        </a>
    </div>
    <div class="btn-group">
        <a href="#" id="submit" class="btn btn-primary">
          <i class="glyphicon glyphicon-send"></i> Send Message
        </a>
    </div>
</div>
```

Next, extend your conversation view to handle the button. Call the handler in the `initialize()` method of the `app.conversation` object (Listing 9-13). Assign a `click` event to the button to process the user input. In the same moment, ask for the current status of the setting and add the class `active` to the button if the user enabled the service prior to this.

Listing 9-13. Location Button Handler (www/js/views/conversation.js)

```
initialize: function() {
    // handle location button
    app.conversation.locationHandler();
},
locationHandler: function() {
    var receiver_id = app.core.getParameterByName('id');
    $('#location').on('click', function(e) {
        e.preventDefault();
        app.modules.location.toggle(receiver_id);
        $('#location').toggleClass('active');
    });
    if(app.modules.location.isEnabled(receiver_id)) {
        $('#location').addClass('active');
    }
}
```

Eventually, in the `addLocation()` method of the `MyParseUser` class, you prevent the geolocation code from being executed if the user did not enable the location service (Listing 9-14).

Listing 9-14. Updated addLocation Method (www/js/models/MyParseMessage.js)

```
addLocation: function(Message) {
    var receiver_id = Message.get('Receiver').id;
    if(!app.modules.location.isEnabled(receiver_id)) {
        return false;
    }
    navigator.geolocation.getCurrentPosition(function(location) {
        console.log(location);
    });
}
```

Background Service for Location Tracking (iOS)

Another interesting, but challenging, use case is to track the user's location in the background. There are many reasons you may want to add a background service to your application, such as if you want to build a running app like the well-known Nike Running app (Figure 9-4). Applications often need to run concurrently with other apps. This next section explores how to do so using the background plug-in.

Figure 9-4. *The Nike Running app tracks your geo location using a background task*

There is one downside for this section: we cover the iOS part only. For an Android implementation of the used plug-in, you cannot use the Parse JavaScript SDK but you can build middleware, which would turn a request defined by the plug-in into Parse data; it's possible, but it's beyond the scope of the book. If you want to build an Android version of this example, please refer to the plug-in documentation.

Plug-in Setup

For this tutorial you'll use the background geolocation plug-in. To install the plug-in, use the `plugin add` command in Listing 9-15. Next, enable the location background mode in Xcode. Navigate to Capabilities of the build target and enable Location updates in the section "Background Modes," as shown in Figure 9-5.

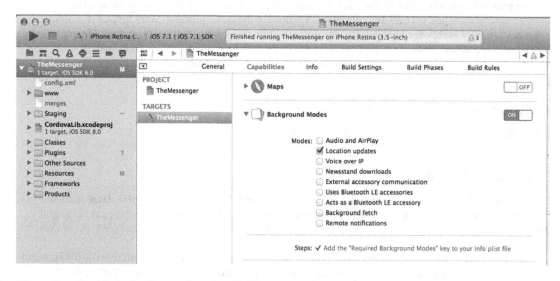

Figure 9-5. Enable the background mode called location updates in Xcode

Listing 9-15. Installing the Plug-in

```
cordova plugin add https://github.com/christocracy/cordova-plugin-background-geolocation.git
```

Next, add a function to call the tracking code in the core of your app (Listing 9-16), for example after you run your access control script `app.core.accessControl()`. Add a new function named `track` to the module `location` (Listing 9-17). For logged-in users, create a reference to the `backgroundGeolocation` plug-in. If you do not add user information to the tracking task, you will get a lot of unusable results.

Listing 9-16. Executing the Tracking Code in Your App Core (www/js/core.js)

```
app.modules.location.track();
```

Listing 9-17. Adding Track Function in the Location Module (www/js/modules/location.js)

```
track: function() {
    if (!Parse.User.current()) {
        return;
    }
    var bgGeo = window.plugins.backgroundGeoLocation;
}
```

Device Identification

Another criterion of the tracking script is the ability to allocate a data stream to one device. Each device has a Universally Unique Identifier (UUID). To get this ID, you need to use another plug-in, the Cordova Device plug-in.

This plug-in defines a global device object, which describes the device's hardware and software. You can get a model or product, like iPhone 5.1 or Nexus One, using device.model. The value is set by the device manufacturer and may be different across versions of the same product. More helpful is probably the value device.platform, which will tell you the device's operating system name. You can implement switches for Android and iOS to adjust your application to the corresponding operating system if needed.

Most important for your goal is the value device.uuid, which will return the UUID. To install the plug-in, use the command shown in Listing 9-18.

Listing 9-18. Adding the PhoneGap Device Plug-in

```
phonegap plugin add org.apache.cordova.device
```

Save Data to Parse

Continue by adding a new function named onSuccess() to save the location to the Parse database inside (!) the track function (Listing 9-19). The function will receive a location object containing latitude and longitude. You'll create a new Parse.Object named "Tracker," and assign a Parse.GeoPoint, the current Parse.User, and the device's UUID.

After executing the save() method, you execute bgGeo.finish() to tell the system that the background task is finished, no matter whether the save() action was successful or not. If you don't do this, you risk having your application terminated by iOS for spending too much time in the background.

Listing 9-19. The Success Callback Function Saves Data to Parse

```
var onSuccess = function(location) {
    var point = new Parse.GeoPoint({
        latitude: location.latitude,
        longitude: location.longitude
    });
    var ParseTracker = Parse.Object.extend("Tracker");
    var Tracker = new ParseTracker();
    Tracker.set("location", point);
    Tracker.set("User", Parse.User.current());
    Tracker.set("uuid ", device.uuid);

    Tracker.save().then(function() {
        bgGeo.finish();
    }).fail(function() {
        bgGeo.finish();
    });
};
```

Furthermore, add an error callback function, which will log the error and report the completion of the background process, too (Listing 9-20).

Listing 9-20. Error Callback Function

```
var onError = function(error) {
    console.log('code: ' + error.code + '\n' +
        'message: ' + error.message + '\n');
    bgGeo.finish();
};
```

The plug-in accepts multiple options regarding the accuracy of the requests as well as for debugging (Listing 9-21). Adjust the options to your needs. For testing purposes, keep the recommended debugging options. While running in the background, app notifications will tell you about the activity of the background task, as shown in Figure 9-6. Add the options object to the track() function as well.

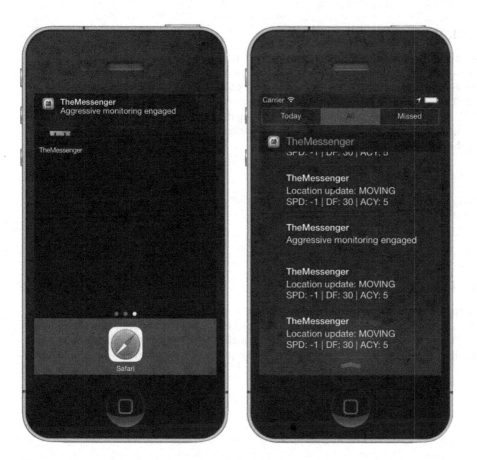

Figure 9-6. *Enable the background mode called location updates in Xcode*

Listing 9-21. Geotracking Plug-in Options

```
var options = {
    desiredAccuracy: 10,
    stationaryRadius: 20,
    distanceFilter: 30,
    notificationTitle: 'Background tracking',
    notificationText: 'ENABLED',
    activityType: 'AutomotiveNavigation',
    debug: true,
    stopOnTerminate: false
};
```

Running Background Task

Before calling the plug-in, make sure that the getCurrentPosition() of the geolocation plug-in is called at least once. Otherwise, you could run into the issue that the user did not grant the location permissions. If you are using the iOS simulator, constantly check your location information, which you can change in Debug ➤ Location. The simulator might reset this information after you build your application.

As a last step (Listing 9-22), configure the plug-in by passing the onSuccess and onError as well as the options object to the function bgGeo.configure(). Start the background task via bgGeo.start(). You may end the task using the command bgGeo.stop().

Listing 9-22. Configuring and Starting the Background Task

```
window.navigator.geolocation.getCurrentPosition(function(location) {
    bgGeo.configure(onSuccess, onError, options);
    bgGeo.start();
});
```

Testing Your Results

As in the other tutorials, it's now time to test the application and review the results in the Parse Data browser (see Figure 9-7). Beside using the simulator and adding fake locations, deploy the application to your phone and test it in the real world. Start the app and go running in the park or take a ride on the subway. Seeing real-world results will help you to adjust your application code to your real needs and motivate you to build more.

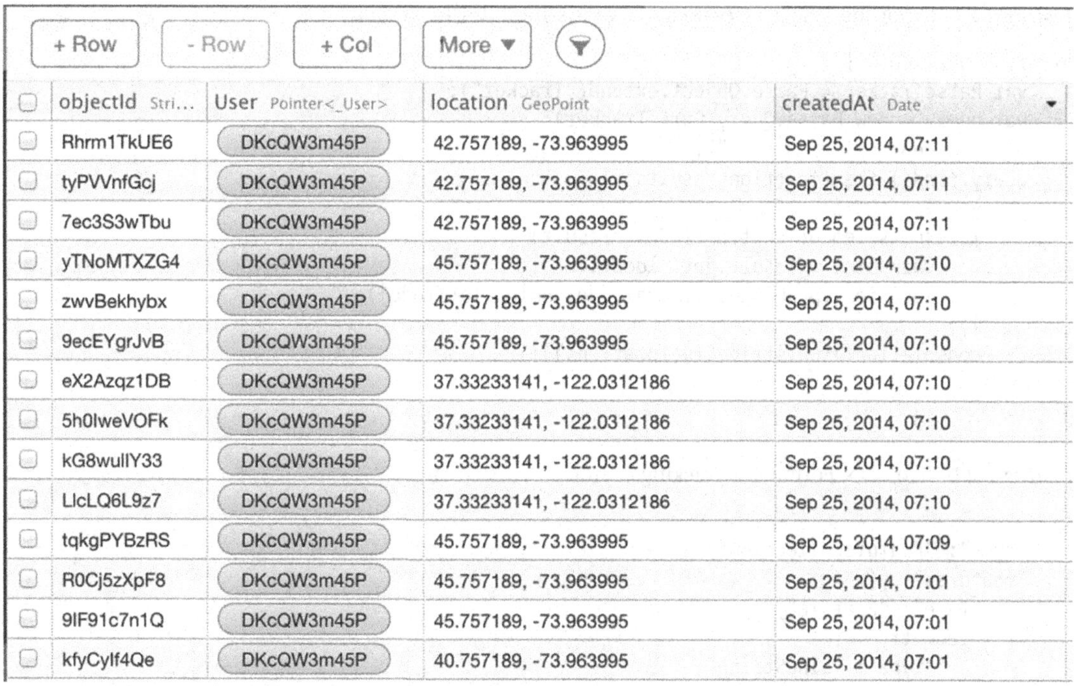

	objectId Stri...	User Pointer<_User>	location GeoPoint	createdAt Date ▼
☐	Rhrm1TkUE6	DKcQW3m45P	42.757189, -73.963995	Sep 25, 2014, 07:11
☐	tyPVVnfGcj	DKcQW3m45P	42.757189, -73.963995	Sep 25, 2014, 07:11
☐	7ec3S3wTbu	DKcQW3m45P	42.757189, -73.963995	Sep 25, 2014, 07:11
☐	yTNoMTXZG4	DKcQW3m45P	45.757189, -73.963995	Sep 25, 2014, 07:10
☐	zwvBekhybx	DKcQW3m45P	45.757189, -73.963995	Sep 25, 2014, 07:10
☐	9ecEYgrJvB	DKcQW3m45P	45.757189, -73.963995	Sep 25, 2014, 07:10
☐	eX2Azqz1DB	DKcQW3m45P	37.33233141, -122.0312186	Sep 25, 2014, 07:10
☐	5h0lweVOFk	DKcQW3m45P	37.33233141, -122.0312186	Sep 25, 2014, 07:10
☐	kG8wullY33	DKcQW3m45P	37.33233141, -122.0312186	Sep 25, 2014, 07:10
☐	LlcLQ6L9z7	DKcQW3m45P	37.33233141, -122.0312186	Sep 25, 2014, 07:10
☐	tqkgPYBzRS	DKcQW3m45P	45.757189, -73.963995	Sep 25, 2014, 07:09
☐	R0Cj5zXpF8	DKcQW3m45P	45.757189, -73.963995	Sep 25, 2014, 07:01
☐	9lF91c7n1Q	DKcQW3m45P	45.757189, -73.963995	Sep 25, 2014, 07:01
☐	kfyCylf4Qe	DKcQW3m45P	40.757189, -73.963995	Sep 25, 2014, 07:01

Figure 9-7. *Tracking results in the Parse Data browser*

Furthermore, use tools like Mapbox, Google Maps, Github's geoJSON mapping, or CartoDB (which we'll introduce in the next section) to visualize your tracking results. Later in this chapter we'll help you display geolocation data on a map inside your application.

Excursion: CartoDB

A big part of building good apps is testing them. This is especially difficult in the case of geodata. Those numbers often don't say a lot to us. Yet there is a tool to help us: CartoDB. CartoDB is a Software as a Service cloud computing platform that provides mapping tools for the Web. You can sign up for a free account on www.cartodb.com.

Next, you need to prepare your test data. CartoDB accepts different file formats. You are using the geoJSON format because you can easily create an export using the Parse JavaScript SDK. Query your results as shown in Listing 9-23, apply filters if needed, and print the result to your console. Add the script to your location module and call the function app.modules.location.export() at any place of your application (after Parse is loaded). Create a new file (named data.geoJSON) based on the structure of Listing 9-24 and, instead of your example values, use the console output as value for the key coordinates.

Listing 9-23. Exporting Tracked Geopoints (www/js/modules/location.js)

```
export: function() {
    var ParseTracker = Parse.Object.extend("Tracker");
    var query = new Parse.Query(ParseTracker);
    query.ascending("createdAt");
    query.find().then(function(results) {
        var locations = [];
        $(results).each(function(index, result) {
            var point = result.get('location');
            locations.push([point.longitude, point.latitude]);
        });
        console.log(JSON.stringify(locations));
    });
}
```

Listing 9-24. GeoJSON-Formatted Tracking Results

```
{
    "type": "FeatureCollection",
    "features": [{
        "type": "Feature",
        "geometry": {
            "type": "LineString",
            "coordinates": [
                [-73.972727, 40.765815],
                [-73.972984, 40.768936],
                [-73.970581, 40.771048],
                [-73.968586, 40.772787],
                [-73.969787, 40.773502],
                [-73.972427, 40.773762],
                [-73.975323, 40.774851]
            ]
        }
    }]
}
```

Create a new table in CartoDB and use the created file as the data source. Your result should look something like Figure 9-8, showing your own tracking results.

Figure 9-8. GeoJSON Import to CartoDB

■ **Tip** You can export your geolocation data by using the option More ➤ Export Class in the Parse Data Browser.

Geocoding

In the leading part of this chapter, you captured the user's location and attached their information to a message. Before displaying this location using a map, you'll start with an easier but still very helpful feature: converting the geographic coordinates into a location name, which could be the name of a city, like New York City.

Doing this will help you and the user a lot. Displaying and loading a map view is an expensive task. Using a text value to serve an abstract description of a location will be a sufficient piece of information for a user to determine whether they want to know more about the actual location. If so, they'll be able to tap the location and get a detailed map view, which we'll explain in Chapter 10.

Furthermore, you'll have the ability to display multiple locations within one view. You'll combine the map information with other elements of your application. In your case, you'll use the location name as a label right next to each message.

Mapbox

Both for converting the user's geolocation into an actual location or city name and displaying maps inside your application, you'll use the service Mapbox shown in Figure 9-9 (www.mapbox.com/). For the development phase or small apps, Mapbox is free to use. For traffic-heavy apps, Mapbox offers paid plans ranging from $5 to $499 a month.

Figure 9-9. *Mapbox home page*

One of the big strengths of the Mapbox visualization software is the ability to easily customize the styling of your map. So instead of having the same style as every other app, you can add a custom taste to yours.

■ **Note**   If you are familiar with the Google Maps SDK, you can use this one instead. The Mapbox JavaScript SDK structure is similar to Google's. Transferring between each other is a mostly frictionless process.

The Mapbox Platform

As with Parse, Mapbox requires you to create an account to use their services. Yet there is a structural difference, which is the distinction between projects and application tokens. A project is the representation of a map styling configuration; in addition it may contain data like markers or lines. Next, your account will have one default application instance, which may possess one or several application tokens.

When adding a map to your application, you use a combination of a project ID (we could also say "map ID") and an access token to identify your application. To use web services like geocoding, you just need to identify using an *access token*.

There are two types of access tokens: *public* and *secret* access tokens. Secret tokens are required when you want to make edits to your map via the Mapbox API. Thus they should be used in environments where they can be kept secret, such as in a native mobile application. As your feature will only need reading permissions, you can use either a public or a secret access token.

Mapbox Account and Project Setup

Head over to www.mapbox.com/ and sign up for a free account. Mapbox will automatically create a new project named "My First Map." This map will contain a marker based on your location. Either remove the marker in the data section of the map settings or create a new map to make sure you start with a fresh and clean map.

Write down the map ID, which you can find in the project list view or when you access the map styling view, as shown in Figure 9-10. Next, get your (secret) application access token. You can find it in the section Account ➤ Apps (www.mapbox.com/account/apps/).

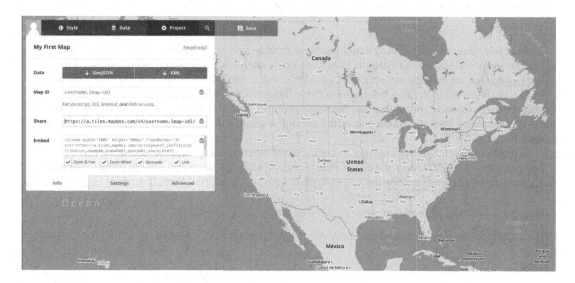

Figure 9-10. *The Mapbox styling view*

Geocoding in the Parse Cloud

Mapbox's geocoding service is a classic web service. This means you will send an HTTP request containing location information to Mapbox and will get back a response. Since you already saved the geolocation information to the Parse database, and this request will require additional network resources, you will not run this process on your client application, but in the Parse Cloud.

■ **Note**   Before moving on, you quickly need to set up a Parse cloud code instance in your development environment. We describe the process of setting up Parse cloud code and deploying code in Chapter 3. In short, run `parse new ProjectName` to create a new local Parse cloud code instance. You will find all cloud code files in the directory `ProjectName/cloud/`. Run `parse deploy` in the project directory to deploy code to the Parse cloud. In your example, you used the project name `TheMessengerCloud`.

Adding a Location to a Message

You already know the `Parse.Cloud.afterSave()` method from previous chapters. It will be executed every time the corresponding object is saved. You could use this method to invoke the geocoding process. After sending a `Message`, you add the location information to the `Message` object, save it, get the location name, and save the `Message` object again. At the root level, a cloud function for the `Message` object looks like Listing 9-25.

Listing 9-25. Handling Operations After Saving an Object

```
Parse.Cloud.afterSave("Message", function(request) {
  // Code executed after saving the Message object
});
```

Using this route, you can already anticipate some trouble: saving the `Message` object as part of an `afterSave` event will end up in an infinite loop *if* you don't catch it by some exception rule. Next, if you update a message, for example as being read, you don't need to update the location name again and again.

To avoid handling such cases, you define a Parse cloud function which you trigger immediately after getting the user's location and adding it to the `Message` object. This way, the only dependency created is the necessity of having a network connection, which should be granted as sending messages requires a network connection as well.

As shown in Listing 9-26, you can define such a cloud function using `Parse.Cloud.define` (`'example_name'`). The function will contain the process of adding a location name. To invoke the cloud function by the client (your application), you simply call `Parse.Cloud.run('function_name')`.

Listing 9-26. Defining a Cloud Function (TheMessengerCloud/cloud/main.js)

```
Parse.Cloud.define("MessageAddLocationName", function(request, response) {

});
```

To match your plan, this should happen in the function `addLocation()` of the `MyParseMessage` class. To identify the message to be updated, you pass the `Message.id` as parameter to the cloud function call (Listing 9-27).

Listing 9-27. Text (www/js/models/MyParseMessage.js)

```
Message.save().then(function() {
    Parse.Cloud.run('MessageAddLocationName', {
        id: Message.id
    });
});
```

Recreating the Message Instance

Once the cloud function `MessageAddLocationName` is called, you need to recreate the instance of the corresponding `Message` object. You run a simple query on the `Message` table using the ID passed as parameter. Doing this, you seamlessly check whether the `Message` actually has a `location` value attached to it. If not, there is no need, or possibility, to add a location name. You can see an example implementation of this process in Listing 9-28.

Listing 9-28. Text cloud/cloud/main.js

```
var query = new Parse.Query("Message");
query.get(request.params.id, function(Message) {
    var location = Message.get('location');
    if (!location) {
        return response.error("No location provided");
    }
}).fail(function(error) {
    response.error(error);
});
```

■ **Tip**   Debugging code in the Parse cloud is a difficult job. Test the code of your cloud function locally in a web browser before running it in the cloud.

Converting the Geolocation into a Location Name

Earlier in this chapter, we introduced the Mapbox service, and you created an account as well as a Mapbox application access token. In this next step, you'll use their geocoding API to convert the message's geolocation into a location name.

The Mapbox geocoding API is a simple HTTP service. This means you can use any technology that supports the HTTP protocol to use the service. It's perfect for your case because the Parse cloud includes a networking module with which you can interface programmatically.

The method therefore is named Parse.Cloud.httpRequest and allows you to send HTTP requests to any HTTP server. It behaves similar to the jQuery.ajax() method, where you define a URL to be requested, add arguments, and execute more code once the request is done. All options are passed using an options object to the method call. There is a limit of executing two HTTP requests at the same time. Any additional requests will be queued up.

Defining an HTTP GET Request

The most common request you will probably do is am HTTP GET request, such as reading data like a news feed from a service. You pass a URL to the method using the key url. You can also add query arguments using the params key. As with other Parse objects, you can define a success and error function to run after the request has completed. The example provided in Listing 9-29 invokes an HTTP request to the URL http://www.google.com/search?q=phonegap.

Listing 9-29. Sending an HTTP Request Using the Parse Networking Module

```
Parse.Cloud.httpRequest({
  url: 'http://www.google.com/search',
  params: {
    q : 'phonegap'
  },
```

```
  success: function(httpResponse) {
    console.log(httpResponse.text);
  },
  error: function(httpResponse) {
    console.error('Request failed with response code ' + httpResponse.status);
  }
});
```

POST Requests and HTTP Headers

You may also use other HTTP request methods like POST or DELETE. If you want to send a POST request to a server, you have to use the key body to pass data to the target server. In addition, you can use the key headers to define HTTP headers, as shown in Listing 9-30.

Listing 9-30. Sending a POST Request

```
Parse.Cloud.httpRequest({
  method: 'POST',
  headers: {
    'Content-Type': 'application/json;charset=utf-8'
  },
  url: 'http://www.domain.com/path',
  body: {
    key: 'value'
  },
  success: function(httpResponse) {
    console.log(httpResponse.text);
  },
  error: function(httpResponse) {
    console.error('Request failed with response code ' + httpResponse.status);
  }
});
```

Geocoding Methods

After this short crash course for the Parse Cloud Networking Module, you are ready to access the Mapbox Geocoding API. The API offers so-called forward and reverse geocoding.

Forward Geocoding

Forward geocoding is the process of translating a location name-based query (e.g. New+York+City) into a **geoposition** (which would be [40.78853, -73.946246] for New York City). Besides your query, you need to define a dataset to run this query against. These datasets are called index. The different indexes are shown in Table 9-1.

Table 9-1. *Mapbox Geocoding Indexes*

Index	Features
mapbox.places-v1	Full geocoding stack (default)
mapbox.places-country-v1	Countries
mapbox.places-province-v1	Provinces
mapbox.places-postcode-v1	Postal codes
mapbox.places-city-v1	Cities
mapbox.places-addresses-v1	US addresses

The format for any request looks like the snippet in Listing 9-31. A "New York City" example is shown in Listing 9-32. A request response will contain a feature dataset that best matches the input query text. It may include one or more results ordered by relevance. Listing 9-33 shows a response example.

■ **Note**   The order of latitude and longitude is inversed: the first value of the response array -73.946246 is the longitude, the second value of 40.78853 is the latitude.

Listing 9-31. Forward Geocoding API URL Structure

```
http://api.tiles.mapbox.com/v4/geocode/{index}/{query}.json?access_token={access-token}
```

Listing 9-32. Forward Geocoding API URL Example Using New York City

```
http://api.tiles.mapbox.com/v4/geocode/mapbox.places-city-v1/New+York+City.json?access_
token={access-token}
```

Listing 9-33. Mapbox API Response Example

```
{
    type: "FeatureCollection",
    query: ["new", "york", "city"],
    features: [{
        id: "city.10001",
        type: "Feature",
        text: "New York",
        place:name: "New York",
        relevance: 1,
        center: [-73.946246, 40.78853],
        geometry: {
            type: "Point",
            coordinates: [-73.946246, 40.78853]
        },
        bbox: [
-74.0472935031892, 40.68391219248488,
-73.91057831367289, 40.877656790011784
        ],
```

```
        properties: {
            title: "New York,NY,NYC"
        }
    }],
    attribution: ""
}
```

Reverse Geocoding

The second API method, which you'll actually need for your app's purposes, is reverse geocoding. In a reverse geocoding request, you provide latitude and longitude coordinates to obtain a more standardized, abstract geo object, like a ZIP code, a street address, or a city name.

For these requests, you can use the Mapbox geocoding indexes like mapbox.places-country-v1 as well. This means you can use a very precise geoposition just to determine whether a user is in one country or another. The response includes at most one result from each geocoding index.

The format for a reverse geocoding request is shown in Listing 9-34. As with the request, the order for latitude and longitude is inversed.

Listing 9-34. Forward Geocoding API URL Structure

```
http://api.tiles.mapbox.com/v4/geocode/{index}/{longitude},{latitude}.json?access_
token={access-token}
```

Combining Parse and Mapbox

Now that you understand the Parse Networking Module and the Mapbox Geocoding API, let's bring these technologies to life. Head back to the Parse cloud function MessageAddLocationName.

After getting the Message object, send an HTTP request to the Mapbox API, as shown in Listing 9-35. By choosing the index mapbox.places-city-v1 you make sure that the first and only result is a city name. Use the access token created in the beginning of this section in params.

Listing 9-35. Running an HTTP Request to the Mapbox API in the Cloud (TheMessengerCloud/cloud/main.js)

```
Parse.Cloud.httpRequest({
    url: 'http://api.tiles.mapbox.com/v4/geocode/mapbox.places-city-v1/' +
    location.longitude + ',' + location.latitude + '.json',
    params: {
        'access_token': '{access_token}'
    }
}).then(function(httpResponse) {
    // Note: The API response handling method
    // will be populated later in this chatper
}).then(function() {
    // Send a success response if the location name was added
    response.success("Location name added ");
});
```

■ **Tip** `Parse.Cloud` classes are only accessible in a Parse cloud environment. To test the code used in combination with these methods locally, you need to simulate their behavior. This sounds more complicated than it actually is. For example, replace the `Parse.Cloud.httpRequest` by using a jQuery call (e.g. `jQuery.load()`). This way you can test whether you are using the right arguments and debug the API response in your browser before using Parse's `Cloud` code.

Parsing Geodata

The API response `httpResponse` will look like Listing 9-33, yet it will show a geoposition instead of a string value for the key query. To convert the response into a JavaScript object, use the method `JSON.parse()`. The first element of the array `features` will contain the location name.

Depending on your query type, the values for `text` and `place:name` will behave differently. In your example, they're the same, yet in general `place:name` will be a more detailed value like `New York, 10029, New York, United States`.

Add the values as they fit your needs best to the `Message` object and save it, as shown in Listing 9-36. If no location is found, return an error response using `response.error()`.

Listing 9-36. Converting the API Response and Saving It to the Message Object (TheMessengerCloud/cloud/main.js)

```
var data = JSON.parse(httpResponse.text);

if (!data.features || !data.features[0]) {
    return response.error("Could not add location");
}

Message.set('location_text', data.features[0].text);
Message.set('location_text_long', data.features[0].place:name);
Message.save();

return Message;
```

■ **Tip** After updating your code, don't forget to deploy updates using `parse deploy`. If you run into any issues, you can identify errors taking a look at the logs in the Parse application dashboard (Section: Core ➤ Logs).

Displaying the Location Name

You now want to display the gathered values in the conversation view. You need to assume that some messages won't have a location name to display or won't have location information at all.

To handle these cases in a centralized place, add a function named getLocationText() to the MyParseMessage class (Listing 9-37). If there is a location, add the prefix from... to indicate that the message was sent from the location provided in location_text. For debugging purposes, you return a rounded geo-position for messages having a location. And finally, if there is no location information; the function will return no value.

Add the method to each message block in the conversation template. In preparation for adding a map view, which you'll do later in this chapter, wrap the output with a link including the Message.id as data attribute.

As with any application data, you need a way for the user to be able to view it. Update the conversation view with the returned value of the getLocationText function (Listing 9-38).

Listing 9-37. Handling the Different States of the location_text Value in the MyParseMessage Class (www/js/models/MyParseMessage.js)

```
getLocationText: function() {
    if(this.get('location_text')) {
        return 'from... ' + this.get('location_text');
    }
    if(this.get('location')) {
        return 'from unknown location (' +
Math.round(this.get('location').latitude*100)/100+',' +
Math.round(this.get('location').longitude*100)/100+')';
    }
    return '';
}
```

Listing 9-38. Adding the Location Name Output to the Conversation Template (www/conversation.html)

```
<div class="small">
  {{ getFromNow }}
  {{#if getLocationText }}
    <a href="#" class="location-text" data-id="{{ id }}">
      {{ getLocationText }}
    </a>
  {{/if}}
</div>
```

Testing Your Updates

Rebuild your application and run it. Previously sent messages having location information will show the numeric values. Send some new messages to invoke the location name scripts. Your new messages should display a location name right next to the time information, as shown in Figure 9-11.

Figure 9-11. *The location name is displayed right next to the time information of each message*

Keep in mind that the location information is added *after* you send each message, and will take a few milliseconds to populate. If you added a function to either refresh your latest messages or directly add the new Message to your view, you won't see the location name immediately. You can improve this behavior by re-rendering the messages, or the last message, once the cloud function ran successfully. Listing 9-39 shows an example of such a promise handler.

Listing 9-39. Updating the Message Display After Getting the Message's Location Name (www/js/models/ MyParseMessage.js)

```
Parse.Cloud.run('MessageAddLocationName', {
    id: Message.id
}).then(function() {
    // Refresh Messages
});
```

Summary

This chapter explored the `navigator.geolocation` JavaScript API. With it, you were able to add location-aware services to your application.

Using the `navigator.geolocation.getCurrentPosition()` function, you added the option of sending a message to someone tagged with the location of the sender. In order to access the geoposition from a device, permission must be granted by a user through the device's settings.

Parse uses a special type of data for geodata called GeoPoint. This field stores the latitude and longitude global positions to pinpoint the location of a device. When combined with the navigator's `getCurrentPosition` function, you saved the data necessary to plot a point on a map. After adding location functionality to your application, you added a user interface element so that users could decide to share their location when sending a message.

Using HTML5 `localStorage`, you were able to create a custom module that checked to see if the user allowed access to their location information. This gives you the ability to toggle usage of geopositioning without having the user update their device settings.

You used a background process to constantly monitor a user's position. To use these background modes, you enabled "Location updates" in the Capabilities section of the application settings in Xcode. An example use case for this is a running app where plotting a device's location is used to create a map. Using Parse, you saved the coordinates of the device's location at intervals. The stored geodata can be used to create a track on a map for a visual representation of the device's path.

There are plenty of map services available to developers for visualizing location information. You used one of these mapping services, CartoDB, to create a path using several geopoints and plot them on a map. This could be used to create running, biking, or other forms of tracking applications.

The latitude and longitude values that you collect for each geolocation aren't very user friendly. Using the Mapbox service, you added the ability to translate these values into understandable location names, like `New York City` instead of `40.71448, -74.00598`. With this metadata, you added text to each message sent in the Messenger application.

CHAPTER 10

Map Views

Adding Map Views in PhoneGap –JavaScript vs. Native Maps

Adding a map to your application in PhoneGap can be a challenging and complicated task that has many approaches and solutions. In the end, you can break it down to a simple rule: By using JavaScript-based libraries, you will get the fastest results and feature-rich maps without the hassle of developing a platform specific implementation.

Using native map SDKs via plug-ins will result in a smooth and fast map experience; however, they have a lot of limitations. These limitations include the lack of features, the impossibility to use them directly in your HTML code, and the intense time requirements needed to implement such a solution.

Before jumping into actual code samples, we'll uncover the strengths and weaknesses of each approach so that you can make a decision that fits your needs.

Two Approaches to Adding Map Views

There are two general approaches to adding map views: JavaScript libraries and native map SDKs. In this section, we'll discuss both approaches and provide a recommendation.

JavaScript Map SDKs

As stated, using JavaScript SDKs is a fast and easy solution. As amazing as it seems, there are two downsides to this approach: a lack of performance and the inability for stepless zooming.

All current major web-based map services are based on pixel tiles, which is also known as Web Map Tile Service (WMTS). Each tile is usually a 256x256 pixel-sized, pre-rendered image of a geographic region. The corresponding JavaScript library will arrange and merge those tiles to one map view, based on the zoom and position of the view. If you zoom in, tiles with a higher level of detail are loaded and placed on the map canvas. If you move north, east, south, or west, more tiles are added to either side of the map. Relying on a web browser to deliver a smooth experience can be unpredictable. Download speeds and device-processing power vary between all users, so creating a consistent experience is virtually impossible.

As you can imagine, a world map could be built up by billions of tiny tiles. Usually map services offer about 20 different zoom levels, from 1 (the world view) to 20 (the street view). To truly create a smooth map experience for the user, an entire map of the content would need to be preloaded so that when the user interacts with a new area, the map reacts instantly. While lacking a smooth experience, zooming to a content area in steps, so that loading can occur, is an efficient way to save the user bandwidth.

To create a stepless, smooth experience, you would need an infinite amount of zoom levels, all with content that will need to be fetched from a server and rendered to the user. Long story short: This technology is not made for stepless zooming.

With that said, there *are* solutions that have been emerging recently that aim to create a better map experience for the Web, particular mobile. With JavaScript APIs such as Web Graphics Library (WebGL), interactive 2D and 3D rendering is possible with a web browser.

One of the companies pioneering this effort is *Mapbox*, which you'll learn more about in the next section. For more information on their WebGL maps, check out `mapbox.com/blog/mapbox-gl/`.

Native Map SDKs

To create a smooth, stepless zooming experience, a map service needs to be based on vector tiles instead of pixel tiles. Vector-based tiles are mathematically created and instantly render a location on a map. The Apple Mapkit or Google Maps iOS SDK is an example of this technology. They both allow users to zoom and rotate the map without being forced into predefined zoom levels, as would be the case in a WMTS-based map.

Native map applications are composed of proprietary operations that are designed to run quickly and efficiently, creating a pleasant experience for the user. The rendering of map objects are executed using multiple processes, or threads, that are independent of each other.

For the application you're building in this chapter, the user message interface needs to be shown at all times so that users can still interact with the rest of the application. Integrating a native map into an HTML-based project may take away from the user experience. It would require platform specific plug-ins, unnecessary hacking, and a constant struggle with the limitations of this approach.

Recommendation

So what should *you* do? If you want to create an application that *highly* depends on a map experience (take Foursquare, for example), you need to develop this view in its entirety as a native application—or at *least* the map sections as a native view.

It's a complex topic, but, in short, you can "mix" a PhoneGap application with a native application. This will force you to develop some parts individually for iOS and Android but still give you the opportunity to save time and resources by sharing simple views.

Using a combined native and web application can be done tastefully without compromising the integrity of the app. For example, a native app can choose to manage administrative profile settings hosted on a web site, rather than have a native UI for this. Crafting the right user experience differs from app to app; use your best judgment on which approach to take based on your application.

Anyway, coming back to the strengths of PhoneGap. You can use JavaScript SDKs you already know for adding maps to your application. This approach will work the same as if you would develop a web application. This is perfectly fine as long as you use maps as an addition to your application, and *not* as a core feature. Likewise, if you use map views as static elements, there is no need to install a map plug-in.

Adding a JavaScript Map View

Previously, we captured and displayed the user's location alongside each message. In this next feature update, we'll add an element showing this location on a map in the form of a marker. You can see an example implementation of this feature in Figure 10-1. We won't display the map for every message when rendering the view. Instead, we'll add an event handler to the location name and display the map on click.

Figure 10-1. Example visualization of a map view using Mapbox and OpenStreetMap. The marker indicates the location of the message from where it was sent

■ **Note** Even though adding a map will have a big visual impact on our product, the implementation is very compact and easy. Generally speaking, this is an important aspect for every developer. Complex features—such as getting a user's location, saving it to a database, or using geocoding to add a location name—seem so easy, as their execution is not visual. Yet, as you learned, they require a lot of pieces working together to as expected.

Mapbox JavaScript Library Setup

You can find the latest Mapbox JavaScript and CSS files on the Mapbox developer page: www.mapbox.com/ developers/. Choose the JavaScript library documentation. The Get Started section will tell you the URLs, as shown in Listing 10-1.

Download the files, and then add the CSS file to your HTML views in which you want to add a map view. Do the same for the Mapbox JavaScript file or add it to your JavaScript loader to make the library accessible globally. At the bare minimum, you should add the files to the conversation view `www/conversation.html`. Add a script reference to the page using the following snippet:

```
<script src='https://api.tiles.mapbox.com/mapbox.js/v2.2.0/mapbox.js'></script>
<link href='https://api.tiles.mapbox.com/mapbox.js/v2.2.0/mapbox.css' rel='stylesheet' />
```

Adding a Map to a Message

In the previous section, we wrapped the location name in a `link` tag. First, we'll use this link to add an event handler (Listing 10-1). On click, we will create a new map instance. In our example, we add the `<div>` container, which will host the map canvas on the fly (the moment the location name is selected). You may add it to your `handlebars` template, yet this will cause the effort of targeting, hiding, and showing this element. It's simpler to just inject the map when we need it. Next, we'll add some Twitter Bootstrap styles to the map container. We store the styles in the variable `mapClasses`, as we will dynamically remove and add these classes at a later point.

Listing 10-1. The Event Handler Calling the addMap Function (www/js/views/conversation.js)

```
$('a.location-text').on('click', app.conversation.addMap);
```

Set your Mapbox access token as shown in 10-2 Create a new map instance using `L.mapbox.map`. We use the scope variable `map` to store our map instance. This way, we are able to have multiple map views within one view without causing naming conflicts. If you want to have a global map instance, write the instance to the window object using `window.map` instead.

As our map view is very small, we remove the map controls by setting `zoomControl` to `false`. For this same reason, we disabled map credits by setting the attribute `attributionControl` to `false`. Don't forget to give map credits in some other way; you must comply with the licensing terms of any map data in your application.

Listing 10-2. Adding a Map View to the Message (www/js/views/conversation.js)

```
addMap: function(event) {
    event.preventDefault();
    // Add Map Element
    var mapClasses = 'alert well-sm alert-info';
    $('<div id="mapbox" class="' + mapClasses + '"></div>').insertBefore(this);
    // Set Mapbox Access Token
    L.mapbox.accessToken = '{your-mapbox-access-token}';
    // Create Mapbox Instance
    var map = L.mapbox.map('mapbox', '{your-mapbox-map-id}', {
        zoomControl: false,
        attributionControl: false
    });
}
```

Besides creating an instance of a map, we also want to show something on it: the location of the message from where it was sent. To identify each message in the view, we previously added the `Message.id` as a `data` attribute to the `link` tag.

Instead of loading the corresponding Message object again, we should access the messages data we queried before. To make this data accessible in an organized way, we cache all messages in a new object variable named app.conversation.Messages. We populate the variable in the renderMessages function as shown in Listing 10-3. While doing this, we create a simple message index by using their respective IDs as object keys.

Listing 10-3. Update the renderMessages Method (www/js/views/conversation.js)

```
renderMessages: function() {
    var limit = 5;
    MyParseConversation.getMessages(app.conversation.Receiver,
limit).then(function(Messages) {
// Render Messages ...
        $(Messages).each(function(index, Message) {
            app.conversation.Messages[Message.id] = Message;
        });
    });
}
```

Now that we are able to access each message's information via the Message.id, we can set the map center to the message's location and chose an appropriate zoom level using the method map.setView(location, zoom). The marker is being added via the method L.mapbox.featureLayer(options).addTo(map), as shown in Listing 10-4.

The options object will contain a complex set of variables. The most important value for our purpose is geometry.coordinates. It contains an array of the user's locations. Note that the order of latitude and longitude is inverted in this case. The function map.setView() uses the default notation. Use properties.title to display the sender name and properties.description to display the message body.

Listing 10-4. Place a Position on a Map Based on the Selected Parse Message (www/js/views/conversation.js)

```
var Message = app.conversation.Messages[$(this).data('id')];
map.setView([Message.get('location').latitude, Message.get('location').longitude], 14);

L.mapbox.featureLayer({
    type: 'Feature',
    geometry: {
        type: 'Point',
        coordinates: [
            Message.get('location').longitude,
            Message.get('location').latitude
        ]
    },
    properties: {
        title: Message.get('sender').get('first_name'),
        description: Message.get('message_body'),
        'marker-size': 'large',
        'marker-color': '#BE9A6B',
        'marker-symbol': 'post'
    }
}).addTo(map);
```

Adding Map Controls

Although the map we currently have would already be good to use, let's add some extra options and make it special. We'll add an event handler to remove the map once it's tapped. Typically, users might expect a full-screen view once they tap the map, yet we will handle such a view by adding a corresponding button at a later point in this chapter. Furthermore, we'll disable dragging and other touch events as shown in Listing 10-5.

To avoid having multiple maps opened at the same time, we destroy an existing instance by removing the respective map container before creating a new one (Listing 10-6).

Listing 10-5. Disable Any Map Interaction (www/js/views/conversation.js)

```
// Remove Map on Click
map.on('click', function(e) {
    map.remove();
    $('#mapbox').remove();
});
// Disable drag and zoom handlers.
map.dragging.disable();
map.touchZoom.disable();
map.doubleClickZoom.disable();
// Disable tap handler, if present.
if (map.tap) map.tap.disable();
```

Listing 10-6. Destroy the Existing Map Container before Creating a New One (www/js/views/conversation.js)

```
addMap: function(event) {
    event.preventDefault();
    if ($('#mapbox').length) {
        $('#mapbox').remove();
    }
    // ...
```

Adding a Full-Screen Mode

When it comes down to it, the map view is just way too small to add any interactions such as panning and zooming. Instead, we want to reserve all those features for a full-screen view. Luckily, Mapbox—or, more accurately, the Leaflet library, which is the base for the Mapbox library—offers a plug-in to add this feature.

First, download the plug-in CSS and JavaScript files (Listing 10-7) from Github: https://github.com/Leaflet/Leaflet.fullscreen. This plug-in will add a full-screen button to your map via the method L.control.fullscreen().addTo(map) (Listing 10-8). Next, add a handler for the event fullscreenchange to the map (Listing 10-9). It is being called once the full-screen mode is either opened or closed. Finally, reset the map position when the view changes and add or remove events as well as styling.

Listing 10-7. Mapbox / Leaflet Full-Screen Plug-in JavaScript and CSS Files

```
<script src="https://api.tiles.mapbox.com/mapbox.js/plugins/leaflet-fullscreen/v0.0.3/
Leaflet.fullscreen.min.js"></script>
<link href="https://api.tiles.mapbox.com/mapbox.js/plugins/leaflet-fullscreen/v0.0.3/
leaflet.fullscreen.css" rel="stylesheet" />
```

Listing 10-8. Adding a Full-Screen Button via the Leaflet Full-Screen Plug-in (www/js/views/conversation.js)

```
L.control.fullscreen().addTo(map);
```

Listing 10-9. Switching between Inline Mode and Full-Screen Mode via the `fullscreenchange` event (www/js/views/conversation.js)

```
map.on('fullscreenchange', function(e) {
    map.setView([Message.get('location').latitude,
Message.get('location').longitude]);
    if (map.isFullscreen()) {
        $('#mapbox').removeClass(mapClasses);
        map.dragging.enable();
        map.touchZoom.enable();
    } else {
        $('#mapbox').addClass(mapClasses);
        map.dragging.disable();
        map.touchZoom.disable();
    }
});
```

Testing the Map View

Now reap the fruit of your labor: Tapping on the location name should open a map view below your message, as in the example visualization (Figure 10-2). On the left is a user's message displayed above the icon. The right image shows a zoomed-in view. Common map gestures (pinch, zoom, tap, and so on) are available in this view. The will be displayed in the top left corner of the map. You can see an illustration of the full-screen mode in Figure 10-2 as well.

Figure 10-2. Example of a Map Full-Screen View (Map Credits: Mapbox / OpenStreetMap)

Adding a Native Map View

Earlier, we mentioned some of the challenges and user flow interruptions when trying to combine a native map view in a PhoneGap application. Although generally not recommended, we wanted to offer a basic example so that you are able to devise which approach best fits for your application.

In our example, we'll be using a plug-in enabling the use of the Google Maps Android SDK v2 and Google Maps SDK for iOS in JavaScript. You can find more information about this plug-in on Github: https://github.com/wf9a5m75/phonegap-googlemaps-plugin.

GOOGLE MAPS API KEYS

Before installing the plug-in, you need to create new Google API keys. For either Android or iOS, you need to follow these initial steps:

1. Go to the Google APIs Console (https://code.google.com/apis/console/)

2. Register your project

3. Turn on Google Maps Android API v2

4. Turn on Google Maps SDK for iOS

5. Go to your project's API & auth ➤ Credentials page

If you want to add the plug-in for Android, execute the following steps:

1. Get your SHA-1 fingerprint as shown:

   Using a Mac:

   ```
   keytool -list -v -keystore ~/.android/debug.keystore -alias androiddebugkey
   -storepass android -keypass android
   ```

   Using Windows:

   ```
   C:\{YOUR-APP-PATH}\platforms\android> keytool -list -v -keystore
   "%USERPROFILE%\.android\debug.keystore" -alias androiddebugkey -storepass
   android -keypass android
   ```

2. Click Create New Key and choose Android Key

3. In the resulting dialog, enter the SHA-1 fingerprint, then a semicolon, and then your application's package name

4. Write down the API Key

For iOS, execute the following steps:

1. Click the Create New Key button and choose iOS Key

2. Enter one or more bundle identifiers as listed in your application's .plist file (com.fernandezalber.themessenger)

3. Write down the API Key

Here, we generated a Google API key that we'll be using for our application.

Google Developers Console

Projects	Public API access	Key for Android applications	
apress-parse-phon...	Use of this key does not require any user action or consent, does not grant access to any account information, and is not used for authorization.	API KEY	AIzaSyCpfIz8cQN2xP98NvH8545ec9f3XXJmDp8
Overview		ANDROID APPLICATIONS	C6:40:E5:6C:42:B1:FC:33:FA:9A:AC:A0:C1:D2:64:B2:D5:B5:19:CE;com.fernandezalber.themessenger
Permissions	Learn more		
Billing & settings		ACTIVATION DATE	Oct 4, 2014 12:50 PM
APIs & auth	Create new Key	ACTIVATED BY	name@domain.com (you)
APIs			
Credentials		Edit allowed Android applications Regenerate key Delete	
Consent screen			
Push		Key for iOS applications	
Monitoring			
Dashboards & alerts		API KEY	AIzaSyDJKN2liury2bdzCzDZ0xxXtQZsFUq0J7Y
Source Code		IOS APPLICATIONS	com.fernandezalber.themessenger
Browse			
Releases		ACTIVATION DATE	Aug 24, 2014 6:34 PM
Developer tools		ACTIVATED BY	name@domain.com (you)
Compute			
Storage			
Big Data		Edit allowed iOS applications Regenerate key Delete	

Google Maps Plug-in Installation

To install the plug-in based on your operating system, run the command in Listing 10-10 in your project directory. Adjust the placeholder for API_KEY_FOR_ANDROID and API_KEY_FOR_IOS according to the keys created in the previous exercise.

Listing 10-10. Install Google Maps Plug-in

```
cordova plugin add plugin.google.maps --variable API_KEY_FOR_ANDROID="{android-client-
secret}" --variable API_KEY_FOR_IOS="{ios-client-secret}"
```

Google Maps View

To position your map, you can use HTML elements and CSS. The plug-in will measure the position and size of your container and place the native map in lieu of your HTML element.

However, there is one important limitation: The native map view will be placed "below" your web view. The layer arrangement is demonstrated in Figure 10-3.

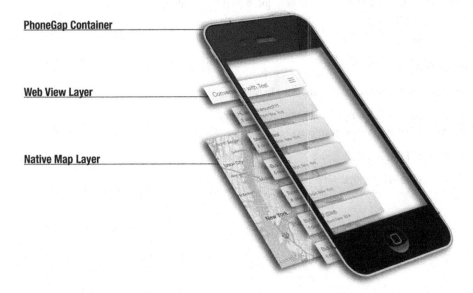

Figure 10-3. *The native map layer will be positioned behind your web view (for example, the conversation template). Solid elements will overcast the map*

As a result, the area where the map is placed needs to be transparent! Background colors, gradients, images, or any other CSS properties creating some kind of colored canvas (for example, a colored border) are not allowed in the same area the map is displayed in. Any non-transparent element will cover the map. Therefore, if you want to wrap with any visual elements, be very careful.

Google Maps Implementation

After installing the plug-in and learning about the technical limitations, we are ready to add a map container to our application.

In particular, the goal of this section will be to replace the newly created JavaScript-based map view with a native map view. We will face one issue while doing this: If we place the map in the same place as the JavaScript map, it won't be visible as each message container holds a background color, or rather a background gradient.

If you want to keep the current position, you will need to remove the background colors from your message boxes. We have decided to follow a different approach. To keep our message styling, we will have one large map container and remove the conversation view for the moment we show the map.

As a first step, add a map container to the conversation template, as shown in Listing 10-11. Right below the map, we will show a Close Map button. Use CSS styles to position your map, as demonstrated in Listing 10-12.

Listing 10-11. Add Map Container (www/conversation.html)

```
<div id="myMap"></div>
<a href="#" id="closeMyMap" class="btn btn-primary">Close Map</a>
```

Listing 10-12. Add Map Container CSS Styles (www/css/styles.css)

```
#myMap {
    display: none;
    position: fixed;
    background: red;
    top: 60px;
    left: 10px;
    bottom: 55px;
    right: 10px;
}
#closeMyMap {
    display: none;
    position: fixed;
    left: 10px;
    bottom: 10px;
    right: 10px;
}
```

Google Maps Module

To keep things in order, we create a new JavaScript module named map.js in the directory www/js/modules and add it to the JavaScript file loader.

In this module, we will use a code organization concept of the same name, the "Module Pattern." The Module Pattern overcomes some of the limitations of the object literal (which we used in the previous chapters) by offering privacy for variables and functions while exposing a public API, if desired. Among other features, we will also avoid long variable names. You can read more about the pattern in the jQuery "Code Organization" documentation: http://learn.jquery.com/code-organization/concepts/.

As shown in Listing 10-13, add the starting structure to your module file map.js. We will explain each function in the following sections.

Listing 10-13. Maps Module (www/js/modules/maps.js)

```
app.modules.map = (function() {

    // Module Variables
    var map, Message;

    // Initialize Module
    var _init = function() {};

    // Event for "Close Map" Button
    var closeEvent = function() {};

    // Convert a Message Location into a Gmaps Location
    var getGLocationFromMessage = function() {};

    // Get a new Map Instance
    var getMap = function() {};

    // Call when Map is Ready
    var onMapReady = function() {};

    // Hide Conversation and Show Map
    var switchView = function() {};

    // Make _init() function accessible form outside
    return {
        init: _init
    };

})();
```

Hiding the Conversation View

In the first function switchView(), we hide the conversation view and make the map view and Close Map button visible (Listing 10-14). We'll call this function from the initialize function.

Listing 10-14. Switch from Conversation to Map View

```
var switchView = function() {
    $('.container').hide();
    $('#myMap, #closeMyMap').css('display', 'block');
};
```

Google Maps Instance

Next, we create a new map instance. Use the #myMap element as virtual container for the map. We as the container we chose. Keep in mind that the actual map view is not "inside" this container, but behind it. If you chose not to use a fixed position for the map container element, the native map view would hold a natural scroll behavior, which means it would scroll in the same way because it would be an HTML inside your body (even though it isn't).

234

You can control map settings by passing an object containing configuration values to the instance method, as shown in Listing 10-15.

Listing 10-15. Create New Map Instance

```
var getMap = function() {
    map = plugin.google.maps.Map.getMap($('#myMap')[0], {
        'controls': {
            'compass': true,
            'myLocationButton': true,
            'zoom': true
        }
    });
};
```

Google Maps "GeoPoint"

Just like with Parse, there is a GeoPoint object in the Google Maps API. The name for the corresponding object type is LatLng. Given that all points on the map will be based on the GeoPoint value of the Message object, we will add a function to create a LatLng object based on a Message object (Listing 10-16).

Listing 10-16. Create a New Geolocation Object

```
var getGLocationFromMessage = function(Message) {
    return new plugin.google.maps.LatLng(
    Message.get('location').latitude,
    Message.get('location').longitude);
};
```

Localizing the Message Location

Our map shouldn't just show any location—it should show the location of the message from where it was sent. Once the map view is loaded, it's time to set the position. We can catch the corresponding event MAP_READY by adding an event listener to the map object: map.addEventListener(plugin.google.maps. event.MAP_READY, callback). We will add this call at a later point in the initialize function.

Setting the position of the map (also known as the map's center point) can be done in different ways, yet the best way to do it is using a "camera" animation. The correspondent function animateCamera will enable you to control both the target position—for which we'll use the getGLocationFromMessage() function—and how to get there. You can change the animation duration, the camera angle, and so forth. Listing 10-17 provides an example.

Listing 10-17. Zoom to the Message Location

```
var onMapReady = function(map) {
    map.animateCamera({
        'target': getGLocationFromMessage(Message),
        'zoom': 15,
        'duration': 3000,
        'tilt': 0,
        'bearing': 0
    });
};
```

Closing the Map View

Second to last, we add an event handler for the Close Map button (Listing 10-18). Aside from destroying the map instance, we also want to restore the conversation view.

Listing 10-18. Close the Map on Button Tap

```
var closeEvent = function() {
   $('#closeMyMap').on('tap click', function() {
      $('.container').show();
      $('#myMap, #closeMyMap').css('display', 'none');
      map.remove();
   });
};
```

Initializing the Map View

Before making a first test of the map view, we need to populate the _init() function. It will have a Message object as argument that we save to the local scope. We then switch the view and create a new map instance while adding the needed event listeners, as demonstrated in Listing 10-19.

In the bottom part of our map module, the _init() function is exposed to the global scope using the name init. Hence, we can call it using app.modules.map.init(). Update your addMap function to match Listing 10-20.

You are now ready to test your native map view. You won't see a marker yet; you will add this in the following section.

Listing 10-19. Zoom to the Message Location and Add a Marker

```
var _init = function(_Message) {
   Message = _Message;
   switchView();
   getMap();
   closeEvent();
   map.addEventListener(plugin.google.maps.event.MAP_READY, onMapReady);
};
```

Listing 10-20. Updated addMap Function Calling the Map Module (js/views/conversation.js)

```
addMap: function(event) {
   event.preventDefault();
   var Message = app.conversation.Messages[$(this).data('id')];
   app.modules.map.init(Message);
}
```

Handling Layer Conflicts

If you opened the navigation menu while showing the native map view, you probably noticed one issue: The navigation links aren't clickable! Instead, all events are passed on to the map.

There are two ways to change this behavior. If elements like buttons, inputs, or links are placed inside the map container, the elements are placed in front of the map and are delegated to listen to all potential events as you are used to. We show an example placement of such a button in Figure 10-4.

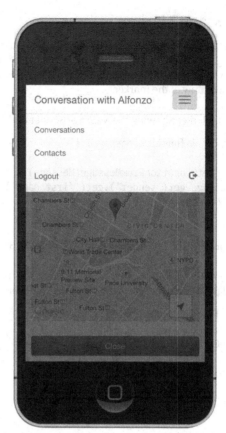

Figure 10-4. A map view possessing a button element living inside the map container (left) and the navigation menu above the map view (right)

Yet as the navigation menu (right in Figure 10-4) is placed outside of the map view—and we don't want to change this—we have to follow the second approach. You can remove the map event watcher by calling setClickable(false) on the map instance. We will do this once the navigation menu is shown, and undo this action when it's hidden again. At this juncture, we also add a backdrop layer to cover the **momentary** inactive map elements (Listing 10-21).

Listing 10-21. Disable the Map Event Handlers When the Navigation Menu Is Shown

```
$('#navigation').on('hide.bs.collapse', function () {
    map.setClickable(true);
    $('.modal-backdrop').remove();
});
$('#navigation').on('show.bs.collapse', function () {
    map.setClickable(false);
    $('body').append('<div class="modal-backdrop fade in"
style="z-index: 999"></div>');
});
```

Adding a Message Marker

Adding a marker for the Message object is a very simple task. Just use the Message object to create a new Google Maps LatLng object and use it for the method map.addMarker(), as demonstrated in Listing 10-22. In the same way as the JavaScript implementation, we use the message sender's name and the message body for the information window of the marker.

Listing 10-22. Add a Marker Showing the Message Sender and Body

```
var addMessageMarker = function(Message) {
    map.addMarker({
        'position': getGLocationFromMessage(Message),
        'title': Message.get('sender').get('first_name'),
        'snippet': Message.get('message_body')
    });
};
```

Call the function *after* the map view is ready (Listing 10-23). You can see an example of the final result in Figure 10-5.

Listing 10-23. Add the Marker as Part of the "Map Ready" Event Callback

```
var onMapReady = function(_map) {
    addMessageMarker(Message);
    // map.animateCamera() ...
});
```

Figure 10-5. *Google Maps view example on iOS*

Geo Queries

Last but not least is the topic of Parse Geo Queries. Geo Queries are a very helpful tool when building location services. An example case would be to find nearby pizza delivery services.

Using Parse makes this once challenging task a dead simple one. You don't need to care about scalability, indexing, speed, caching, and so forth. Parse will do it for you.

Radial and Box Queries

There are two general approaches to set limits for geo queries: using a radius or a "box." In other words, you could either use a circle or a square. Depending on your use-case, either of the two will give you a better result. You can see an illustration of both approaches in Figure 10-6.

Figure 10-6. *A radial geo query (left) in comparison to a box geo query (right)*

Radial queries should be used if the center of a query is the most important element. For example, if you want to get the nearest subway stations in relation to the user's current position, a radial query may be more appropriate. Parse offers different filters for this approach: `Parse.Query.withinKilometers()` and `Parse.Query.withinMiles()`. In addition, you can use the method `Parse.Query.near()`, which will essentially do the same, but use an infinite value for the radius and return nearby results first.

Box queries are the best fit if you want a result to match a quadrangular view (for example, to show all subway stations that fit into your current map view). The method, therefore, is called `Parse.Query.withinGeoBox()`.

■ **Note**   The Geo Queries tutorial is based on the "Google Maps View" tutorial referred to earlier in this chapter, so make sure it's completed before starting this lesson.

Getting Nearby Messages

As a half-practical example, we'll get all messages close to the current map view. For testing purposes, we will query all messages that exist in the database. In a "real" application, you should only display messages that belong to the *current* user. You can set access rules for your messages using `Parse.ACL`. You can learn more about securing Parse objects here: `https://parse.com/docs/js/guide#security`.

We begin by updating the map module variables defined in the head of the module to Listing 10-24. We'll need to store some values such as which message markers had been added to the map and whether we are currently in a process of loading data from Parse.

Listing 10-24. Add the variables message_ids and loading (www/js/modules/map.js)

```
var map, Message, message_ids = [], loading = false;
```

Next, we extend the map-ready event handler, as shown in Listing 10-25. If the map camera changes, we need to get the map center and subsequently invoke a geo query (Listing 10-26). Once you start a query, save the status in the variable loading to avoid running multiple queries at the same time. Add the function getMapCenter and all following functions to the body of your module app.modules.map.

Listing 10-25. Update the onMapReady Function

```
var onMapReady = function(_map) {
    // Keep existing code...
    map.animateCamera(options, function() {
        map.on(plugin.google.maps.event.CAMERA_CHANGE, getMapCenter);
    });
});
```

Listing 10-26. After Getting the Map Center Run

```
var getMapCenter = function(position) {
    if (loading) {
        return;
    }
    loading = true;
    getMessagesNearBy(position).then(addMarkersToMap);
};
```

Once we know the center of the map, we can convert the Google Maps position into a Parse GeoPoint. Use either the method near(), withinMiles() or withinKilometers() to filter the Message table. We show the syntax of all methods in Listing 10-27. The callback function addMarkersToMap() for the query promise had already been defined in Listing 10-27. In this function, cycle through all results and verify that there is no marker for the corresponding message on the map. If not, add a new marker (Listing 10-28). When you have finished loading messages and adding markers, reset the loading value to false.

Listing 10-27. Convert Google Maps Position into Parse GeoPoint and Query Messages near Current Position

```
var getMessagesNearBy = function(position) {
    var currentPosition = new Parse.GeoPoint({
        latitude: position.target.lat,
        longitude: position.target.lng
    });
    var query = new Parse.Query(MyParseMessage);
    query.near("location", currentPosition);
```

```
    // Alternatives:
    // query.withinMiles("location", currentPosition, 3);
    // query.withinKilometers("location", currentPosition, 5);
    query.limit(10);
    return query.find();
};
```

Listing 10-28. Add Message Markers to the Map

```
var addMarkersToMap = function(Messages) {
    $.each(Messages, function(index, Message) {
        if ($.inArray(Message.id, message_ids) > -1) {
            return;
        }
        message_ids.push(Message.id);
        addMessageMarker(Message);
    });
    loading = false;
};
```

Getting Messages within Map Bounds

Getting messages within the map bounds will follow the same structure as getting nearby messages. Yet, instead of using the map center as base for our query, we will use the visible map area—the "map bounds"—for the geo query.

Replace the getMapCenter callback with a new function named getVisibleRegion. The plug-in function of the same name will return latitude and longitude values for the northeast and southwest corner points of the map view (Listing 10-29).

Listing 10-29. Query Messages near Current Position

```
var onMapReady = function(_map) {
    // Keep existing code...
    // Replace getMapCenter with getVisibleRegion
    map.animateCamera(options, function() {
        map.on(plugin.google.maps.event.CAMERA_CHANGE, getVisibleRegion);
    });
});
```

In the callback shown in Listing 10-30, we execute the query function getMessagesWithinBounds(). In our getVisibleRegion function, call the map method getVisibleRegion. The object latLngBounds contains the methods northeast and southwest, which you will convert into two new Parse.GeoPoint objects. This will then be used as arguments for the filter query.withinGeoBox() (Listing 10-31).

Listing 10-30. Get the Map Bounds

```
var getVisibleRegion = function(position) {
    if (loading) {
        return;
    }
    loading = true;
    map.getVisibleRegion(function(latLngBounds) {
        getMessagesWithinBounds(latLngBounds).then(addMarkersToMap);
    });
};
```

Listing 10-31. Query Messages within a Given Box

```
var getMessagesWithinBounds = function(latLngBounds) {
    var southwest = new Parse.GeoPoint(latLngBounds.southwest.lat,
latLngBounds.southwest.lng);
    var northeast = new Parse.GeoPoint(latLngBounds.northeast.lat,
latLngBounds.northeast.lng);
    var query = new Parse.Query(MyParseMessage);
    query.withinGeoBox("location", southwest, northeast);
    query.limit(10);
    return query.find();
};
```

▪ **Tip**   If you want to calculate the distance between the current position described by GeoPointA and a marker described by GeoPointB, use the method `GeoPointA.milesTo(GeoPointB)`. To get the distance in kilometers or radians, use `kilometersTo()` or `radiansTo()`.

Summary

Going a step further than Chapter 9, this chapter discussed the differences between native and JavaScript map APIs. Using the native device API for maps provides a smoother experience for the user when compared to a JavaScript-based map, an important difference that factors into the experience you want for your users.

Each position on a map has metadata associated with it. Using Parse, we investigated different methods of geo queries and displayed them on a map generated by Google Maps.

We added the option for users to send their current location within a message. By updating our current user interface with this new map feature, we were able to highlight the geolocation capabilities of the application. We're not only saving the position that our users are in, we provide a way for them to view it on a map inside the interface of the message.

In Chapter 11, we combine the usage of your phone's media—both using the camera and existing pictures—with the Parse cloud database.

CHAPTER 11

■ ■ ■

Accessing and Sharing Photos

If a tree falls in a forest and no one is around to hear it, does it make a sound?

During the last ten years, the role of the average Internet user has changed dramatically. Today, practically everyone is a content publisher as well as a consumer. "User Participation" was one of the key phrases of the Web 2.0 era, and this concept applies today for modern mobile applications.

In most applications, having an identity is a basic feature for user participation. Any form of text is typically the most common way of sharing information. We covered creating users and sending text messages in the previous chapters; now let's ramp it up a level and add photos, sounds, and videos to this application.

Since photos are the most shared media type, we will focus on them and touch on some methods for capturing sound and video as well. But why stop there?

Getting back to the forest ... Reality only exists to those who experience it. Digital media allows us to share moments using video, sound, and images. Parse and PhoneGap can help us create that experience.

Using the class `Parse.File`, we'll save photos and other documents to the Parse cloud so users can share them with each other.

We will use the Messenger application so you can see it in action; however, you can apply the introduced examples to any other application.

Enabling Camera Access

The first part of this chapter will discuss accessing photos from a device. Later, you will use what you learned to send the image to another user in the Messenger App. We'll be using the Cordova camera plug-in.

As with most software you'll use, make sure you check out the documentation for quirks on the operating systems you are targeting. You can learn more here: `github.com/apache/cordova-plugin-camera`.

Using this plug-in, we can take *new* photos and access *existing* photos from a device. We'll start by installing it using the terminal command shown in Listing 11-1.

Listing 11-1. Camera Plug-in Installation

```
cordova plugin add org.apache.cordova.camera
```

Using the camera plug-in shares the same requirement as accessing a user's global position in that the user must accept permissions for your application to access camera features.

User Interface for Photo Sharing

Every supported device platform offering a photo or camera feature will have a user interface to manage it. If it doesn't, the plug-in will *attempt* to do it for you. This gives us a programmatic interface to manage the camera, which includes enabling or disabling the flash, setting the focus, and taking photos. There will be another interface to select a photo from one of your albums. An example interface for browsing the albums and photos on iOS is shown in Figure 11-1.

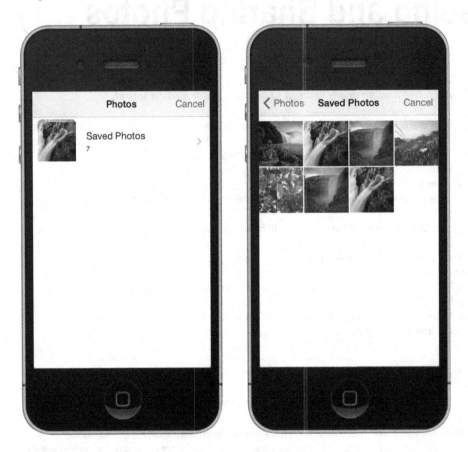

Figure 11-1. Browsing the device's albums and photos

Photo and Camera Button

The first thing users need to be able to do is attach a photo to a message. The right place to start is the conversation view, created in Chapter 8. The users could either use their device's photo library for sharing an existing photo or the camera for sharing a new photo yet to be taken. Hence, we'll add one button for each case to the user interface.

To create compelling buttons quickly and easily, we make use of the Twitter Bootstrap Glyphicon font. Fitting icons for this case are the classes glyphicon-picture and glyphicon-camera. Update your conversation view template using the code in Listing 11-2. You can see the result of this update in Figure 11-2.

Listing 11-2. Add a Picture and Camera Button to Your Conversation View (www/conversation.html)

```
<div class="btn-toolbar" role="toolbar">
  <div class="btn-group">
    <a href="#" id="js-event-use-albums" class="btn btn-default">
      <i class="glyphicon glyphicon-picture"></i>
    </a>
    <a href="#" id="js-event-use-camera" class="btn btn-default">
      <i class="glyphicon glyphicon-camera"></i>
    </a>
  </div>
  <div class="btn-group">
    <a href="#" id="location" class="btn btn-default">
      <i class="glyphicon glyphicon-map-marker"></i>
    </a>
  </div>
  <div class="btn-group">
    <a href="#" id="submit" class="btn btn-primary">
      <i class="glyphicon glyphicon-send"></i>
      Send Message
    </a>
  </div>
</div>
```

Figure 11-2. The picture and camera buttons are shown to the left of the existing button set

JavaScript Module for Accessing Photos and Camera

In this section, we'll add a new module to our application that will handle all photo library and camera interactions. We'll use the namespace app.modules.**pictures** for the module. Just like the location module from Chapter 9, we'll use the module pattern. The basic structure of the pictures module is shown in Listing 11-2.

Create a new module file in www/js/modules/**picture.js** and add the reference to your JavaScript file loader.

This module, shown in Listing 11-3, will contain a function to get a photo from the user's albums—getPhotoFromAlbums—and one to get a photo from the camera—getPhotoFromCamera. Both functions will be part of the returned object and thereby accessible globally.

Furthermore, we will have the non-public functions _getPhoto, _save, and _onFail. The _getPhoto function will capture or get the actual photo, the function _save will save the photo to the Parse database, and _onFail will handle all error cases. We added an underscore as a prefix to highlight that these functions will not be accessible from outside and are intended to be private for the current module.

Listing 11-3. Initial Setup for the Pictures Module (www/js/modules/picture.js)

```
app.modules.pictures = (function() {
    // Wrapper function to get a photo from the device's album(s)
    var getPhotoFromAlbums = function() {};

    // Wrapper function to get a photo via the device's camera
    var getPhotoFromCamera = function() {};

    // Common used function to get a photo from different sources
    var _getPhoto = function() {};

    // Save photo to parse
    var _save = function() {};

    // If something goes wrong...
    var _onFail = function(message) {
        console.log('Error: ' + message);
    };

    // public API
    return {
        getPhotoFromAlbums: getPhotoFromAlbums,
        getPhotoFromCamera: getPhotoFromCamera
    };
})();
```

PhoneGap Camera Plug-in

To get photos from the device's library or camera, we'll be using the plug-in's function `navigator.camera.getPicture()`. This function has three arguments: a `success` callback, an `error` callback, and an `options` object.

Optional Camera Options

The following descriptions explain the plug-in's available `options`:

- `sourceType`: The property `sourceType` will determine whether to use the camera (`CAMERA`), the album browser (`PHOTOLIBRARY`), or a photo-stream (`SAVEDPHOTOALBUM`) of the device. When using these keys, you need to add the prefix namespace `navigator.camera.PictureSourceType`.

  For example, `PHOTOLIBRARY` will use `navigator.camera.PictureSourceType.PHOTOLIBRARY`. The syntax is demonstrated in Listing 11-4 in the following section, "Using the Camera Plug-in."

- `destinationType`: To assign whether the resulting photo should be saved to the filesystem (`FILE_URI`), a native URL (`NATIVE_URI`), or base64-encoded string (`DATA_URL`), use the key `destinationType` and the prefix `navigator.camera.DestinationType`.

- cameraDirection: Modern smartphones usually have two cameras, one on the front and one on the back. Use navigator.camera.Direction.FRONT or navigator.camera.Direction.BACK to target a specific camera.

- encodingType: This value determines whether the captured photo should be compressed or not. Use navigator.camera.EncodingType.JPEG or navigator.camera.EncodingType.PNG to handle this setting.

- quality: Use a value between 0 and 100 to pick the quality of the photo. A value of 100 is typically the full-resolution photo with no loss from file compression, with 0 being the lowest quality setting.

- targetWidth and targetHeight: Use a pixel value for the keys targetWidth and targetHeight to set a maximum width and height for the captured photo. If the photo is bigger than the defined sizes, it will be resized to stay within the limits.

■ **Note** It' is extremely important to set *both* targetWidth and targetHeight. Setting just one value will have no impact on the captured picture. You'll want to choose appropriate values; if you don't set any limits, it might take a long time to upload the captured photo. On the other hand, picking small values will obviously result in low-resolution photos and perhaps a faster experience.

Using the Camera Plug-in

The camera offers some more settings that we'll delve into next. First, update the functions getPhotoFromAlbums and getPhotoFromCamera to define the source (either the photo library or the camera), and then call the _getPhoto function, as shown in Listing 11-4.

Besides the source argument, the _getPhoto function will use a viewCallback variable as second parameter. We assume that after the process of selecting or capturing a photo, the "caller" (which is the conversation view) will do something with it. In our case, this will be the act of attaching the photo result to a message.

Next, and most importantly, the _getPhoto function will capture the actual photo using the function navigator.camera.getPicture(). At this point, we also want to set the options object for configuring settings like the destinationType. We're using DATA_URL, as we don't want to save the picture on the local device, but rather directly send it to Parse.

If you still want to keep a copy of the captured picture on the device, enable the option saveToPhotoAlbum. You can also offer the opportunity to edit the photo before sending by setting the option allowEdit to true. Feel free to experiment with all the options available to suit your needs.

Listing 11-4. Populate Methods in the Picture Module for Getting and Setting a Photo from a User's Camera or Album (www/js/modules/picture.js)

```
var getPhotoFromAlbums = function(viewCallback) {
    _getPhoto(navigator.camera.PictureSourceType.PHOTOLIBRARY, viewCallback);
};
var getPhotoFromCamera = function(viewCallback) {
    _getPhoto(navigator.camera.PictureSourceType.CAMERA, viewCallback);
};
```

```
var _getPhoto = function(source, viewCallback) {
    navigator.camera.getPicture(function(photoData) {
        _save(photoData, viewCallback);
    }, _onFail, {
        allowEdit: true,
        destinationType: navigator.camera.DestinationType.DATA_URL,
        encodingType: navigator.camera.EncodingType.JPEG,
        quality: 40,
        saveToPhotoAlbum: true,
        sourceType: source,
        targetWidth: 1024,
        targetHeight: 1024
    });
};
```

Camera and Photos Permissions

The very first time a source is requested via `navigator.camera.getPicture()`, the application will ask for permissions to do so, as in Figure 11-3. Once a user grants permission, the application will never ask for permissions again (similar to geolocation).

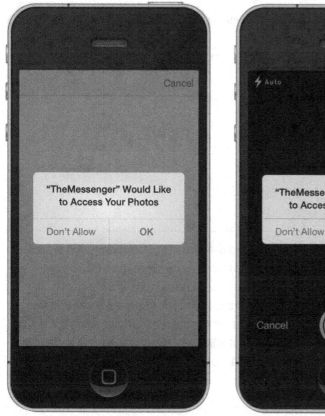

Figure 11-3. *Photos and camera permission requests on iOS*

If a user declines a permission request or disables access via the system's privacy settings, the camera will stay black and, instead of their albums, the user will see an error message. In this case, the _onfail() method will be called. The function argument will contain an error message such as "has no access to assets." Inform your users about the issue and ask them to adjust their privacy settings.

Using Parse Files

A typical PhoneGap application will end here, or require you to set up a server for hosting your files and perhaps use another plug-in to transfer the file to the server. Since we are using Parse, we can skip these steps!

We'll help ourselves and use the Parse.File class for saving image file types to Parse. The class allows us to store data of any file type in the cloud. Aside from photos, we can also use videos, music, or other supported document formats. The maximum size of a file can be ten megabytes.

Saving a Photo to Parse

Since we're using PhoneGap, common input sources include the local filesystem, external sources (like the Facebook API), or the device camera.

Yet you might want to emulate some application behavior in the Web version of your app for testing purposes. To do this, you can use a classic input file element and the script shown in Listing 11-5.

Listing 11-5. New Parse.File Instance Created via an Input Element of the Type "file"

```
<input type="file" id="fileUpload">
<a href="#" onclick="doUpload(); return false">Upload</a>
<script>
    function doUpload() {
        var fileUploadControl = $("#fileUpload")[0];
        if (fileUploadControl.files.length > 0) {
            var file = fileUploadControl.files[0];
            var name = "filename.ext";
            var parseFile = new Parse.File(name, file);
        }
    }
</script>
```

■ **Note** Base64 is a technology to convert binary data into text data. For HTML, this conversation is needed, as it's a text-based file format, and mixing of binary data and text data is generally not possible. The result text will consist of letters, numbers, and the symbols "+", "/", and "=". The downside of this system is the overhead added by the conversion. Base64 encodes each set of three bytes into four bytes. In addition, the output is padded to always be a multiple of four. This means that the size of the Base64 representation is about 30% larger than its binary source. Currently, the Parse JavaScript SDK solely accepts file uploads via Base64 or a classic file input element. In the future, it might be possible to send binary data using the JavaScript FileReader object.

Since we are in the possession of a base64-encoded string from the captured photo by default, we'll use the same format for creating the new `Parse.File` instance. By executing the `save()` method on the `Parse.File` object, we upload the file to the Parse Cloud.

Once the file has been saved to the cloud, it will obtain a unique URL, which we can retrieve using the method `url()` on the `Parse.File` instance.

Immediately after saving the file, the callback function will be executed while passing the `Parse.File` instance to it. (See Listing 11-6.)

Listing 11-6. Saving an Image to Parse (www/js/modules/picture.js)

```
var _save = function(photoData, viewCallback) {
    var parsePhoto = new Parse.File("photo.jpg", {
        base64: photoData
    });
    parsePhoto.save().then(function() {
        console.log(parsePhoto.url());
        viewCallback(parsePhoto);
    }, _onFail);
};
```

Camera and Album Event Handler

After defining the `pictures` module, it's time to put it to use in the view. Then we'll add event handlers to the conversation view buttons with the element ID selectors `#js-event-use-albums` and `#js-event-use-camera`. Each button should call its corresponding function, as demonstrated in Listing 11-7.

Listing 11-7. Attach Event Handlers for Getting Images via the User's Album or Camera (www/js/views/conversation.js)

```
$('#js-event-use-albums').on('click', function(e) {
    e.preventDefault();
    $('form').addClass('uploading');
    app.modules.pictures.getPhotoFromAlbums(function(parsePhoto) {
        // callback
    });
});

$('#js-event-use-camera').on('click', function(e) {
    e.preventDefault();
    $('form').addClass('uploading');
    app.modules.pictures.getPhotoFromCamera(function(parsePhoto) {
        // callback
    });
});
```

Next, we'll add some simple styles (used in Listing 11-8) to let the user know that the file is in the process of uploading to Parse.

Listing 11-8. A New CSS Class for Referencing the Loading Image (www/css/styles.css)

```
.uploading {
  background:transparent url(../img/ajax-loader.gif) no-repeat center;
}
.uploading * {
  opacity: 0.5;
}
```

Photo Capture Callback

In Listing 11-7, we added a placeholder for code (// callback) that should be executed after the photo is captured from the camera or selected from a photo album. In these callbacks you, could either start sending the message immediately or ask the users whether they want to send this picture. We will use the notification plug-in to confirm if the users want to use the image.

To use the notification plug-in, verify that you installed the Cordova Dialogs plug-in (org.apache. cordova.dialogs). An example of this callback function that can be used for the camera functions (getPhotoFromCamera or getPhotoFromAlbums) is shown in Listing 11-9. Eventually, the callback should execute the sendMessage function to invoke sending the message.

Listing 11-9. Asking the User to Confirm the Sending of a Message (www/js/modules/picture.js)

```
navigator.notification.confirm("Do you want to send this picture?", function() {
    app.conversation.sendMessage(parsePhoto);
    $('form').removeClass('uploading');
}, "Confirmation", ['OK', 'Cancel']);
```

Attaching a Photo to a Message

There are only a few small steps left to get the message and its photo to the intended user. First, we'll add a parsePhoto variable as argument of the sendMessage() function in conversation.js (Listing 11-10).

We'll then use it in Message.end() as an argument object. Because we decided to either send a text message or a photo, we only reset the textarea value if there *isn't* a photo. In order to actually use the new photo feature for a message, you need to explicitly add it to the send method of the MyParseMessage class (See listing 11-11).

Listing 11-10. Attaching a Photo (www/js/views/conversation.js)

```
sendMessage: function(parsePhoto) {
    var Message = new MyParseMessage();
    Message.send({
        Receiver: app.conversation.Receiver,
        message_body: !parsePhoto ? $('textarea').val() : null,
        parsePhoto: parsePhoto
    }).then(function() {
        if (!parsePhoto) {
            $('textarea').val('');
        }
        // At this point you should add a script
        // to refresh conversation (messages)
    });
}
```

Listing 11-11. Update to send() Method to Save the Photo (www/js/models/MyParseMessage.js)

```
if (options.parsePhoto) {
    this.set('Photo', options.parsePhoto);
}
```

Sending an image in its original format may be rather large, especially with the cameras available in today's smartphone. Before showing the image in the view, we'll use Cloud Code to resize the image first.

Image Resizing in the Parse Cloud

Sending and receiving images on a slow connection can be frustrating for users. To create a better experience, we'll use Parse's Cloud Code to resize the image smaller *before saving* it to the cloud. To do this, we'll be using the *Parse Image* Cloud Module.

Cloud modules are importable pieces of code written in CommonJS that can be used throughout your application. They are executed on Parse's servers and can be invoked within your code, or they can be used as trigger functions for specific events.

You can write your own cloud module, or use one of the readily available modules provided by Parse. From things such as payment processing using *Stripe* to text messing using *Twilio*, cloud modules are simple, effective ways to get tons of functionality without all the hard work.

First, will add new code that will contain functionality for resizing the image *before* it's saved to Parse. The original image *will,* however, get saved to Parse. We use the resized image for populating the view only.

Next, we'll use the Parse Image module to resize the image before it gets saved to the Message object. Start by editing the main file where we are storing our Cloud Code for Parse (Listing 11-12).

Listing 11-12. Contains Code That Will Resize the User's Image before Saving It to the Cloud (/cloud/cloud/main.js)

```
var ParseImage = require("parse-image");
Parse.Cloud.beforeSave("Message", function(request, response) {
    var Message = request.object;
});
```

Here we start by *requiring* the parse-image module. This allows us to manipulate the image in a number of ways, including cropping and setting the image format. We reference the module using the ParseImage variable.

Using the beforeSave Cloud function, we will alter the image *before* it gets saved to Parse. Inside this function, we use the request argument to store a reference to the object returned in a variable named Message. This variable represents a message that is sent to a user.

Validating Data

As they say in programming, garbage in, garbage out. Before we process any data, let's make sure we know what we're working with.

First, we'll put in some safeguards to only work with valid data (Listing 11-13). This kind of checking helps us weed out any values that would otherwise introduce a new bug in the code.

Listing 11-13. Execute the Function Only If Specific Conditions Are Met

```
// No image attached to the message object
if (!Message.get("Image")) {
  response.success();
  return;
}
// The photo wasn't modified
if (!Message.dirty("Image")) {
  response.success();
  return;
}
```

If there is no image attached to Message, execute the success method of the response object. This essentially does no operation and falls to the return statement, which prevents the function from processing any further instructions.

Next, we use a function named dirty. This is called on the returned object (Message) from the cloud module's response object. The dirty method returns **true** if the object *has* been modified since its last save/ refresh.

Parse Cloud HTTP Request

For this cloud code functionality, we will be using the httpRequest method of the Parse.Cloud object. Before a picture is saved to Parse, we make an HTTP request to Parse (*Cloud Code*), allowing us to preprocess the object (Listing 11-14).

Listing 11-14. Make an HTTP Request to the URL of the Image in the Message

```
Parse.Cloud.httpRequest({
  url: Message.get("Image").url()
});
```

The httpRequest method takes an object as an argument. Using the url property, we supply the value of the image's URL.

After we call the httpRequest function, we'll next call a series of promise functions in succession. Chaining functions together like this is one of the many cool things about the Parse JavaScript API. One after another, we will call functions at different points in the promise chain. Each function will have its own scope and context.

With that said, there will be a lot going on from the time that an image is attached to the object to when it's resized. Follow along in Listing 11-15 with the code comments.

■ **Note**   The Parse.Cloud.**httpRequest** uses the **then** method to process functions asynchronously. The **then** async method returns a *promise* that is fulfilled when the callback is complete. In Listing 11-15, when a then function returns a value, that value can be used inside the *next* then function in the chain, just as long as the promise is successful.

Listing 11-15. Cloud Code to Resize an Image before Saving to Parse

```
Parse.Cloud.httpRequest({
    // Get the url value of the 'Image' property on the Message object
    url: Message.get("Image").url()
}).then(function (response) {
    // Use the parse-image Cloud Module and create a new image
    var image = new Image();
    // Set the data of the image using the response object
    return image.setData(response.buffer);
}).then(function (image) {
    // The argument 'image' refers to returned object from the previous function

    // Select an arbitrary width value
    var width = 400;
    // Calculate our altered image's ratio using actual data from the image
    var ratio = (image.width() / image.height());
    // Based on the ratio, calculate a height
    var height = Math.round(width / ratio);

    /* Add a new property (ThumbnailSize) to the Message object containing
     the details of the thumbnail*/
    Message.set("ThumbnailSize", {
      width: width,
      height: height,
      ratio: ratio
    });
    // Resize the image using the parse-image module's 'scale' function
    return image.scale({
      width: width,
      height: height
    });
}).then(function (image) {
    // 'image' refers to returned object from the previous function (now resized)

    // Make sure it's a JPEG to save disk space and bandwidth
    return image.setFormat("JPEG");
}).then(function (image) {
    // Get the image data in a Buffer
    return image.data();
}).then(function (buffer) {
    // Save the image into a new file
    var base64 = buffer.toString("base64");
    // Create a new file containing the image data
    var resized = new Parse.File("thumbnail.jpg", {
      base64: base64
    });
    // Return the saved and resized image
    return resized.save();
```

```
}).then(function (resized) {
  // Attach the image file to the original object.
  Message.set("thumbnail", resized);
}).then(function (result) {
  // That's it, success!
  response.success();
}, function (error) {
  response.error(error);
});
```

Using the Resized Image

Let's next add a new method to the MyParseMessage object named getThumbnail. This new method will return the image that is inside the returned object. We are going to use it inside the conversation view for displaying. Listings 11-16 and 11-17 demonstrate the code for extending MyParseMessage, followed by updating the view to use our newly created getThumbnail function.

Listing 11-16. Returns the URL of the Resized Thumbnail Image (www/js/models/MyParseMessage.js)

```
var MyParseMessage = Parse.Object.extend('Message', {
  //...
  getThumbnail: function() {
      return this.get('thumbnail') ? '<img src="' + this.get('thumbnail').url() + '" alt=""
class="img-thumbnail" />' : '';
    //...
});
```

Listing 11-17. Updated Conversation Template to Display a Thumbnail of the Image (www/conversation.html)

```
{{ attributes.message_body }}
{{{ getThumbnail }}}
```

By combining Parse's file capabilities, along with the PhoneGap camera plug-in, you are able to extend the application by allowing users to share images. Because Parse is capable of storing many types of media, you could further extend your application by adding video or sound files using a corresponding PhoneGap plug-in. You can learn more about all core and third-party libraries here: build.phonegap.com/plugins.

Summary

This chapter introduced incorporating images into the Messenger App. Using the Cordova camera plug-in, we were able to access images from a device's library, as well as taking a new image. We created a new **pictures** module that contains all code for image-related functions.

Using some of the many options available with the camera plug-in, we were able to determine things like the source and camera direction.

When the plug-in is instantiated by the users, they're asked to accept permissions to use their camera's functionality.

Using the captured image, we attached it to the Message object and saved it to Parse. Parse is able to store base64-encoded Strings. We use this after we resize the image using the *parse-image* cloud module.

■ ■ ■

CHAPTER 12

Network Connection Status

We are always connected... sometimes.

Wouldn't it be nice if you were connected to the Internet 24/7? As magical as that experience may be, it can never fully be achieved. There will come a time in your life when you aren't connected to the Internet. It's like the 80s all over again.

This chapter focuses on the dreadful moment when your user may not have an Internet connection. What is a person to do, read a book or something?

For the Messenger application, you'll notify the user that they will not be able to send messages. Using the Network Information PhoneGap plug-in, you'll be able to detect if the user has an active Internet connection and respond accordingly. Before doing that, you first want to be able to update a person's status when they log in to indicate that they're online.

Code Preparation

Start off by setting up your user class with custom instance methods and class properties. Open the **MayParseUser.js** file. In it, add some new class properties that will allow you to track their status.

Here's an overall view of what you're trying to achieve. The MyParseUser object already has some instance methods that you've used throughout the application. This chapter will use class properties to further extend your object.

To begin, set up some placeholder properties. Update the object with three new properties, as shown in Listing 12-1.

Listing 12-1. Setting Up the MyParseUser Object with Class Properties as Placeholders

```
window.MyParseUser = Parse.User.extend({
    // Instance Methods ...
}, {
    // Class properties
    trackOnlineStatus: function() {
        },
    setOnline: function() {
    },
    setOffline: function() {
    }
});
```

Class Properties

Using class properties on custom Parse objects allows you to extend the functionality of your object. In this case, you want to keep track of a user's status by creating a new object property named **online**. This is a field that is set to true or false (Boolean values) based on whether the user is logged in or not.

When a user logs in, you want to set the online value to true. The two functions setOnline and setOffline toggle this value. The trackOnlineStatus initiates the online status by calling methods from the object itself. You'll call this later, when the user logs in. Fill in the placeholder class methods using the code in Listing 12-2.

Listing 12-2. Populated Class Properties for Tracking a User's Online Status (www/js/models/MyParseUser.js)

```
window.MyParseUser = Parse.User.extend({
    // Instance Methods ...
}, {
    // Class properties
    trackOnlineStatus: function() {
        MyParseUser.setOnline();
    },
    setOnline: function() {
        var User = MyParseUser.current();
        User.set('online', true);
        User.set('last_seen', new Date());
        User.save();
    },
    setOffline: function() {
        var User = MyParseUser.current();
        User.set('online', false);
        User.set('last_seen', new Date());
        User.save();
    }
});
```

Now that there is code in place, you put it to use when the user is logged in. Because your accessControl function gets called on every page, you use it to also call the new MyParseUser.trackOnlineStatus() method, as demonstrated in Listing 12-3.

Listing 12-3. Making a Call to Track the Online Status of the Current User (www/js/core.js)

```
app.core = {
    //...
    accessControl: function() {
        // ...
        // Update User Status
        MyParseUser.trackOnlineStatus();
    }
};
```

Last Seen

Since you now have a way of knowing when a user has last been online, you can use this data to populate the view, allowing for this information to be visible to other users.

Because this functionality is about the current user, you will further extend the MyParseUser class with two new instance methods, isOnline and lastSeenText, as shown in Listing 12-4.

As you might expect, the isOnline function is used to determine if a user is online by checking the user's last_seen time and comparing it with the current time. The span must fall in between two minutes to qualify a user being "online."

Listing 12-4. Instance Methods Added to the MyParseUser Object for Tracking the Online Status of a User

```
window.MyParseUser = Parse.User.extend({
  // Instance Methods
  isOnline: function() {
    var timeout = 120 * 1000; // 120 seconds
    var currentDate = new Date();
    return this.get('online') && (currentDate.getTime() - this.get('last_seen').getTime() <
    timeout);
  },
  lastSeenText: function() {
   var currentDate = new Date();
     return this.get('last_seen') ? moment(this.get('last_seen')).fromNow() : '';
  }
}, {
    // Class properties ...
});
```

Recall that for MyParseUser, the class method setOnline is called when you want to track the user's online status. When a user is logged in, this is the information they see about *other* users in their contacts list. The isOnline function returns a Boolean value based on if user is online and has been last seen at least two minutes ago (timeout). The lastSeenText uses the moment.js library to display the last time the user was online, if they ever were.

Update the Contacts List View

Next, update the view to reflect the data. Your template currently has two columns. Add a new one and add some function calls to update the user interface (Listing 12-5).

Update the second column by adding a call to the lastSeenText function. Add a new column to display an icon that reflects the user's online status. Figure 12-1 shows an example of the new timestamp representing the last time they were seen, or if they are currently online.

Listing 12-5. Update Contacts View, Making Use of the Instance and Class Methods for Tracking a User's Status (www/contacts.html)

```
<td class="small" style="vertical-align: middle">
    <a href="conversation.html?id={{ id }}">
        {{attributes.first_name}}
        {{attributes.last_name}}
    </a>
    <div>{{ lastSeenText }}</div>
</td>
```

```
<td>
    <a href="conversation.html?id={{ id }}">
      {{#if isOnline }}
        <i class="alert alert-success glyphicon glyphicon-stop"></i>
      {{ else }}
        <i class="alert alert-danger glyphicon glyphicon-stop"></i>
      {{/if}}
    </a>
</td>
```

Figure 12-1. UI update based on user instance data

Network Information Plug-in

The previous example showed how to get and set a user's online status. This is only useful if the user has an active Internet connection to be able to save this information to Parse. What if they don't have a connection?

If the user doesn't have a connection, your application can respond by providing a message. This can present a better user experience so they don't go through the frustration of trying to send or receive messages.

You use the Network Information plug-in to determine if the user has an active cellular or WiFi connection. Start by adding the plug-in to the project, as shown in Listing 12-6.

Listing 12-6. Adding the Network Information Plug-in

```
cordova plugin add org.apache.cordova.network-information
```

Update the UI

Now that you have the plug-in in place, you can provide a friendly message to the user about their Internet connection. You'll use two state messages, for **on** or **off** line information (Listing 12-7).

Listing 12-7. The contacts.html Template Updated with Information About the User's Connection

```
<div id="offline-message" class="alert alert-danger" role="alert">
    <strong>Offline</strong><br>
    You cannot send messages at the moment.
</div>
<div class="modal-backdrop fade in"></div>

<div id="online-message" class="alert alert-success" role="alert">
    <strong>Online</strong><br>
    You are back online!
</div>
```

Listening for Updates

Using the new UI elements, you show the message to the user. The Network Information plug-in works by providing two states do the document, online or offline. You add an event listener to the document and respond with the UI accordingly.

You provide the user a message when the application is loaded.

■ **Note**   In order to provide accurate information about the network, you need to continually access the information in intervals. Doing so will not only provide a better experience for the user with respect to providing their status, it also improves your app's chance of acceptance in a marketplaces like the Apple Store, which may choose to reject your application if these considerations aren't addressed.

You won't consistently poll to check for an active Internet connection. However, you may want to consider doing so if your application relies heavily on an Internet connection. Add a new function for each available network status (Listing 12-8).

263

Listing 12-8. Snippet to Get the UI to Respond to the Status of the User's Connection (js/core.js)

```
// Online
document.addEventListener("online", function() {
    MyParseUser.setOnline();
    $('#offline-message').fadeOut();
    $('#online-message').fadeIn();
    window.setTimeout(function() {
        $('#online-message, .modal-backdrop').fadeOut();
    }, 1000);
}, false);
// Offline
document.addEventListener("offline", function() {
    $('#offline-message, .modal-backdrop').fadeIn();
}, false);
```

Figure 12-2 shows the two state messages, based on the connection of the device.

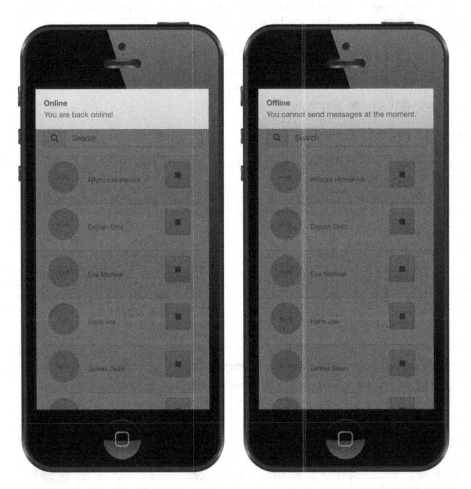

Figure 12-2. *The online and offline messages*

Using the Network Information plug-in, you were able to extend your custom user object to include some functionality for reporting network status information.

You use instance methods to populate the view in your template. With class properties, you set their online status to assist in providing unique messaging based on their connection. Providing alternate experiences for users based on a condition, in your case connectivity, is a good practice and provides a great user experience.

Summary

This chapter covered how to approach user messaging if there is no network connection available. You extended the MyParseUser object by adding class methods for tracking the status of a user. Using the last_seen field, you were able to calculate times to display to the user in a friendly format using moment.js.

As you have experienced, there are many different and unique ways you can integrate PhoneGap plug-ins with Parse. From saving files to updating a user's geographical position on a map, creatively combining different methods can make your applications feature-rich with little effort.

Conclusion

You made it to the end! We hope you ran into bugs, extended the code, and learned something new you can apply to your next project.

We encourage you to keep up-to-date with Parse (blog.parse.com) and PhoneGap (phonegap.com/blog) and continuously improve your skills to create unique applications everyone can enjoy.

Happy Programming!

Index

Get the eBook for only $5!

Why limit yourself?

Now you can take the weightless companion with you wherever you go and access your content on your PC, phone, tablet, or reader.

Since you've purchased this print book, we're happy to offer you the eBook in all 3 formats for just $5.

Convenient and fully searchable, the PDF version enables you to easily find and copy code—or perform examples by quickly toggling between instructions and applications. The MOBI format is ideal for your Kindle, while the ePUB can be utilized on a variety of mobile devices.

To learn more, go to www.apress.com/companion or contact support@apress.com.

Printed in the United States
By Bookmasters